QM

23

D1685782

WITHDRAWN
FROM STOCK
QMUL LIBRARY

The End of Laissez-Faire?

To Elissa, Zadie and Naomi

The End of Laissez-Faire?

On the Durability of Embedded Neoliberalism

Damien Cahill

Senior Lecturer in Political Economy, University of Sydney, Australia

Edward Elgar
PUBLISHING

Cheltenham, UK • Northampton, MA, USA

© Damien Cahill 2014

All rights reserved. No part of this publication may be reproduced, stored in a retrieval system or transmitted in any form or by any means, electronic, mechanical or photocopying, recording, or otherwise without the prior permission of the publisher.

Published by
Edward Elgar Publishing Limited
The Lypiatts
15 Lansdown Road
Cheltenham
Glos GL50 2JA
UK

Edward Elgar Publishing, Inc.
William Pratt House
9 Dewey Court
Northampton
Massachusetts 01060
USA

Paperback edition 2015

A catalogue record for this book
is available from the British Library

Library of Congress Control Number: 2014937773

This book is available electronically in the **Elgar**online
Social and Political Science Subject Collection
DOI 10.4337/9781781000281

ISBN 978 1 78100 027 4 (cased)
ISBN 978 1 78536 643 7 (paperback)

Typeset by Columns Design XML Ltd, Reading
Printed and bound by CPI Group (UK) Ltd, Croydon, CR0 4YY

Contents

Acknowledgements

This book is the product of several years of intellectual labour, and thanks are due to the many people who helped me to complete it. Apologies to anyone who I have inadvertently missed.

Initial work on the book was done during a period of sabbatical in 2011. Thanks to the University of Sydney which funded this. Big thanks to Adam Morton, Andreas Bieler, Sara Motta, Tony Burns and others at the Centre for the Study of Social and Global Justice at the University of Nottingham, as well as to William Carroll and Daniel Fridman at the Sociology Department, University of Victoria, Canada and Ben Spies-Butcher, Pauline Johnson, Michael Fine, Shaun Wilson and Justine Lloyd in the Sociology Department at Macquarie University for hosting me, going out of your way to make me feel welcome and providing such a stimulating environment in which to think.

Thanks to scholars at the University of Sydney and beyond, who, through collegial discussion, have helped me to formulate the arguments contained in this book: Martijn Konings, Bill Dunn, Joy Paton, Gillian Hewitson, Mike Beggs, Tom Barnes, Dick Bryan, Frank Stilwell, Liz Hill, Diarmuid Maguire, Evan Jones, John Mikler, Stephen Castles, Raewyn Connell, Nour Dados, Jean Parker, James Goodman, Jane Andrew, Tim DiMuzio, Anthony Ashbolt, Nick Southall, Mark Gawne, Joe Collins, Liz Humphrys, Tad Tietze, Jamie Peck, Fred Block, Greg Albo, Leo Panitch and Alfredo Saad-Filho.

Thanks to students in Political Economy at the University of Sydney from whom I continue to learn, and who continue to knock me over with their insights.

Thanks to Liz Humphrys, Barney Lewer and Tom Barnes who provided invaluable research assistance for this book. Special thanks are due to David Primrose who in addition to research assistance also offered valuable comments on the manuscript as a whole and provided the index.

Thanks to my comrades in the National Tertiary Education Union, and the student activists at the University of Sydney who, during the period in which I wrote this book, stood up against two major attacks upon the working conditions of staff at the University of Sydney and engaged in a successful fight against actually existing neoliberalism.

Some of the ideas in this book were first developed in: Damien Cahill, 'The Embedded Neoliberal Economy' in Damien Cahill, Lindy Edwards and Frank Stilwell (eds), *Neoliberalism: Beyond the Free Market* (Edward Elgar, 2012); Damien Cahill, 'Always Embedded Neoliberalism and the Global Financial Crisis' in Kate Macdonald, Shelley Marshall and Sanjay Pinto (eds), *New Visions for Market Governance: Crisis and Renewal*; Tom Barnes and Damien Cahill, 'Marxist Class Analysis: A Living Tradition in Australian Scholarship', *Journal of Australian Political Economy*, 70, 2012; Damien Cahill, 'Beyond Neoliberalism? Crisis and the Prospects for Progressive Alternatives', *New Political Science*, 33(4), 2011; Damien Cahill, 'Actually Existing Neoliberalism and the Global Economic Crisis', *Labour and Industry*, 20(3), 2010; Damien Cahill, 'Is Neoliberalism History?' *Social Alternatives*, 28(1), 2009; Damien Cahill, 'Labo(u)r, the Boom and the Prospects for an Alternative to Neo-Liberalism', *Journal of Australian Political Economy*, 61, 2008; Damien Cahill, 'Ideas-Centred Explanations of the Rise of Neoliberalism: A Critique', *Australian Journal of Political Science*, 48(1), 2013, pp. 71–84. While this book is an original contribution to the study of neoliberalism, some passages from those works appear in the current volume.

Thanks to Louella, Wal, Damien, Lucinda, Dylan (and Heath!) for your warmth over many years (and for looking after my girls!).

Thanks to Jenny and Jamie for always being there for me.

Thanks to Mum, Dad, Rae and Tim for your unquestioning support.

To Elissa, Zadie and Naomi, thanks for everything, but especially for your patience and your love. I'll be home soon.

Introduction

When the global financial crisis hit in 2007, many believed it sounded the death knell for neoliberalism. Several years on and an end to the crisis is nowhere in sight. Neoliberalism, moreover, appears to be alive and well as states respond to the ongoing crisis with privatisation, austerity programmes and attacks upon the rights of labour.

This book examines why neoliberalism has proven to be so durable in the face of crisis, and why those who predicted its collapse got it so wrong. It argues that the commentators who thought the crisis heralded the death of neoliberalism fundamentally misunderstood the very nature of neoliberalism. They assumed that the major neoliberal policy changes that swept the capitalist world during the last three decades simply mirrored the agenda advocated by influential neoliberal polemicists and intellectuals such as Milton Friedman, Friedrich von Hayek and the various think tanks and foundations which disseminated their ideas. Many commentators mistakenly believed the capitalist world economy had come to resemble the free market, small government *laissez-faire* vision of such neoliberal thinkers and think tanks. And, if neoliberalism was understood as being about reducing the size of the state and its regulation of markets, then it was only natural that the nationalisations and bailout measures adopted by states to deal with the global financial crisis would be interpreted as a shift away from neoliberalism.

This book argues that such an understanding reflects an idealist, or ideas-centred, conception of reality, in that it interprets human society as a reflection of the dominant ideas used to explain it, and views ideas as the main drivers of political and economic change. More importantly, the book argues that such idealist assumptions about neoliberalism do not withstand scrutiny against empirical evidence. They offer an unhelpful portrayal of the dynamics of neoliberalism in practice and, consequently, an unrealistic vision of the way out of neoliberalism.

In contrast this book argues that, while neoliberal ideas are important, any account which puts them at the centre of its analysis is insufficient for understanding the major changes to capitalist states and economies during the last three decades. Instead, the book offers an alternative, materialist interpretation of neoliberalism. Human society is understood not as a reflection of dominant ideas about it, but rather as constituted by historically specific institutions and social relations which structure people's everyday lives. The book argues that neoliberalism in practice, as distinct from neoliberal ideas, is best understood as an evolving, socially embedded, policy regime, emerging at the end of the twentieth century. As a policy regime, neoliberalism is defined by microeconomic policies of privatisation, marketisation and deregulation as well as macroeconomic policies of inflation-targeting. The emergence of this regime entailed a radical transformation of the ways in which states regulated the economy, society and indeed, their own internal operations.

If something is embedded it is 'fixed firmly in a surrounding mass'. So, to be 'socially embedded' is to be fixed firmly in the surrounding *social* mass. The book argues that neoliberalism is embedded in three distinct, but related social spheres: class relations, institutions and ideological norms. Together these spheres form a social structure that supported the revival of business profitability after the economic crisis that beset the global capitalist economy in the 1970s and that was manifest in 'stagflation' – low or negative growth accompanied by rising unemployment and inflation – and that have continued to facilitate capital accumulation on a global scale ever since. Moreover, it will be argued that, while embedded neoliberalism is beset with internal contradictions that ultimately provided the preconditions for the current global financial crisis, the socially embedded nature of the neoliberal policy regime has made it highly resistant to retrenchment.

The concept that capitalist economies are socially embedded is most often associated with Karl Polanyi, but it is also evident in the broad traditions of Institutionalist and Marxist political economy. This book draws heavily upon these traditions in order to put forward a more useful understanding of neoliberalism to that proffered by the dominant idealist explanation. It argues that ideas are but one social institution in which neoliberalism is embedded and, even then, the relationship between neoliberal doctrines and neoliberal practices needs to be traced very carefully. Through a critique of dominant progressive narratives about neoliberalism and the crisis, this book establishes the platform for a more useful investigation of the foundations of neoliberalism, the reasons for its durability in the face of crisis, and a consideration of the prospects for moving beyond the neoliberal organisation of states and economies.

Chapter 1 outlines the idealist, or ideas-centred, conception of neoliberalism. It identifies two main assumptions that structure such discussions of neoliberalism: that the world has become a mirror of fundamentalist neoliberal doctrine; and that the rise of neoliberal policy regimes was the result of the direct influence of this doctrine and the intellectuals and think tanks which promoted it. In Chapters 2 and 3, the book identifies the major problems with the idealist understanding of neoliberalism and its demise. Chapter 2 demonstrates that the idealist thesis fails to account for the expansion of both the economic size and the regulatory scope of capitalist states during the neoliberal era. It argues that it is useful to delineate 'actually existing neoliberalism' from the normative prescriptions of neoliberal polemicists. Chapter 3 shows that there is very little evidence to support the idealist claim that it was the influence of fundamentalist neoliberal ideas and think tanks that drove the neoliberal policy revolution and, indeed, that there is considerable evidence that other factors, including the political mobilisation by corporations and the imperative for capitalist states to ensure the profitability of businesses, were more directly influential in pushing policy makers towards neoliberalism.

Chapter 4 outlines the concept of 'always embedded neoliberalism' as an alternative to the idealist understanding. It argues that capitalist economies have always depended upon a range of social relations and institutions, including the state, for their operation and constitution. Just as capitalism has always been embedded in social institutions and class relations, so too, it is argued, has 'actually existing neoliberalism' – a historically specific manifestation of the capitalist economy – from its very beginning been always socially embedded. It is argued that the socially embedded nature of neoliberalism helps explain its durability in the face of crisis, but also points towards the possibilities of a non-neoliberal politics.

Chapters 5, 6 and 7 detail the three major mechanisms through which neoliberalism is socially embedded. Chapter 5 outlines the class-embedded nature of neoliberalism. It describes the new patterns of class power which underpinned the neoliberal response to the stagflation of the 1970s and how these have subsequently continued to shape the prevailing political economic configurations of capitalism. The chapter identifies a shift in political and industrial power away from labour to the owners of productive resources and argues that the profit-making strategies of business are premised on the continuation of such arrangements. Thus businesses and their representative bodies are likely to preference neoliberal arrangements in their policy advocacy.

Chapter 6 examines the ways in which neoliberalism is institutionally embedded, particularly through state rules which privilege neoliberal forms of regulation. This chapter assists an understanding of the persistence and expansion of the state during the neoliberal era. As well as 'rolling back' many of the regulations characteristic of the post-World War Two Keynesian era, from the 1970s onwards states also 'rolled out' new forms of regulation and institutions which underpinned the operation of newly 'deregulated' or privatised industries.

Chapter 7 returns to the topic of fundamentalist neoliberal ideas, arguing that they provide the basis for a set of neoliberal ideological norms which form the dominant discursive framework through which political elites across most capitalist nation-states organise and justify their policy agendas. Thus, it is argued that neoliberalism is ideologically embedded at the elite level, albeit this ideology has been less successful at colonising the realm of 'common sense' among the vast bulk of the human population. Indeed, the chapter also outlines the recurrent resistance and opposition to neoliberal policies which show that although neoliberalism is ideologically embedded, this is a contested hegemony.

The final chapter examines the effects of the global financial crisis upon always embedded neoliberalism and examines the prospects for alternatives to neoliberalism. It argues that the institutions and class relations which drove and sustained neoliberalism for 30 years remain largely intact. While the legitimacy of neoliberal ideology has suffered as a result of the crisis, this has not yet been translated into a coherent and widely-supported anti-neoliberal agenda. Indeed, neoliberal policies are once again being relied upon by states and supra-national institutions to deal with the ongoing global economic instability. Nonetheless, it is argued that the weakening of neoliberal ideology and the implementation of neoliberal austerity policies of governments open up a window of opportunity for change. However because neoliberalism is underpinned by more than merely ideas, so is the roll-back of neoliberalism only likely if anti-neoliberal ideas are underpinned by an anti-neoliberal politics. Therefore the chapter pays attention to the need for political mobilisation in pursuit of a post-neoliberal politics, and the need to embed alternative logics within the apparatuses of the state to secure the durability of a post-neoliberal order.

The ambition of this book is to provide a more useful understanding of neoliberalism than the idealist conception which currently dominates progressive critiques. It is an unfortunate fact that the idealist interpretation of neoliberalism offers unfounded optimism to progressive forces about the imminent decline of neoliberalism. Regulation designed to rescue neoliberalism is mistaken for a wholesale retreat from neoliberalism. Moreover, the idealist interpretation holds out the false promise of a relatively easy road to overcome neoliberalism. It suggests that progressive forces just need to put together the right combination of ideas, and that policy makers just need to realise that they have been living under a neoliberal delusion for 30 years, for neoliberalism to give way to a more rational and humane social democratic order. If only that were true! It is hoped that this book provides the basis for a more thoroughgoing critique of neoliberalism that allows progressive forces to navigate the combination of forces ranged against alternative proposals for ordering the economy along more socially just lines, and thereby develop strategies that have a realistic prospect for moving beyond neoliberalism.

1. The idealist view of neoliberalism

In April 2009, well-known Marxist historian Eric Hobsbawm predicted that the global financial crisis heralded the end of the neoliberal era. He wrote that 'the global free market [had] imploded' and that '[w]e don't yet know how grave and lasting the consequences of the present world crisis will be, but they certainly mark the end of the sort of free-market capitalism that captured the world and its governments in the years since Margaret Thatcher and Ronald Reagan' (Hobsbawm 2009).

In one sense, Hobsbawm's prognosis was understandable. When Hobsbawm wrote this article, the global economy had, in the space of less than two years, plunged into a crisis, the magnitude of which was only matched by the Great Depression of the 1930s. Unemployment was on the rise, aggregate demand and economic growth were plummeting, private sector credit had all but dried up and governments had launched massive rescue packages to bail out private sector companies, including the nationalisation of some of the world's largest corporations – a move that just a couple of years previously would have been considered virtually unthinkable. Given this, it was perhaps reasonable of Hobsbawm to conclude that he was witnessing a turning point in the global capitalist economy.

Yet, the way in which Hobsbawm described the neoliberal era that preceded the global financial crisis – as an era of 'free market capitalism' – suggests another reason for his optimism that the crisis represented not only a turning point for capitalism, but also an endpoint for neoliberalism. Hobsbawm's argument and language reflect the tenor of many other commentators on the implications of the crisis for neoliberalism. They share an assumption that the major neoliberal changes to states and economies since the 1970s resulted in a system of free market capitalism. They assumed, whether implicitly or explicitly, that the world had come to resemble the utopian prescriptions for state retrenchment outlined by fundamentalist neoliberal intellectuals, like Milton Friedman and Friedrich von Hayek. Neoliberal ideas about how economies ought to be organised were held to be synonymous with the way economies actually were organised. Such assumptions mean that arguments of this type are properly characterised as idealist, or ideas-centred. This means they take reality to be a reflection of dominant ideas about it. It was on the basis of such assumptions that many commentators interpreted the fiscal packages, bank nationalisations and financial stability regulations which states implemented after the onset of the global financial crisis as a 'return to regulation' (Helleiner 2008) and therefore as constituting the end of the unregulated, free market era.

Moreover, another pervasive idealist assumption was often embedded in discussions of the future of neoliberalism in the wake of the crisis. This too is evident in Hobsbawm's article. According to Hobsbawm (2009), the last three decades were characterised by 'attempts to realise' in 'pure form' a 'totally unrestricted and uncontrolled free market capitalist economy', much as Soviet apparatchiks had supposedly attempted to realise the totally planned economy of Marxist theory. Not only is neoliberal policy assumed to mirror neoliberal normative prescriptions, but neoliberalism is understood as a fundamentalist doctrine that drove changes to the state and economy during the past three decades. According to this view, it was the influence of a utopian free market vision that swayed political elites to adopt neoliberal policies. Such reasoning is also idealist. It puts ideas at the centre of its explanation by assuming that ideas are the primary force driving political and economic change.

That Hobsbawm, a Marxist and otherwise committed materialist, should base his arguments upon idealist assumptions might seem odd. After all, idealism and materialism are antithetical forms of analysis. That this is the case, however, would seem to reflect just how deeply entrenched is the idealist assumption in contemporary discussions of neoliberalism and its future.

This chapter analyses the idealist arguments at the heart of contemporary discussions of neoliberalism. It demonstrates that they have a long lineage within analyses of neoliberalism. By identifying the idealist predisposition of much contemporary debate, this chapter lays the groundwork for 'clearing the decks' of some of the pervasive and unhelpful assumptions about the nature of neoliberalism in order to put forward a more useful understanding of neoliberalism and its future prospects in the context of the current crisis. The chapter first shows the ways in which the assumption that capitalist economies have come to mirror fundamentalist neoliberal doctrine shapes debates about neoliberalism and the global financial crisis. It then demonstrates how the assumption that the rise of a neoliberal policy regime was driven by the direct influence of fundamentalist neoliberal doctrines and the intellectuals and think tanks that promoted it is also deeply ingrained within discussions of the implications of the global financial crisis for the future of neoliberalism.

NEOLIBERALISM AS A REFLECTION OF NEOLIBERAL IDEAS

As a set of ideas (as distinct from a policy regime), neoliberalism (like all theories of society) is diverse and, as shall be discussed in Chapter 3, there is disagreement among its adherents as to ontological and normative principles (that is, disagreement about 'what is' and 'what should be'). Nonetheless, it is possible to identify the core features of neoliberal doctrine.

First, the neoliberal understanding of the world develops its analysis through the use of methodological individualism. This means that the individual is taken to be the basic unit of analysis. Moreover, the individual is conceived of in a particular way: self-interested (that is, not other-regarding); rational (that is, the individual understands and acts according to their own preferences); and utility (pleasure/satisfaction) maximising.

Second, the preservation of the liberty of the individual (typically conceived of negatively as freedom from coercion) should be the ultimate goal of society and government.

Third, markets are understood as spheres of voluntary exchange between such individuals. Because no rational self-interested individual would voluntarily engage in a disadvantageous exchange, if markets are freed from exogenous impediments and restrictions such as states and trade unions, market transactions, by definition, benefit both parties and ensure that individuals are able to satisfy their preferences. Moreover, free competitive markets also guarantee economic efficiency.

Therefore, free competitive markets are understood to be the most efficient and the most moral (because they preserve individual liberty), form of social organisation. Neoliberals therefore advocate the devolution of as many state functions as possible to market exchanges. This is the conceptual origin of their advocacy of policies of privatisation, deregulation and marketisation.

Those who advocate such arguments are properly called 'fundamentalist' or 'doctrinaire' neoliberals because they observe strict maintenance to the fundamental doctrines of neoliberalism. Publicly, fundamentalist neoliberals, and the think tanks that proselytised their ideas, came to be associated with not only the transfer of services once provided directly by the state to the private sector, but also calls for reductions in the economic size of the state. Thus, with some justification, neoliberal doctrine has come to be associated with advocacy of a small, *laissez-faire* state (as discussed in Chapter 3, this common public image of fundamentalist neoliberals is an accurate depiction of the ideas advocated by Milton Friedman and many neoliberal think tanks, but it is less accurate a characterisation of Friedrich von Hayek, which is an important distinction in understanding the ideological nature of neoliberal doctrine).

It was this small state ideal which many progressive scholars and commentators believed had become reality in the neoliberal era. As with Hobsbawm, the assumption that neoliberalism in practice mirrored the policy programme advocated by fundamentalist neoliberal intellectuals and think tanks informed the predictions by legions of progressive commentators that the onset of the global financial crisis heralded the imminent demise of neoliberalism. One striking example of this was the essay published by then Australian Prime Minister, Kevin Rudd, in the progressive *The Monthly* magazine that achieved international exposure when condensed and republished in the French newspaper, *Le Monde*. It argued that the current global financial crisis exposes the failings of neoliberalism, which he also refers to as 'free-market fundamentalism, extreme capitalism and excessive greed' (Rudd 2009: 20). 'In the past year', wrote Rudd, 'we have seen how unchecked market forces have brought capitalism to the precipice' (p. 22). As a consequence, the 'ideological legitimacy' of neoliberalism is now destroyed (p. 29). For Rudd, neoliberalism is understood as the triumph of the free market, or unregulated capitalism, underpinned by a slimmed-down version of the state. Therefore, he argues, 'With the demise of neoliberalism, the role of the state has once more been recognized as fundamental' (p. 25).

Similar sentiments are evident in Will Hutton's (2008) contention that policy responses to the financial crisis marked a return to Keynesian-style 'managed capitalism' – implying that, in the previous neoliberal era, capitalism was somehow unregulated and not managed by the state. When conservative French President Nicolas Sarkozy announced in 2008 that '*laissez-faire* is finished', he was expressing a synonymous view (Vucheva 2008).

Arguments such as these implicitly treat neoliberal theory, and the policy practices of neoliberal governments, as synonymous. In describing neoliberalism as a system of 'free market capitalism', they tend to accept the normative vision of the state and economy, proffered by neoliberal polemicists such as Milton Friedman and Friedrich von Hayek, as the actual state of affairs that prevailed in most capitalist countries during the last two to three decades. They view neoliberalism as a diminution of the state and a withering of its regulatory 'intervention' in capitalist economies, as advocated by neoliberal fundamentalists. Such a perspective takes as an accurate description of the neoliberal era the visions of Milton and Rose Friedman, for example of 'a society that relies primarily upon voluntary cooperation to organize both economic and other activity' (Friedman and Friedman 1980: 58), whereby the government is limited such that it only:

> maintained law and order, defined property rights, served as a means whereby we could modify property rights and other rules of the economic game, adjudicated disputes about the interpretation of the rules, enforced contracts, promoted competition, provided a monetary framework, engaged in activities to counter technical monopolies and to overcome neighborhood effects widely regarded as sufficiently important to justify government intervention, and … supplemented private charity and the private family in protecting the irresponsible, whether madman or child. (Friedman 2002: 34)

In viewing neoliberal policy practices as simply a reflection of neoliberal ideas, such accounts, as Panitch and Konings (2009: 68) argue, 'analyse the … dynamics of the past decades within the terms of that era's hegemonic self-representation'.

States versus Markets

Similarly widespread, and also evident in predictions of neoliberalism's demise, is the assumption of markets and states as separate and antithetical social spheres, where the history of the capitalist economy is understood as progressing through alternating periods in which either one or the other dominates (see Radice 2010: 34–5). This perspective leads to the view of neoliberalism as a 'retreat of the state' (Strange 1996) and the triumph of the market. Such assumptions are evident, for example, in commentaries on neoliberalism and the crisis by Nobel Laureate and high-profile progressive economist, Joseph Stiglitz, who (2010: xii) argues that:

> Economies need a balance between the role of markets and the role of government – with important contributions by nonmarket and nongovernmental institutions. In the last twenty-five years, America lost that balance, and it pushed its unbalanced perspective on countries around the world.

According to this view, responses to the crisis represent the early stirrings of a shift back toward states reasserting their dominance over markets.

This idea that states and markets are separate and antithetical spheres of human conduct is deeply embedded in neoliberal thought and in neoclassical economics, with which neoliberalism shares key foundational assumptions. It is expressed in the common rhetorical device used by neoliberals that when governments regulate markets they 'interfere' or 'intervene'. One can see this, for example, in the following statement by Terry Miller (2009), editor of the Heritage Foundation's (perhaps the world's leading neoliberal think tank) *Index of Economic Freedom* report:

> the first responsibility of policy makers in leading economies, especially in a time of downturn or crisis, is to preserve the capitalist system and to do no harm. Markets are by and large self-correcting. Government interventions, which are almost always designed to restore or protect the status quo ante, impede the corrective action of the market and thus slow recovery.

> The record of government interference in the economy, whether in the United States or in countries around the world, is not pretty.

To 'interfere' or 'intervene' is to 'come in as an extraneous factor or thing'. Thus, to describe state regulation as intervention necessarily implies that markets exist separately to states, and that when governments regulate, they distort the otherwise natural workings of markets. As Jones (1984: 54) rightly points out:

> 'Government intervention' is contemporary orthodox language for the *presence* of the State in the capitalist economy. The label has powerful connotations – there is the tacit presumption that the state is, in some sense, 'outside' the economic sphere; that the State's role in the economic sphere is 'unnatural'; and that the workings of the economic sphere have been 'distorted' by the State's role.

One can readily see how this emerges from the conceptual foundations of neoliberal doctrine. If markets are understood as self-regulating spheres of freedom in which rational individuals with unique and subjective preferences voluntarily interact for mutual advantage, then the state regulation of markets is an exogenous interference with an otherwise natural realm of human conduct. Thus, neoliberal discourse implicitly posits states and markets as separate and distinct entities. One can see this dichotomous form of thinking, for example, in Hayek's conception of markets as a form of 'spontaneous order' in contrast to states which he views as a deliberately constructed institution (Hayek 1973, 1978), or in Friedman's statement that:

> Fundamentally, there are only two ways of coordinating the activity of millions. One is central direction involving the use of coercion – the technique of the army

and of the modern totalitarian state. The other is voluntary cooperation of individuals – the technique of the market place. (Friedman 2002: 13)

As shall be discussed in later chapters, such discourses mischaracterise the nature of capitalist states and markets (see also Harcourt 2011). Moreover, while the discourse of 'government intervention' is a hallmark of neoliberal fundamentalist discourse, there is nonetheless significant conceptual slippage in the ways that neoliberal fundamentalists deploy the concept of the state, which imbues neoliberal doctrine with an inherent malleability which, as discussed in Chapter 7, is crucial to its development as an ideology that is used to justify neoliberal policy regimes. For now, however, it is sufficient to note that those who assume that states and markets are separate and antithetical spheres are actually assuming that the world mirrors the foundational ideas of neoclassical and neoliberal thought. Evidently, idealist assumptions run deep in discussions of neoliberalism.

Neoliberalism as 'Disembedding'

This idealist conceptual framework also underlies the understanding of neoliberalism as a process by which the economy is 'disembedded' from its social support structures. Like other idealist assumptions already discussed, such a discourse has been a feature of critical analyses of neoliberalism both prior to and during the current crisis. While ultimately derived from the work of Karl Polanyi, this discourse typically contrasts neoliberalism with John Ruggie's concept of the 'embedded liberalism' of the post-World War Two era of capital accumulation, in which the state played a 'mediating role ... between market and society' (Ruggie 1982: 392) through capital controls, currency regulation and a growing welfare state. Whereas the golden age of capitalism is understood as a period in which the economy was embedded in social institutions, the neoliberal era, in contrast, is often presumed to have been characterised by the freeing of the economy from such socially imposed constraints and thus disembedded from its social moorings. This argument is exemplified by Best (2003: 369–70): 'Since the collapse of the Bretton Woods exchange rate system in the early 1970s there has been a gradual and practical move to disembedded liberal finance from its political and social contexts'. As shall be discussed in Chapter 4 such approaches are, at best, partial readings of Polanyi, and rather unhelpful ones for deciphering the real world of neoliberalism.

Once again, these assumptions lead to the view that neoliberalism is best described as a system of *laissez-faire*, in which political economic change is substantially driven by and reflective of the normative prescriptions of neoliberal polemicists. As with other idealist approaches, the understanding of neoliberalism as a process of disembedding leads to an interpretation of the state regulations implemented in the wake of the crisis as constituting the end of neoliberalism. If neoliberalism is viewed as a retreat of the state, and thus as a disembedding of the economy from society, then the state's re-entry into the economic arena is likely to be interpreted as marking a re-embedding of the economy and thus the beginning of the end of neoliberalism. This is precisely the line of argument taken by Altvater who, like Hobsbawm, is also a Marxist and, one might have thought, normally averse to idealist theorising. After describing neoliberalism as a system of disembedded financial markets he argues that as a result of the crisis and subsequent state interventions, 'the inherent tendency of disembedding markets from society and nature has halted' (Altvater 2009: 82). Once again, this underscores the pervasiveness of ideas-centred approaches to understanding neoliberalism and its future in the wake of the global financial crisis.

NEOLIBERALISM AS THE ROLL-OUT OF NEOLIBERAL DOCTRINE

So far this chapter has argued that many predictions of neoliberalism's demise in the wake of the global financial crisis rely upon the assumption that neoliberal changes to the state and economy reflect the normative prescriptions of neoliberal fundamentalists. It has been argued that this assumption is idealist because it takes the world to be a reflection of dominant ideas about it.

However, there is a second category of idealist assumptions underpinning many of the predictions that the global financial crisis marks the end of neoliberalism. This is the assumption that the neoliberal policy revolution was driven by the influence of fundamentalist neoliberal ideas – that neoliberal policy practices are causally related to the neoliberal ideas expounded by the likes of Milton Friedman, Friedrich von Hayek and other fundamentalist polemicists, and proselytised through think tanks and similar organisations such as the Mont Pelerin Society, the Heritage Foundation or the Institute of Economic Affairs. The two idealist assumptions are often closely related: the former holds that the world is a reflection of neoliberal ideas, while the latter holds that changes to the world were driven by such ideas.

The second category of idealism is evident in the work of many of the commentators already mentioned. As noted earlier, Hobsbawm makes this assumption when he writes about neoliberalism as an attempt to realise in 'pure form' a particular 'way of thinking' about the economy. In doing so, Hobsbawm implicitly posits neoliberalism as operating at the level of ideas which policy makers then come under the sway of, driving them to mould the world according to such utopian models. Similarly, Joseph Stiglitz (2008) – another who assumes economic practice follows economic theory – describes neoliberalism as a 'grab-bag of ideas based on the fundamentalist notion that markets are self-correcting' and that '[i]t was this market fundamentalism that underlay Thatcherism, Reaganomics and the so-called "Washington Consensus" in favour of privatization, liberalization, and independent central banks focusing single-mindedly on inflation'. Fellow Nobel Laureate, Paul Krugman, adheres to a similar conceptual logic. He describes Reaganism (which can, reasonably, be taken to be a proxy for neoliberalism) as a 'zombie doctrine: even though it should be dead, it keeps on coming' (Krugman 2009). In describing neoliberalism as a 'doctrine', Krugman understands it as operating at the level of ideas. He goes on to write that 'the New Deal regulations that had prevented banking crises for half a century' were 'dismantled' by 'politicians in the thrall of Reaganite ideology'. Thus, according to Krugman, neoliberal policy changes reflect the influence of neoliberal doctrine.

In predictions of the demise of neoliberalism such assumptions allow commentators to argue that the global financial crisis has discredited neoliberal ideas, which therefore opens space for a new set of ideas to take their place as the guiding vision of policy practice. For example, Australian progressive critic of neoliberalism, Robert Manne (2010: 18), describes neoliberalism as a 'faith' and a 'secular religion'. He and fellow author David McKnight argue that 'the only reason neoliberalism is still with us is because the Left have not presented a coherent alternative' (Manne and McKnight 2010: 2), clearly positing causation primarily at the level of ideas. From this perspective, economic policy and practice are conceptualised as being grounded in the application of theoretical principles. If those theoretical principles are found to be wanting, then they are assumed to be replaced by a more cohesive set of principles.

Like the assumption that neoliberal policy practices reflect the normative prescriptions of neoliberal polemicists, the assumption that such ideas are causally related to neoliberal change was deeply ingrained in discussions of neoliberalism prior to the onset of the current crisis. Even David Harvey, a Marxist, foregrounds the causal power of fundamentalist neoliberal ideas in the introduction to his *A Brief History of Neoliberalism* (published prior to the crisis in 2005): 'Volcker and Thatcher both plucked from the shadows of relative obscurity a particular doctrine that went under the name of "neoliberalism" and transformed it into the central guiding principle of economic thought and management' (Harvey 2005: 2). As discussed in later chapters, Harvey does not adopt this position consistently, and one might therefore explain it away simply as intellectual slippage. Indeed Harvey's story of the rise of neoliberalism is largely told through a class-based analytical lens. Nonetheless, that Harvey, who like Hobsbawm, otherwise adopts materialist forms of analysis, simultaneously deploys an ideas-centred explanation of political change, indicates how pervasive and unexamined such assumptions are in discussions of neoliberalism.

This assumption that neoliberalism in practice is the result of the application of fundamentalist neoliberal doctrines is also evident in Naomi Klein's well-known *The Shock Doctrine: The Rise of Disaster Capitalism*. Klein (2007) asserts the primacy of neoliberal ideas in explaining the major transformations to the state and economy since the 1970s. She argues that fundamentalist economists such as Milton Fried-man, and those trained by them, used economic and political crises, as well as natural disasters, to impose their fundamentalist neoliberal blueprints upon unsuspecting societies. Similarly, Pierre Bourdieu presents neoliberalism in practice as a product of fundamentalist neoliberal ideas. He wrote of 'The movement ... towards the neoliberal utopia of a pure, perfect market' and that the 'neoliberal programme tends overall to favour the separation between the economy and social realities and so to construct, in reality, an economic system corresponding to the theoretical description' (Bourdieu 1998: 96).

Although not sharing the radical critique of neoliberalism found in the work of Harvey, Klein or Bourdieu, Richard Cockett's *Thinking the Unthinkable: Think Tanks and the Economic Counter-Revolution 1931– 1983*, which did much to draw attention to the evolution of neoliberal think tanks in Britain, is based upon similar assumptions regarding the driving forces behind neoliberalism. Cockett (1995: 4–5) argues that neoliberal think tanks 'did as much intellectually to convert a generation of "opinion-formers" and politicians to a new set of ideas as the Fabians had done with a former generation at the turn of the century'. While Cockett (1995: 7) does acknowledge that the Thatcher government 'only achieved a limited success in implementing these ideas', his dominant narrative is that the new right think tanks converted the Tory leadership in Britain to neoliberalism. Thus, Cockett contends that neoliberal think tanks provided the impetus for the neoliberal shift in British economic policy in the 1980s.

Many contemporary critics of neoliberalism seem to share this view. Susan George (1997: 48), for example, argues that neoliberalism came to dominate economic policy due to the work of neoliberal think tanks: 'The victory of neoliberalism is the result of fifty years of intellectual work, now widely reflected in the media, politics, and the programs of international organisations'. George (1997: 48) contends that the investment by conservative elites in neoliberal think tanks paid off in the form of a transformation of the 'intellectual and psychological' landscape in favour of neoliberalism, which then led to a transformation of the 'economic, political and social landscape'.

Although his modern followers seem to have averred from describing neoliberalism in doctrinal terms, preferring instead to conceive of neoliberalism as a set of governmental practices (Dean 2012), Foucault's *Lectures on Biopolitics* suggest he too saw a link between neoliberal theory and emerging neoliberal technologies of government (Foucault 2008).

It is perhaps not surprising that neoliberal ideas, intellectuals and think tanks have come to be identified so closely with the neoliberal policy revolution which swept the capitalist world from the 1970s onwards. Friedrich von Hayek, one of the key figures of the 'neoliberal thought collective', argued that ideas were the key to policy change. The ability of 'socialism', he contended in the 1940s, to become 'a determining influence on politics' (Hayek 1960: 371) was due primarily to the ability of intellectuals – 'professional second hand dealers in ideas' (ibid.) – to organise political opinion. Hayek therefore called upon 'true liberal[s]' (p. 384) to learn from the success of their enemies and mobilise ideas in a similar fashion. This position is very close to that outlined by one of Hayek's chief intellectual adversaries, John Maynard Keynes, who, in the *General Theory of Employment, Interest and Money*, made the following well-known claim:

> [T]he ideas of economists and political philosophers, both when they are right and when they are wrong, are more powerful than is commonly understood. Indeed the world is ruled by little else. Madmen in authority, who hear voices in the air, are distilling their frenzy from some academic scribbler of a few years back. I am sure that the power of vested interests is vastly exaggerated compared with the gradual encroachment of ideas. ... soon or late, it is ideas, not vested interests, which are dangerous for good and evil. (Keynes 1964: 383)

This passage is often quoted as confirmation of the importance of ideas to the neoliberal policy revolution: just as a generation of intellectuals learned from Keynes the power of economic ideas and organised to shape the 'Keynesian' order of 'embedded liberalism' in the post-World War Two era, so, it is assumed, did neoliberal intellectuals learn the same

lesson and organised in the wake of the stagflationary crisis of the 1970s
to transform states and economies in the image of their own anti-
Keynesian, normative neoliberal visions. That this quote from Keynes
hangs on the wall of the Institute of Economic Affairs (IEA), Britain's
oldest and leading neoliberal think tank, no doubt adds weight to this
argument in the minds of its adherents (Cockett 1994: 139). As discussed
in the following chapters, however, such assumptions about the causal
role of fundamentalist neoliberal ideas paint an overly simplistic picture
of the forces that drove neoliberalism and that continue to re-shape it
today. A more satisfactory account of neoliberalism requires that attention be paid to the complex relationships between neoliberal ideas,
institutions and changing patterns of class relations in the capitalist world
economy from the 1970s onwards.

CONCLUSION

This chapter has argued that many of the predictions that neoliberalism
faces imminent demise because of the global financial crisis are based
upon idealist assumptions about the nature of neoliberalism.

Two idealist assumptions about the nature of neoliberalism were
identified. First, many authors assume that neoliberalism in practice
entailed the spread of free market capitalism as advocated by neoliberal
polemicists. In essence they assumed that the political economy had
come to mirror dominant ideas about how it should be organised. It was
only on the basis of such assumptions that they could argue that the
government regulations and nationalisations which followed the sub-
prime crisis and subsequent financial contagion of 2007–08 constituted
the end of neoliberalism.

Second, many authors also assume that the implementation of neoliberal policies was driven by the influence of those same fundamentalist
neoliberal ideas over policy makers. They implicitly drew a line of direct
causation from ideas, thinkers and think tanks to political economic
change. It was on this basis that they could argue that, because neoliberal
ideas had been delegitimated by the crisis, neoliberalism was at an end.
Furthermore, it allowed them to argue that all that was needed for the rise
of a new progressive non-neoliberal form of policy making was for the
development of a coherent alternative set of progressive non-neoliberal
ideas.

The next two chapters subject these assumptions to scrutiny. It is
argued that there is little empirical evidence to support such idealist
assumptions about neoliberalism and, indeed, that there is much evidence

which directly contradicts them. This has implications for how we think about neoliberalism. As this chapter has suggested, idealist assumptions about neoliberalism are pervasive. Therefore, a more satisfactory conception of neoliberalism is required before we can speculate on its likely future in the wake of the global financial crisis.

2.   Actually existing neoliberalism

This chapter assesses the validity of the idealist understanding of the nature of neoliberalism. It examines the trajectory of the size of the state and of state regulation of the economy over the last four decades in order to test the assumption that the neoliberal era was characterised by a diminished state presence in the economy. In particular, the concept of 'actually existing neoliberalism' is used to highlight the discrepancy between the utopian visions of neoliberal theorists and the realities of neoliberalism in practice. While noting the correlations evident between neoliberal normative prescriptions and the policy trajectories of capitalist states at a very broad level of analysis, the chapter nonetheless also demonstrates the existence of significant discrepancies between neoliberal theory and practice with respect to the size and scope of the state. Empirical evidence from international comparative studies is used to illustrate that, during the neoliberal era, the economic size of states was not diminished when measured in terms of relative expenditure. Furthermore, the extensive programmes of deregulation, privatisation and marketisation carried out by most capitalist states during the last 30 years resulted not in a diminution of the regulatory reach of states, but in the concurrent implementation of a host of new regulations and agencies to govern the markets transformed and created through neoliberalism. The coercion used by states against those opposed to neoliberal measures is further evidence against the argument that the neoliberal era entailed a retreat of the state, as is the persistence of universalist institutions, such as socialised education and healthcare, in the neoliberal era. The implication of the argument developed in this chapter is that new regulations enacted since the global financial crisis are not, in and of themselves, sufficient conditions to pronounce the death of neoliberalism because the neoliberal era itself was characterised by extensive state regulation and activity.

CORRELATIONS BETWEEN NEOLIBERAL THEORY AND PRACTICE

What marked as distinct the movement which promoted fundamentalist neoliberal doctrine was its advocacy of the policy suite of privatisation, deregulation and marketisation as a way of devolving government provision of services to the private sector, introducing competition into state-dominated services and freeing private sector agents from the restrictions imposed by state regulations. It was through this policy suite that the fundamentalist neoliberals envisaged their utopia of a market-dominated society being realised.

At first glance, there appear to be strong correlations between the normative agenda advocated by neoliberal intellectuals and the policy trajectories of capitalist states globally since the 1970s. During this period, capitalist states were increasingly transformed through the policy suite of privatisation, deregulation and marketisation. While such corre-lations obscure the more fundamental discrepancies between neoliberal theory and policy practices, they are nonetheless worth examining for two main reasons. First, such correlations provide a useful 'first cut' indication of the broad parameters of the neoliberal policy regime that has become dominant within capitalist states. Much more detail will be added to this first cut throughout the book, but it does, nonetheless, provide a useful starting point for discussing 'actually existing neoliber-alism'. Second, examination and recognition of such correlations as do exist between neoliberal theory and practice highlights, on the one hand, that ideas-centred understandings of neoliberalism are based upon an understandable, though limited, reading of observable phenomena, which helps to explain the durability of such interpretations. On the other hand, however, it also sets the scene for a more detailed examination of 'actually existing neoliberalism', which in turn paves the way for a critique of ideas-centred accounts.

Empirical evidence showing the extent privatisation, deregulation and marketisation offers a sense of such correlations as do exist between neoliberal theory and practice as well as of the global spread of the neoliberal policy regime. On the privatisation front, for example, between 1977 and 1999 there were 1415 full or partial privatisations of state-owned assets in the advanced capitalist countries alone. In North America and the Caribbean countries there were 126 privatisations. Latin Ameri-can countries engaged in 424 privatisations. Sub-Saharan Africa experi-enced 146 privatisations. In the Middle East and North Africa there were 149 privatisations. Across Asia there were 448 privatisations, and in

Central and Eastern Europe and the former USSR countries there were 919 privatisations after the collapse of communism, between 1990 and 2001. The peak of global privatisation in terms of both incidence and revenue was the 1990s. Although there is both a temporal and geographic unevenness to these privatisations, the data points to a global neoliberal policy trend.[1] By the 1990s, in both developed and less developed nations and among democratic and dictatorial regimes, as well as conservative and social democratic governments, the neoliberal policy prescription of privatisation had become a state policy norm.

At least in developing economies, the extent of the spread of neoliberal polices of deregulation is indicated by the number of structural adjustment programmes coordinated by the IMF. Under the 1985 'Baker Plan', the IMF was transformed into an institution that required countries in receipt of financial assistance to restructure their economies through privatisation and the deregulation of trade and finance (Chorev and Babb 2009: 468–9). As discussed in more detail in Chapter 6, from 1985 the IMF became an institutional agent of the expanded reproduction of neoliberalism. Between 1986 and 2000 the IMF approved the use of its Structural Adjustment or Enhanced Structural Adjustment Facilities for 131 programmes in over 50 countries (Barro and Lee 2002: 36; IMF 2004).

More broadly, perhaps the most significant indicator of the neoliberal turn in policy was the dismantling of the 'Bretton Woods' system of currency and financial controls. From the 1970s countries began to deregulate the cross-border flow of finance and lift some restrictions on financial transactions, instruments and institutions within their borders. This broke with the 'financial repression' of the post-World War Two era. As Helleiner (1994: 146) notes, 'by the early 1990s, the restrictive Bretton Woods financial order had been completely overturned and an almost fully liberalised pattern of financial relations had emerged between advanced industrial states, giving market operators a degree of freedom unparalleled since the 1920s'. But it was not only the advanced capitalist economies that exhibited a taste for neoliberal financial deregulation. Many developing countries also went down this path (Williamson and Mahar 1998: 12). Concurrently, national currencies moved to floating rates. This dismantled the fixed exchange rate system that was a hallmark restriction of the post-war era. The extent of this neoliberal policy transformation is noted by IMF figures that '97 percent of its member countries in 1970 were classified as having a pegged exchange rate; by 1980, that share had declined to 39 percent, and in 1999 it was down to only 11 percent' (Reinhart 2000: 65).

DISCREPANCIES BETWEEN NEOLIBERAL THEORY AND PRACTICE

The Transformation of States

Clearly, since the 1970s there has been a general embrace by policy makers of the broad policy mechanisms advocated by fundamentalist neoliberal intellectuals. However, this is not a sufficient condition for proclaiming this period as a triumph of free markets or *laissez-faire*. While the roll-out of privatisation and deregulation may superficially appear to be synonymous with a retreat of the state, when this policy history is probed in more detail the picture that emerges is quite different.

While states were certainly transformed during this period, they were not retrenched. To sketch the nature of this transformation, the following discussion will focus upon changes to the economic size and regulatory scope of states, the coercive powers and actions of states, and the persistence of universalist-based institutions within states.

Had the neoliberal era been characterised by a retreat of the state, one would expect to find government expenditure diminishing over this period. It is therefore worth examining the trajectory of government expenditure as a proportion of GDP during this period. This is a reasonable proxy for the economic size of the state as it measures government expenditure relative to the national economy as a whole (Cohen and Centeno 2006: 37). Moreover, as Cohen and Centeno (ibid.) argue, 'much government spending is dedicated to redistributive transfers, which constitute nonmarket transactions (and hence market distortions in neoliberal thinking). If governments were dedicating themselves to promoting the market as a mechanism of allocation, we would expect these transfer payments and, in turn, government expenditures to decline'.

In determining whether state expenditure declined during the neoliberal era one is confronted with the perennial problem of when to begin and end the time-series. One starting point would be the early 1970s, for this was when the government of the USA ended the convertability of dollars into gold, floated its currency and began the process of financial deregulation. It was also when the military dictatorship in Chile began its neoliberal economic agenda. If this is taken as the starting point of the neoliberal era, then it is clear that the neoliberal era was one during which there was a significant increase in the relative economic size of the state, at least in the advanced capitalist countries. As Sanz and Velázquez (2007: 917) report, 'in the period 1970–1997, government expenditure as a share of GDP in the OECD countries increased from 30.5% in 1970 to 43.3% in 1997'.

However, while neoliberalism as a state policy regime certainly began in the 1970s, it was not until the 1980s that neoliberal policies came to occupy a central place in the policy agendas of major states. If we examine data from 1980 onwards the picture is somewhat different, but still contradicts the state retrenchment thesis. Cohen and Centeno, for example, have analysed government expenditure as a proportion of GDP in 101 countries from 1980 to 2000. Average expenditure in 1980, across all 101 states, was 15.6 per cent of GDP in 1980, 15.6 per cent in 1990 and 14.8 per cent by 2000 (Cohen and Centeno 2006: 37–8). Despite the slight decline, given the margin for error this paints a picture of remarkable stability in the relative economic size of states globally during the neoliberal era. Moreover, according to Cohen and Centeno's data, it was primarily the states that began the neoliberal era with higher relative public expenditure (above the 95th percentile) that experienced a decline in spending during this period (ibid.). Cohen and Centeno argue there is very little regional variation to these results. In the Middle East and North Africa, there was a decline in relative state expenditure during the 1980s, but this picked up during the 1990s. In Latin America and the Caribbean, there was a decline during the 1990s, but this had returned to its 1980 level by 2000. The OECD states 'are remarkably stable and show no downward trend at all' (pp. 38–9). Thus, if the 1980s (or even the early 1990s) are taken as the beginning of the neoliberal era, then it is clear that it is wrong to argue that a retrenchment of state expenditure occurred. Rather, there was a plateauing, on average, of state expenditure during this period. As Cohen and Centeno (pp. 39–40) state: 'Overall, these data cast serious doubt on the notion that there was a significant change in government spending because of neoliberalism ... we find little evidence for a major overhaul of the size of government budgets during the 1980s and 1990s as neoliberal programmes were applied throughout the world'. To be sure, the rate of state expenditure growth slowed during this period, but this is quite contrary to the depiction of the neoliberal era as one of *laissez-faire* and small and shrinking states.

Furthermore, within state budgets, there have been increases to expenditure even in areas that have been subject to significant neoliberalisation. Healthcare in the USA and Australia is a good example. In 2008, people in the USA were primarily reliant upon private health insurance, with only 24 per cent covered by government schemes and 15 per cent completely uninsured. Yet, even with this extensively marketised system of private health insurance, government health expenditure in the USA was the highest in the world at 16 per cent of GDP, a figure that had been 'increasing at rates well above increases in national income' (Thomson et al. 2010: 56). In 1960 this figure stood at 5 percent of GDP, and in 2000 at 14 percent (Auerback and Wray 2010: 4). A similar pattern is evident in Australia where the federal government introduced subsidies to expand the market for private health insurance in 1998. After the introduction of this subsidy and the expansion of the market for private health insurance, federal government health expenditure as a proportion of GDP increased from 3.7 per cent in 1996–1997 to 4.3 per cent in 2001–2002 (Segal 2004: 13).

It is also worth investigating the regulatory scope of states to determine whether this too was denuded during the neoliberal era, as this era's own 'hegemonic representation' (Panitch and Konings 2009: 68) would have it. Were the three decades prior to the global financial crisis characterised by the reign of 'free market capitalism' and the 'withering away of the state', then one would expect the regulatory scope of the state to have declined.

Empirical studies suggest, however, that this normative vision is not matched by the histories of states during the neoliberal era. This is highlighted in the pioneering work by David Levi-Faur and colleagues. One such study (Jordana et al. 2011) examined the establishment of new 'autonomous regulatory agencies' across 48 countries (all of Latin America and the OECD) and 15 sectors from 1966 to 2007. It found that the annual rate of regulatory agency set-up increased during the neo-liberal era. Prior to the 1980s, new agencies were established at a rate of less than five per year. Thereafter the rate increased to over 15 per year, with a peak of over 20 per year from 1995 to 2001 (Jordana et al. 2011: 1344). The authors therefore argue that these trends point towards 'rebureaucratization and, consequently, expansion in the regulatory capacities of the state' (ibid.).

Levi-Faur's (2005) study of the electricity and telecommunications sectors across 171 countries from 1980 to 2002 shows that the incidence of privatisation was almost matched by the incidence of new regulatory agencies in these sectors during the 1980s and some of the 1990s. Moreover, by the late 1990s new regulatory agencies were outstripping privatisations in the global telecommunications sector, as well as in the electricity sector by 2000 (Levi-Faur 2005: 18–19). This reflects 'the intimate relations between one of the major features of the neoliberal agenda – privatization – and the rise of regulatory institutions' (p. 19).

This 'intimate relationship' between neoliberalism and regulation is borne out by examination of an arena of deregulation often considered to be the *sine qua non* of neoliberalism: financial deregulation. Such an investigation confirms Vogel's (1996: 3) contention that 'what we have

witnessed has been reregulation, not deregulation. That is, the governments of the advanced industrial countries have reorganised their control
of private sector behaviour, but not substantially reduced the level of
regulation'. Thus, the key problematic surrounding regulation is not
simply a quantitative one of whether there has been more or less
regulation, but rather requires a more qualitative analysis of the changing
nature of policy and the ways it enables and constrains particular
economic agents and interests.

With respect to the floating of national currencies, for example, the
formal position of nation-states and their formal recognition by the IMF
as having floating currencies, often disguises what in practice is a regime
of currency manipulation. Reinhart (2000: 65) argues this forcefully:
'Countries that say they allow their exchange rates to fluctuate mostly do
not'. In fact many countries continue to use foreign and domestic
currency reserves and interest rate settings to lower the variability of their
exchange rate. This leads Reinhart to conclude, '[t]he low relative
exchange-rate variability is the deliberate result of policy actions to
stabilize the exchange rate' (p. 65). Beyond these cases, however, even
for those countries considered to be 'committed floaters, such as the
United States, Australia and Japan', it is not unknown for states to take
action designed to affect the exchange rate.

Looking at the experience of the USA, whence originated the wave of
financial deregulation that swept the world from the 1970s onwards,
three broad trends are evident that undermine the claim that neoliberalism entailed an evacuation of the state's presence within the economy
and point to the intimate relationship between neoliberalism and institutional regulation. First, a host of new regulations and regulatory institutions were created to facilitate and respond to new freedoms for finance
capital, the use of new financial instruments and new practices for
governing national currencies and their trade. Such developments are
perhaps what led Donald Mackenzie (2005: 569) to remark that 'modern
American financial markets are almost certainly the most highly regulated markets in history, if regulation is measured on volume (number of
pages) of rules, probably also if measured by extent of surveillance, and
possibly even by vigour of enforcement'. Such regulation was manifest,
for example, in new institutions such as the Commodity Futures Trading
Commission, established in 1974 which, as Panitch and Konings (2009:
69) point out, both regulated and facilitated the development of derivatives, often considered the exemplar of footloose speculative financial
capital. It was also evident in state regulations specifically designed to
quarantine from scrutiny and create new markets for new financial
products, such as the *Commodity Futures Modernisation Act* passed by

Congress in 2000 which 'essentially exempted derivatives and other exotic instruments from regulation by the agencies that regulated more conventional financial assets' (Hacker and Pierson 2010: 195). The strong arm of the state was also apparent when the Clinton government instructed Fannie Mae and Freddy Mac to extend their securitisation of mortgages for low-income households (Konings 2011: 146–7). This built upon the earlier 1977 *Community Reinvestment Act* which required these government sponsored enterprises to 'underwrite home loans by banks in poor communities' (Panitch and Konings 2009: 73). At the international level too, states continued to perform a crucial role in regulating money and finance throughout the neoliberal era. The breakdown of the strict currency controls of the Bretton Woods era did not mean an end to state involvement in influencing exchange rates or global financial markets and institutions. At the Plaza and Louvre agreements of 1985 and 1987, representatives from the world's largest economies agreed first to a devaluation of the US dollar and subsequently attempted to halt its fall in value (Helleiner 1994: 183–4; Konings 2011: 142). The first was achieved through direct involvement in currency markets, and the second through a restructuring of fiscal policy in the major economies. Similarly through the Basel agreements, rules were developed for minimal capital holding requirements for banks across the major economies (Abdelal 2007: 88).

Second, long before the onset of the global financial crisis in 2007, the state effectively underwrote the viability of the financial sector through, for example, deposit guarantees and the direct provision or facilitation of bailout packages for failing financial institutions. In contrast to the idea of the neoliberal era being one during which the provision of state welfare became denuded, the volatility facilitated through financial deregulation created the conditions whereby directing corporate welfare to the financial sector became a normal part of the activities of the US state. As Konings points out, the suite of legislation often seen as marking the turning point in the slide toward financial deregulation, not only removed some restrictions upon the conduct of financial institutions but also 'extended the coverage of deposit insurance and enhanced the powers of the Federal reserve' (Konings 2011: 135). State support for the finance sector of the US economy would later come in the form of more direct provision of assistance by bailing out institutions during the Savings and Loans crisis of the mid-1980s, and later facilitating a bailout package for the Long Term Capital Management Fund in 1998.

Third, the neoliberal era witnessed, and indeed financial deregulation brought about, new freedoms for the US state. Most particularly, it significantly freed the state from fiscal constraint with successive US administrations able to finance mounting deficits through the sale of securities to burgeoning financial markets (Konings 2011: 139). Thus, rather than restraining Leviathan, the neoliberal era enabled its continued expansion.

These are but a few examples of the centrality of an activist state to processes of financial deregulation which are most commonly conceptualised as exemplifying the retreat of the state from the economy. As is clear, quite the opposite is the case in practice. These should not be viewed as irrational or politically opportunistic departures from otherwise sound neoliberal economic policy. Rather they need to be understood as integral to the new dynamics of a neoliberalised financial sector.

State Coercion

If neoliberalism had meant a reduction in the state's interference in the lives of individuals, then one would expect to find a reduction in state coercion during the neoliberal era. Yet, examination of the historical record demonstrates that state-led coercion is a necessary, albeit uneven, element of neoliberal state and economic transformations. The sometimes intimate link between state coercion and neoliberal transformation is apparent in one of the earliest neoliberal regimes – the Pinochet dictatorship in Chile, 1973–1990. Pinochet implemented a programme of privatisation and deregulation, alongside violent repression of opposition (Klein 2007: 75–128). As Etchemendy (2004: 275) notes, 'In Chile, repression of unions accompanied the economic liberalization process'. During the period of neoliberal governance, 'more than 3,200 people were disappeared or executed, at least 80,000 were imprisoned, and 200,000 fled the country for political reasons' (Klein 2007: 77).

State coercion has also followed the implementation of structural adjustment programmes, through which international lending organisations, the International Monetary Fund and the World Bank obliged debtor nations – mainly developing economies – to implement extensive programmes of neoliberalisation as a condition of financial assistance. Cross-country analyses by Abouharb and Cingranelli (2007) of 431 IMF and 442 World Bank neoliberal structural adjustment programmes throughout the 1980s and 1990s found that human rights abuses – including torture, extra-judicial killing, political imprisonment and disappearances – became more likely the longer a country spent under a structural adjustment programme. They argue this is attributable to state regimes repressing dissent arising from the implementation of the neoliberal programmes and the social and economic dislocation such programmes cause.

While state coercion linked to neoliberalism has been most widespread in developing economies, states in advanced capitalist economies have also regularly engaged in coercion of civil society as part of implementing neoliberal agendas. Labour unions have been a common target of such coercion. On the one hand, 'labour market deregulation' has often entailed restrictions being placed upon the ability of workers to take collective action of various types, and limitations upon the representative capacities of unions. Both of these constitute state coercion of individuals as they entail an outside entity limiting, without consent, the liberty of an individual to engage in their chosen course of action. Additionally, such regulations typically apply only to a particular class of individuals – workers – and not to others. On the other hand, neoliberal regimes in advanced capitalist economies have also employed more direct forms of coercion against organised labour, including the use of police and the army for strike breaking, the gaoling of unionists and the deregistration of unions.

Three Anglophone countries – Australia, Britain and the USA – that have experienced profound neoliberalisation of their industrial relations systems – provide useful illustrations of these trends. The regulatory and coercive elements of neoliberal labour market deregulation have been evident in Australia since the shift under the Labor government to 'enterprise bargaining' in the 1990s. Enterprise bargaining on the one hand entailed the beginning of the 'roll-back' of Australia's historic institutions of arbitration through the devolution of bargaining from the industry to the enterprise level. The crucial role of the state in this process is captured by the phrase commonly used to describe it: 'managed decentralism' (Gahan and Pekarek 2012). Part of the 'roll-out' of new regulations to facilitate enterprise bargaining was the codification of the right to strike via the *Industrial Relations Reform Act 1993*. However, as White (2005) notes, this also had the effect of limiting legitimate industrial action to periods of enterprise bargaining, therefore restricting the ability of organised labour to pursue industrial action. The conservative Howard Government's *Workplace Relations Act 1996* placed further restrictions upon organised labour and extended the roll-back of Australia's historical system of centralised arbitration as embodied in the Australian Industrial Relations Commission (AIRC). The latter was achieved, as Teicher et al. (2006: 4) argue, by 'restricting its arbitral powers to 20 allowable matters' and through the roll-out of the new institutions of the Office of the Employment Advocate and Australian Workplace Agreements (AWAs), which enabled individual employment contracts outside of collective agreements and which 'marginalised' the AIRC. In 2005 the apogee of this process arrived in the form of

Workchoices, through the *Workplace Relations Amendment Act 2005*. *Workchoices* curtailed the legitimate activities of unions even further, introduced a broader range of penalties to be applied against unions, gave the relevant Minister greater discretionary power to intervene in industrial disputes and introduced a range of 'prohibited content' provisions relating to trade unions. It also removed restrictions upon employers by reducing the number of allowable award matters and introducing five minimum conditions to which AWAs had to adhere (Ellem 2006: 211–13; Cooper and Ellem 2008: 542–4). Such across the board changes to the regulations governing the employment relationship occurred alongside interventions by the state against the power of unions within specific industries, including construction, stevedoring and higher education.

Several scholars have noted the centrality of the state to the neoliberalisation of the Australian industrial relations system and therefore the unhelpful nature of the term 'deregulation' as a description of such processes. As Ellem argued in the context of *Workchoices*, 'Governments in Australia talk of the free market, deregulation, and now choice, but they act in highly interventionist and prescriptive ways' (Ellem 2006: 216). We are surely then best advised to conclude with Anderson that:

> Deregulation really means a market re-regulation to guarantee new and profitable markets to large corporations, and a social re-regulation to restrict the meaning of citizenship, where this conflicts with the delivery of profitable markets to large corporations. (Anderson 1999: 18)

Alongside such legislative changes that have restricted the rights of labour in a general sense, there are also several examples of government interventions designed to weaken or curtail the activities of specific unions. In 1989, for example, the Federal Labor government used the air force to break a strike being conducted by commercial air pilots. It was the longest continuous use of the military against unions in the country's history (Norrington 1990; Burgess and Sappey 1992). Importantly the targeted union was attempting to break free of the restraints imposed upon unions through the Accord agreement between the government and the peak trade union body, the Australian Council of Trade Unions (ACTU) – an agreement which facilitated the neoliberalisation of the Australian state and economy by locking in the trade union movement as partners in a process of neoliberal restructuring (Cahill 2008b: 325–9). In 1998, the Conservative Coalition government led by John Howard worked closely with employers in an attempt to destroy the power of the Maritime Union of Australia, one of the country's historically strong, left-wing, and more militant trade unions (Svensen 1998). Unionised stevedores were locked out of ports across Australia and replaced with non-union workers. Private security guards and police were used to enforce this lockout. It was the most significant industrial confrontation of the 11 years of Conservative government and only ended when the Federal Court ruled that the unionised workers had been dismissed unlawfully and therefore could return to work. However, upon doing so they were forced to accept more flexible working arrangements, thus extending the process of neoliberalisation. Other moves by the Conservative government to curtail the activities of specific unions included the creation of the Building Industry Task Force in 2002, with wide-ranging powers aimed at curtailing the rights of unionised workers in the construction industry, and the establishment of the Higher Education Workplace Relations Requirements, which tied universities' funding to their restriction of trade union rights and activities.

The Reagan Government also used coercive tactics against organised labour. The most obvious example of this was the Professional Air Traffic Controllers Organization (PATCO) dispute of 1981, in which the government confronted the union, sacking striking workers and gaoling its activists (Arnesen 2007: 1123–6). The effect of this dispute was not only to intimidate other unions from taking industrial action but also to legitimise the use of 'permanent replacements' for striking workers (Silvers and Slavkin 2009: 306). However, active coercion of organised labour by the Reagan administration was not limited to this high-profile confrontation. In what proved to be a more far-reaching episode, Reagan used Presidential appointment of anti-union activists to the National Labor Relations Board (NLRB) to restrict and coerce trade unions further, in a campaign of 'active regulatory constraint' (Farber and Western 2002: 392) against organised labour. Although, as Levy (1985: 270) points out, this campaign was 'carried out without any legislative change or rule making authority', it was nonetheless a process by which the state actively regulated organised labour and constituted in Levy's (1985: 269) words 'an unprecedented assault on this country's labor laws'. While the appearance of deregulation proper is given by the fact that the Board 'refrained almost entirely from using the powers it did have to address employer interference with workers rights under the National Labor Relations Act' (Silvers and Slavkin 2009: 306), this superficial appearance belies the many concrete rulings and decisions by the Board which reshaped the regulation of unions and labour relations during the Reagan era and beyond. Such rulings included the legitimation of employer surveillance and interrogation of, and retaliation for, workers' union activities (Levy 1985: 299).

In the mid-1980s, too, the Thatcher government in Britain used the coercive powers of the state, including the police and secret services, to undermine the powerful National Union of Miners (NUM). Not only did this enable the eventual privatisation of coal mines but, by defeating the NUM, Thatcher also weakened the broader labour movement, paving the way for further neoliberal measures (Harvey 2005: 59). As with other Anglo-Saxon neoliberal regimes, this occurred during 'a long period during which a succession of legal changes had greatly increased constraints on collective action and collective organisation' (Brown et al. 2000: 613). Moreover, the New Labour government which succeeded the Thatcher/Major regimes continued this process introducing new regulations which circumscribed the ability of workers to organise collectively even as they enacted some new protections for workers, including a national minimum wage and protection against dismissal for lawful strikers (Smith and Morton 2006: 402–11).

Recent state assaults upon civil liberties, undertaken in the name of the 'war on terror', provide further illustrations of the intimate links between neoliberalism and coercion. Most obviously, the US-led invasion of Iraq was an example of 'neoliberalism by other means' (Lafer 2004: 325). Invasion, and the deaths of what has been estimated at over 600,000 Iraqis (Burnham et al. 2006) enabled the US administration to neoliberalise the Iraqi state: 'public empoyees have lost their jobs and have seen their civil service rights undermined; state industries have been put on the auction block to be privatized; public subsidies have been cut; taxes cut or eliminated completely; and markets opened to foreign capital' (Lafer 2004: 327; see also Klein 2007: 325–82). Prior to the US invasion, significant state ownership of industry persisted in Iraq. As in Chile, it was only through ultra violence that a neoliberal programme of state and economic restructuring was enabled. Perhaps less obviously, the war on terror has been used to justify the expansion of neoliberal coercion within advanced capitalist countries. This is particularly noticeable in the USA, whereby under the pretext of securing the country from terrorist attack, the Bush administration further restricted the trade union rights of public sector workers (Lafer 2004).

Regulatory Unevenness

Despite widespread neoliberalisation during the last three decades, universalist and decommodified state institutions and services persisted. This further confounds the notion that the neoliberal era is simply about the diminution of the state and the rise of free markets. Decommodification entails quarantining services from market dependence. By providing services on a universalist basis, states ensure that the price mechanism is not the factor determining use. Both of these are clearly contrary to the normative neoliberal vision of market provision. Yet, such principles were evident across the advanced capitalist countries during the neo-liberal era. Perhaps the most common example of the persistence of universalist institutions is healthcare. Many OECD countries (including Australia, Britain, Sweden, France, New Zealand, Norway, Canada and Denmark) continued, during the neoliberal era, to fund healthcare systems based upon the principle of universal access (Thomson et al. 2010).

Moreover, welfare expenditure in the OECD countries increased as a share of GDP during the neoliberal era (Swank and Martin 2001). Indeed, it seems that increases to health and welfare expenditure largely drove the broader increase to state expenditure from the 1970s to the 1990s. Health and social welfare expenditures accounted for over 85 per cent of the increases to government expenditure as a proportion of GDP in the OECD nations between 1970 and 1997 (Sanz and Velázquez 2007: 917).

THE CONCEPT OF 'ACTUALLY EXISTING NEOLIBERALISM'

Clearly there are significant discrepancies between the normative vision of neoliberalism as an era of free markets and small states and the reality of neoliberalism in practice. It order to distinguish between the normative visions of neoliberal polemicists and the policy realities of the neoliberal era, it is useful to refer to the latter as 'actually existing neoliberalism'. The term captures the disjunction whereby:

> while neoliberalism aspires to create a 'utopia' of free markets liberated from all forms of state interference, it has in practice entailed a dramatic intensification of coercive, disciplinary forms of state intervention in order to impose market rule. (Brenner and Theodore 2002: 352)

It prompts recognition that neoliberal doctrine and neoliberal policy practices are not synonymous, and that the popular conception of neoliberalism as free markets mystifies the actual trajectory of state transformations during the last three decades.

The concept alludes to 'actually existing socialism', a concept developed by dissident Socialists during the cold war who wished to maintain their allegiance to the ideals of socialism, as expounded by Marx and

Engels, but who nonetheless viewed the regimes of Eastern Europe which carried the name socialism as a distortion of and unrepresentative of those ideals (Bahro 1977: 3). Those who used the term 'actually existing neoliberalism' are critical of both neoliberal ideas and policy practices, yet in order to have a clear-sighted analysis of neoliberalism wish to avoid reifying neoliberal ideas. The concept of actually existing neoliberalism recognises that the last 30 years of global history have not simply mirrored normative prescriptions of neoliberal polemicists about how societies and economies should be organised. To speak of actually existing neoliberalism is not to deny the correlations that, as has been demonstrated, do exist between neoliberal normative theory and the policy practices of capitalist states since the 1970s, limited though they are. Rather, the concept opens up the possibility of a more complex and nuanced appreciation of the messy, uneven and multicausal nature of political economic change.

As shall be discussed in the next chapter, part of the explanation for departures of actually existing neoliberalism from the normative prescriptions of neoliberal theory is the utopian character of neoliberal ideas. Put simply, they are largely unsuitable as detailed policy blueprints and make unrealistic assumptions about crucial elements of capitalist societies, their constitution and dynamics. However, another source of the discrepancy between normative neoliberal theory and actually existing neoliberalism is the nature of neoliberal change itself. As Peck and Tickell (2002) argue, actually existing neoliberalism 'should be understood as a process, not an "end state"' (p. 383). Neoliberalism, or 'neoliberalisation', is an ongoing process of institutional transformation, involving both destruction and reconstruction of regulatory architectures, and the overlaying of these upon existing institutions. Such a 'processual conception' (ibid.) helps to begin to explain not only the departure of neoliberal practices from utopian neoliberal discourses, but also the uneven character of neoliberal change. Such unevenness is highlighted, for example, in Fourcade-Gourinchas and Babb's (2002) study of the development of neoliberalism across four countries – Britain, Chile, Mexico and France – which suggests, in their words, two distinct 'routes' to neoliberalism. One, manifest in Britain and Chile was an '"ideological road" to neoliberalism' while the other was a 'pragmatic transition' as exemplified by the experiences of Mexico and France (Fourcade-Gourinchas and Babb 2002: 570). Both, they argue, were the product of the inherited institutional environments of those countries and the ways in which these mediated and shaped political agency. Similarly, Monica Prasad (2006) argues that different institutional environments explain different roads to neoliberalism. Others write of 'variegated neoliberalism' (Macartney 2011) and 'varieties of neoliberalism' (Cerny 2008). Each of these examples points to the difficulty, at best, of mapping neoliberal ideas onto actually existing neoliberal policies and institutional transformations.

Because processes of neoliberal transformation occur in real-world institutional environments, they are necessarily conditioned, enabled and limited by inherited political economic institutional environments. While one element of this process has been the 'roll-back' of such institutional environments and the 'roll-out' of new neoliberal forms of regulation (Peck and Tickell 2002: 384), the path-dependent nature of political economic institutions sometimes pushes against or mutates such projects. Although we might be able to identify a 'metalogic' (p. 383) of actually existing neoliberalism globally, contextualising processes of neoliberalisation helps explain the 'uneven geographical development' of neoliberalism (Harvey 2005) its uneven 'geography of state regulation' (Brenner and Theodore 2002: 356) and its uneven temporal development.

CONCLUSION

This chapter has demonstrated that the ideas-centred understanding of neoliberalism is fundamentally flawed because it erroneously assumes that the last four decades witnessed the realisation of the small-state normative agenda advocated by fundamentalist neoliberal intellectuals. While, at a very broad level of analysis, correlations certainly exist between neoliberal theory and practice, to focus on this level alone ignores the significant discrepancies between the role for the state as advocated by fundamentalist neoliberals and the trajectory of states in the neoliberal era. A more detailed analysis has revealed that states were transformed, not retrenched in the neoliberal era. Moreover, states were central to the roll-out and expanded reproduction of the neoliberal policy regime. The concept of 'actually existing neoliberalism' was introduced as a useful way of recognising the discrepancies between neoliberal theory and practice. This concept will be further elaborated in subsequent chapters, as part of a more detailed examination of the ways in which the neoliberal policy regime has become deeply embedded and entrenched in a particular set of institutional structures, class relations and ideological norms. It will be argued that this provides neoliberalism with significant inertia and durability. Before exploring the socially embedded nature of neoliberalism more fully, however, it is necessary to focus critical attention on the other key assumption underpinning the ideas-centred analysis of neoliberalism: that fundamentalist neoliberal intellectuals were the primary social force responsible for the neoliberal transformation of states and economies. This will allow for a 'clearing of the decks' of the more unhelpful assumptions characteristic of the dominant progressive accounts of neoliberalism and allow for a more thoroughgoing analysis of the relationship between neoliberal ideas and neoliberal policy regimes.

NOTE

1. All data is from Bortolotti and Siniscalco (2004: 1–4; 21–44).

3. Did neoliberal ideas create the neoliberal state and economy?

INTRODUCTION

Having interrogated the assumption that state policies in the neoliberal era were a reflection of the normative visions of fundamentalist neoliberal theorists, a critical gaze can now be turned to the assumption that the neoliberal transformation of capitalist states and economies from the 1970s was primarily due to the direct influence of fundamentalist neoliberal ideas. This assumption is widespread in discussions of neoliberalism among both scholars and journalists alike.

This chapter tests the validity of the idealist assumption that neoliberalism in practice was caused by the influence of neoliberal ideas – particularly by the influence of neoliberal think tanks and theorists. It begins by considering what substance there might be to this argument by examining the emergence of the source of fundamentalist neoliberal ideas and their proselytisation – the fundamentalist neoliberal movement, or 'thought collective'. It then discusses possible transmission mechanisms for such neoliberal ideas from the movement to policy makers. The chapter then considers a range of contrary evidence to the thesis of ideational causation, and argues that the evidence for the idealist assumption turns out to be quite slim. Finally, the chapter asks 'what was the influence of neoliberal ideas if not as blueprints for policy transformation?' and answers that they have been more influential as legitimating frameworks for neoliberal agendas than as the main forces driving such agendas.

ASSESSING IDEATIONAL CAUSATION

For the idealist thesis that neoliberal ideas drove the neoliberal policy revolution to hold weight, three conditions must be satisfied. First, it must be demonstrated that states and the way they regulate the economy came to resemble the normative prescriptions of neoliberal ideologies during the neoliberal era. Second, potential mechanisms must be identified for the transmission of neoliberal ideas from their proponents (fundamentalist neoliberal intellectuals and think tanks) to policy makers. Third, it must be demonstrated that such potential transmission mechanisms were activated – that such mechanisms influenced the conduct of policy makers in such a way that policy was shaped according to the normative ideas of neoliberal polemicists. Each of these conditions will be critically examined in turn. It will be argued that none of these conditions can be plausibly said to have operated with sufficient strength to support the thesis of ideational causation as the chief explanation for neoliberal policy change.

Correlations between Prescription and Practice

As noted in the previous chapter, there is at least a superficial correspondence between the normative prescriptions of the radical neoliberals and the major policy changes that swept capitalist states during the three decades prior to the global financial crisis. The radical neoliberals called publicly for the transfer of government activities to the private sector through policies of privatisation, deregulation and marketisation and indeed, from the 1970s onwards, states' policies increasingly came to resemble this agenda until such practices became the norm among political elites. Yet, as also noted in the previous chapter, a closer examination of the normative rhetoric of the radical neoliberals against the trajectories of most capitalist states also reveals significant discrepancies between the two. Most importantly, again as noted in the previous chapter, the size and scope of the state did not diminish during the neoliberal era. Indeed, in some areas the size and scope of the state actually increased, and there is evidence that neoliberal policies of privatisation and deregulation were, at least in part, responsible for this expansion.

These observations, in and of themselves, cast significant doubt upon claims that fundamentalist neoliberal ideas, or the neoliberal 'thought collective', drove the neoliberal policy revolution. For if the real world of state–economy relations did not come to resemble the ideal hoped for by the radical neoliberal intellectuals, then it seems difficult to sustain the argument that policy makers had come under the influence of neoliberal intellectuals and were essentially implementing their blueprints for change. This diminishes the case for fundamentalist neoliberal intellectuals being the primary driving force behind the major policy shift within capitalist states since the 1970s. For, if there is only a weak correlation between normative prescription and political economic change, then it is difficult to sustain the case that the former was responsible for the latter.

However, there is a possible objection to this line of reasoning. Some scholars argue that the proposition that radical neoliberals advocated a winding back of the state is false, and that the characterisation of neoliberal intellectuals and think tanks as advocates of small government is incorrect, but that fundamentalist neoliberal intellectuals were nonetheless widely influential over policy makers. If this argument is correct, then the apparent discrepancy between neoliberal theory and practice would prove to be a misnomer, as would the weak correlation between neoliberal theory and practice that has been outlined so far. If true, it bolsters the credibility of the idealist account of the rise of neoliberalism and undermines the central line of argument developed in this book.

It is therefore useful to tease out this line of reasoning in more detail. Such a position is put forcefully by Philip Mirowski (2009) in *The Road From Mont Pelerin: The Making of the Neoliberal Thought Collective*, his well-known book co-edited with Dieter Plehwe, as well as in his more recent book *Never Let a Serious Crisis go to Waste: How Neoliberalism Survived the Financial Meltdown*. Mirowski argues that fundamentalist neoliberal intellectuals were not really interested in winding back the state. Rather, while advocating a minimal state agenda in public, in private they were well aware of the need for a strong state to bring about an expansion of market rule, at the expense of democracy. This is Mirowski's concept of the '"double truth" doctrine: one truth for the masses/participants and another for those at the top' (Mirowski 2009: 426). Thus, according to Mirowski, there is no contradiction between neoliberal theory and practice:

> Apparently, one could reconcile oneself to live in a world where quantitatively more state apparat abided with quantitatively less slavery (or serfdom), which should quell the rather naïve hand-wringing one sometimes encounters, complaining that a quarter-century of neoliberal ascendancy has done little to reduce the size of the state, no matter how you choose to measure it. (Mirowski 2009: 441)

For Mirowski, then, those who question the influence of fundamentalist neoliberals based upon the lack of alignment between their advocacy and the policy practices of neoliberal governments mischaracterise the agenda of the fundamentalist neoliberals. According to this argument, evidence of a highly regulating neoliberal state, in which government expenditure was not retrenched, does nothing to discount the influence of fundamentalist neoliberal intellectuals. Rather, according to Mirowski, this was precisely what they intended.

It is worth examining this argument more closely, and to do so requires a more detailed discussion of the ideas of fundamentalist neoliberal intellectuals and the movement and think tanks through which they were proselytised. What were the key normative propositions of leading fundamentalist neoliberal intellectuals, Hayek and Friedman, and the dynamics and organisational elements of the movement through which neoliberal ideas were supposedly so influential? How well do they conform to the 'double truth' concept as put forward by Mirowski?

Fundamentalist neoliberal ideas have been proselytised primarily by a movement or 'thought collective' comprising mainly of professional intellectuals but also of some journalists, managers and owners of capital. Unlike the more traditional social movements, this neoliberal movement is drawn almost exclusively from elite social strata. Moreover, it is sustained by ongoing corporate support (Beder 2000; Cahill 2002; Krugman 2009: 10; Phillips-Fein 2009). As Dean (2012: 73) argues, it is a 'militant movement' with a 'frontal character', in the vanguard of the push to dismantle – primarily through privatisation, deregulation and marketisation – what they view as the collectivist consensus and institutions that had dominated political life during much of the twentieth century.

In this goal Hayek's (1944) *The Road to Serfdom* serves as a talisman. Dedicated 'To the Socialists of all Parties' it sounded a warning that the predilection for economic planning, so evident in 1944 when it was published, and when governments had mobilised economic resources fully for war, risked plunging democratic societies towards totalitarianism, irrespective of the political persuasion of the governing party. Mirowski and Plehwe's (2009) description of this movement as the 'neoliberal thought collective' is therefore apt, highlighting the contradiction of a movement defined by its antipathy towards collectivism but reliant upon the principles of collective organising to promote its message. Plehwe (2009: 4) outlines how the thought collective grew from its origins in the Mont Pelerin Society in the 1940s into a global 'network of organised neoliberal intellectuals … and a closely related network of neoliberal partisan think tanks' including the Heritage Foundation, Institute of Economic Affairs, The Fraser Institute and the Centre for Independent Studies. Such think tanks provide the organisational backbone for the global fundamentalist neoliberal intellectual movement.

Think tanks proved crucial to the more focused proselytisation of fundamentalist neoliberal ideas among policy makers, business leaders and journalists. Common proselytisation tactics deployed by think tanks include publication of journals and policy briefs, the organisation of seminars and public lectures, writing opinion pieces for major media, providing commentators for television and radio, devoting resources to getting think tank publications and events covered by the mainstream press, accepting positions in government or bureaucracy, granting former politicians or bureaucrats positions within think tanks, inviting policy makers to seminars and workshops and liaising with or lobbying politicians and other policy makers (Abelson 2002: 75–86).

Rather than generating significant new knowledge, neoliberal think tanks are 'second hand dealers in ideas' (Hayek 1949; Desai 1999). As Stone (2007: 72) argues, think tanks are adept at 'recycling' the ideas of others, 'translating dense ideas or abstract theory into sound bites for the media; blue prints for decision-makers; and understandable pamphlets and publications for the educated public'. They took the core propositions of intellectuals such as Hayek and Friedman and distilled them into simpler, often shorter discursive frames and used them to analyse contemporary policy issues. Edwin J. Feulner, President of the Heritage Foundation views his and other neoliberal think tanks as 'help[ing] to translate the works of academics into background papers, issues briefs, monographs, journal articles, congressional testimony and conference topics' (Feulner 1985: 24). According to Feulner (p. 24), Heritage would apply the 'briefcase test' to its publications – '[t]he study should be as brief as possible … we try to limit our Backgrounders to ten pages – a document which stands a much greater chance of being put into the briefcase and read *before* the debate than a book which generally ends up on a bookshelf'. Such brevity, according to Stone (2007), is built upon by 'repetition. The constant restatement of policy message via different formats and products – seminars, conferences, workshops, policy briefs, web-sites, books – broadcasts and amplifies policy research'.

In distilling the arguments of complex theorists into simple propositions and frames, neoliberal think tanks tend to adhere to the image of neoliberalism as represented by the idealist assumptions examined in previous chapters. Theirs was a call for reducing state spending and state regulation of the economy. It was an agenda that promoted the radical retrenchment of state provision and social protection through deregulation, privatisation and marketisation. The Heritage Foundation provides a useful illustration. Its publications are replete with titles espousing the small state agenda: 'Cutting the U.S. Budget Would Help the Economy Grow'; 'A Moral Case Against Big Government'; 'How to Roll Back the Administrative State'; and 'The New New Left: The Politics of Ever-Expanding Government' (Malanga 2006; Messmore 2007; Moffit 2011; Boccia 2013). A recent Heritage report offers a flavour of the small government rhetoric of the neoliberal thought collective:

> Government spending should be significantly reduced ... For most of America's history, the aggregate burden of government was below 10 percent of GDP. This level of government was consistent with the beliefs of America's founders. As the IMF has explained, 'classical economists and political philosophers generally advocated the minimal state – they saw the government's role as limited to national defense, police, and administration'. America's policy of limited government certainly was conducive to economic expansion. In the days before income tax and excessive government, America moved from agricultural poverty to middle-class prosperity.
>
> Reducing government to 10 percent of GDP might be a very optimistic target, but shrinking the size of government should be a major goal for policymakers. (Mitchell 2005)

Activists within the thought collective are also inspired by Hayek's call to 'train an army of fighters for freedom' (Cockett 1995: 104). Hence they also deploy discursive frames to discredit their opponents who they view as the 'new class' of tertiary educated professionals who benefit from an enlarged welfare state and use their privileged positions to attack the central values and institutions of the liberal civilisation (see Feulner 1985; Ehrenreich 1990; Cahill 2001, 2004; Blumenthal 2008). Neoliberal think tanks thereby cast progressives as 'special interests' and denigrate their legitimacy.

In all of this the neoliberal think tanks globally tended to exhibit a high degree of homogeneity. However, this should not obscure the very real differences that existed within the movement of neoliberal intellectuals, particularly among its leading theorists. When gathered privately, away from the public gaze, disagreements, arguments and fallings out were not uncommon. Most particularly, within the Mont Pelerin Society, the epicentre of the neoliberal intellectual movement, while discussion was 'mostly convivial' (Peck 2010: 51) there were also 'struggles and even purges' (Mirowski 2009: 418). Mises, for example, famously 'stormed out' of one meeting session of which Milton Friedman was chair and yelled 'You're all a bunch of Socialists' (Cockett 1994: 114). Furthermore, during the late 1950s and early 1960s the Society was consumed by internal conflict, which was partly due to issues of personality, partly to questions of tactics, with a minority favouring a more proselytising and advocacy role for the Society than was entailed in Hayek's preferred course of 'winning the battle of ideas'. This resulted in the resignation of several key members from the Society in 1961 (Hartwell 1995: 100–124).

Moreover, because it was a 'political movement informed by distinctive and sometimes contradictory, intellectual currents' (Paton 2012: 90) – including classical liberalism, libertarianism, neoclassical economics and the anti-rationalist Austrian economics – a degree of incoherence and tension was inevitable, manifesting in 'disparate attitudes about government, the role of markets, and the balance to be struck between economic freedom and political justice' (ibid.: 101). While there was often 'consensus on first principles' (Peck 2010: 51) and 'Mont Peleirn did eventually forge agreement on some fundamentals' (Mirowski 2009: 418), they 'were divided over the character of any positive neoliberal program' (Peck 2010: 53), and over appropriate limits upon the state.

Such differences are evident in the work of Friedman and Hayek, for example, and it is worth contrasting these different approaches in order to draw out the different conceptions of the proper role of the state in the economy which permeated the movement and which render problematic any simple story of ideational causation as an explanation of neoliberal change. Milton Friedman was probably the best known of all the fundamentalist neoliberal intellectuals and also the one who had the most direct involvement with key policy makers. Like other leading neoliberal intellectuals Friedman was well-known within the economics profession and achieved the highest honours of that discipline being awarded the Swedish Bank Prize for Economics in Memory of Alfred Nobel. Unlike other fundamentalist neoliberal intellectuals, however, Friedman was also a high-profile political and economic commentator during the 1970s and 1980s. Not only did he publish several bestselling neoliberal polemical tracts (including *Capitalism and Freedom* which has sold over 500,000 copies and has never been out of print since its first publication (van Horn and Mirowski 2009: 167)) he also had his own ten-part television series in 1980, *Free to Choose*, based upon the bestselling book co-authored with his wife Rose, and had a regular column in *Newsweek*. Much of his discourse therefore was targeted at a broad audience and indeed had quite a populist free market character.

Like other fundamentalist neoliberals, Friedman argued that markets are the most efficient way to organise society, preserve individual freedom and unleash the creative powers of individuals, thus facilitating human progress (Friedman 2002: 2–3). His was an elaboration of the foundational principles of neoclassical economics and their application to normative questions. According to Friedman, markets protected individual freedom by limiting concentrations of power and in allowing for the satisfaction of the multitude of individual preferences existing within society at any given time (Friedman 2002: 15). Friedman's ideal society, then, was one based upon free markets.

Friedman was quite clear that government needed to be limited and restrained in order for his ideal free market system to be attained. Such limits applied to both the economic size and the regulatory scope of government. Friedman argued that the role of government should be limited to three functions: the construction, maintenance and enforcement of a system of rules that would allow markets to operate; the provision of services in a very limited range of circumstances where technical monopolies or 'neighbourhood effects' prevailed; and on paternalistic grounds to protect 'non-responsible individuals', such as children and the insane who were not able to recognise and act upon their own preferences (Friedman 2002: 33–4). While there is of course a degree of ambiguity as to what the proper size of the state should be when one allows for the state to provide services in the presence of technical monopolies and neighbourhood effects, Friedman was quite clear that his normative vision entailed a significant cut to the economic size of government. An indication of this can be gleaned from *Capitalism and Freedom* in which Friedman (2002: 35–6) argues that his ideal government 'would have clearly limited functions and would refrain from a host of activities that are now undertaken by Federal and State governments in the United States, and their counterparts in other Western countries', and proceeds to list 'some activities currently undertaken by government in the US, that cannot, so far as I can see, validly be justified', including price controls, tariffs, quotas, controls on outputs, rent controls, minimum wage rates, interest rate ceilings, 'detailed regulation of industries', state control of radio and television, social security, occupational licensing, public housing, conscription, national parks and toll roads, but adds that '[t]his list is far from comprehensive'. Not only did he pioneer the advocacy of policies of deregulation, privatisation and vouchers (Friedman 2002: 89–99), he also argued that a free society was one in which the size of government had been limited to about 12 per cent of GDP (Friedman n.d.). Indeed, at the height of the neoliberal era, Friedman would argue that the major capitalist economies still embodied the principle of 'creeping or stagnant socialism' (Friedman 2002: viii) because state expenditure had not been retrenched to his preferred level. Friedman also pioneered the doctrine of monetarism, arguing that central banks should target the quantity of money in an economy, rather than the exchange rate, interest rates, or even the price level, and have as their aim a steady increase in the supply of money (Friedman 1968). Moreover, he called for the development of rules for the conduct of monetary policy which would remove policy discretion from monetary authorities (Friedman 2002: 51–5).

Overall then, while Friedman certainly saw an ongoing role for government in bringing about his desired free market utopia, this was unambiguously a limited role entailing a quantitative reduction in government spending and the wide ranging transfer of government functions to the private sector. Where government was allowed to operate, it was to be strictly controlled by rules.

This vision stands in contrast to that of Hayek who, although sharing broadly similar conceptual foundations to Friedman, potentially justified a much more expansive role for the state in regulating the economy. A brief examination of Hayek's views of the role of the state in *The Constitution of Liberty* serves to illustrate this point. For Hayek, the good society is one measured against a negative conception of liberty 'in which coercion of some by others is reduced as much as is possible' (Hayek 2009: 11). The best way of achieving this state of liberty, according to Hayek, is by allowing humans to interact voluntarily. Because markets enable people to secure their interests through voluntary interaction, Hayek argues that markets are the most appropriate way of arranging human affairs. In general, the role for the state in such a liberal order is to provide the rule of law which protects 'the known private spheres of the individuals against interference by others and delimiting these private spheres' (Hayek 2009: 20). The rule of law also provides legal frameworks to underpin the operation of markets, such as the enforcement of contracts and the ability to 'own and acquire property' (p. 19). Hayek admits that state coercion of individuals is inevitable, but argues that this should be limited 'to instances where it is required to prevent coercion by private persons' (p. 20). So far, this resembles the basic normative proposition recognisable from the publications of neo-liberal think tanks.

However, Hayek also allows for a potentially much greater role for the state than is suggested by the 'freedom from coercion' principle. He argues that so long as state-coercive rules are 'known general rules', widely understood and not applicable to particular classes of individual, then they are permissible. In this case, coercion is justified because the individual is able to predict that certain types of action will lead to coercive responses by the state and therefore 'the individual never need by coerced unless he has placed himself in a position where he knows that he will be coerced' (Hayek 2009: 20). Yet, one can imagine many types of state regulation that might constitute 'known rules' and yet would contravene an indivudual's 'free action', which 'presupposes the existence of a known sphere in which the circumstances cannot be so shaped by another person so as to leave one only that choice prescribed by the other' (Hayek 2009: 19). Thus begins the process whereby *The Constitution of Liberty* legitimates a host of seemingly illiberal state activities. Indeed, Hayek (p. 190) allows that '[e]ven the most fundamental principles of a free society, however, may have to be temporarily sacrificed when, but only when, it is a question of preserving liberty in the long run, as in the case of war'.

Moreover, Hayek (2009: 202) argues against the principle of *laissez-faire* as a guiding doctrine of government. Because markets are the best mechanisms for allowing individuals to pursue their own interests, a host of government measures might be appropriate to provide an environment in which markets, and hence liberty, can flourish. While he is opposed to 'all controls of prices and quantities' (p. 200), as well as government monopolies (p. 196), he concludes that 'it is the character, rather than the volume of government activity that is important' (p. 194). Clearly, this is significantly different to the normative agenda advocated by Friedman.

Citing Adam Smith, Hayek argues that government might have a legitimate role in providing a range of 'public amenities' that are clearly in the 'interest of all' but which private enterprise would not find it profitable to undertake (Hayek 2009: 196, 226). Nonetheless, he also argues that these are best provided by local rather than national authorities, and has a general preference for decentralised forms of government and against supra-national bodies (pp. 226, 229–30). Hayek reserves some of his strongest criticisms for trade unions, and what he describes as their powers to coerce other workers (p. 235). However, he also argues that, were these powers to be rescinded (through the imposition of voluntary unionism, for example), 'the coercion of employers would lose most of its objectionable character' (ibid.). While he believes that workers in some occupations should be prohibited from striking, he also says that in general, '[n]either the right of voluntary agreement between workers nor even their right to withhold their services in concert is in question (ibid.).

What emerges then is a normative agenda somewhat at odds with the characterisations of neoliberalism, by idealist critics, as a doctrine of *laissez-faire*. But it also differs from the rather rigid and dogmatic formulations of the neoliberal think tanks, which generally advocated simply reducing regulation and government expenditure. Hayek's work is much less a policy blueprint (other than his preferred system of taxation, where he favoured a flat rate that mirrored the rate of government expenditure as a proportion of total economic activity (Hayek 2009: 280)) than a general philosophy, but one that is flexible enough to allow for so many extraordinary circumstances in which state activity is legitimate as to justify all manner of state forms, so long as they support the capitalist organisation of society. Certainly they differed from the view that the size and scope should simply be reduced, however, as Keynes perceptively noted to Hayek '[y]ou agree that the line has to be drawn somewhere [regarding the scope of the state], and that the logical extreme is not possible. But you give us no guidance whatsoever as to where to draw it' (in Peck 2010: 48).

In their most public manifestation, then – the proselytising activities of the think tanks – the neoliberals tended to be quite coherent in their policy advocacy of, and normative commitments to, reducing the size and scope of government within the economy. Moreover, such a position was consistent with the most high-profile and publicly visible of the fundamentalist neoliberal intellectuals, Milton Friedman. However, there are clearly differences between the normative visions of Friedman and Hayek regarding the proper role and scope and size of the state. Behind closed doors, within the invite only confines of forums such as Mont Pelerin, disagreement and difference was not uncommon. In this sense Mirowski is correct to describe a neoliberal 'double truth' – 'one truth for the masses/participants and another for those at the top' (Mirowski 2009: 426).

However, it is quite misleading to claim, as Mirowski does, that this double truth was primarily strategic – a deliberate plot by the neoliberals to deceive the public as to their true intentions which were to impose by subterfuge an enlarged state supporting market rule. Certainly there was a strategic element to the rhetoric of neoliberal think tanks. Feulner's admissions, quoted earlier, demonstrate the think tanks were aware that to influence political debate required the ideas of neoliberal theorists to be selectively appropriated and framed in ways that gave them greatest appeal and resonated with public values. This certainly means that the subtleties and nuances characteristic of some of the more complex neoliberal theorists, such as Hayek, are rarely represented in the public discourse of the think tanks. Nonetheless, this need not lead to the conclusion that those who met secretly through the Mont Pelerin Society were in agreement that an expanded form of state would be necessary in order to guarantee the kinds of market freedoms they wished to see. Rather, within the neoliberal movement there were disagreements about the proper role of the state, which existed alongside some shared commitments to fundamental principles as well as a broad anti-collectivist vision that processes which extended market provision were desirable.

The biggest problem with Mirowski's position is that for the 'double-truth' argument to hold requires the operation of an extraordinary conspiracy. It requires a sustained disciplined approach by intellectuals to deliberately engage in propaganda in public, while flatly contradicting such public pronouncements in private. Indeed, Mirowski suggests that Hayek deliberately set out to deceive the public as to the ambitions of the neoliberal thought collective:

> Hayek hit upon the brilliant notion of developing the 'double truth' doctrine of neoliberalism – namely, an elite would be tutored to understand the deliciously transgressive Schmittian necessity of repressing democracy, while the masses would be regaled with ripping tales of 'rolling back the nanny state' and being set 'free to choose' – by convening a closed Leninist organisation of counter-intellectuals. (Mirowski 2009: 444–5)

One can readily concede that the fundamentalist neoliberals were aware of the need to tailor their messages to a broad public. Indeed, the quotes earlier from Feulner bear out this point. However, Mirowski's 'double truth' argument assumes the existence of a sustained deception whereby aspirations expressed in private discussions are knowingly far removed from those expressed in public. While this is theoretically possible, its plausibility in practice must surely be questioned. Such a line of reasoning shares the weakness with Naomi Klein's 'Shock Doctrine' thesis in that it 'imbues neoliberal policies with a strategic coherence they never possessed in practice' (Davidson 2010: 16). The plausibility of the 'double truth' argument is further undermined by the passion with which the neoliberal fundamentalists put their normative commitments to winding back the state to a minimal level – which suggests a deeply held commitment to such ideals rather than a merely pragmatic commitment to them for the purposes of public propaganda.

For the 'double truth' argument to hold also requires that the influence of the neoliberal movement proceeded primarily from the invitation-only, closed-door discussions of Mont Pelerin and other semi-clandestine associations, with the massive and more substantial public output of think tanks being merely smokescreens and ideological cover for the main game which was the insinuation of secretive ideas into networks of power. One must ask the question: why would think tanks pour so many of their resources into producing publications and giving speeches which were *not* designed to influence public policy? Indeed, the double truth doctrine falls down when it is realised that much of the output of neoliberal think tanks was aimed at policy makers, not the general public. What is one to make, for example, of the Heritage Foundation's well-known and elaborate *Mandate for Leadership* series of publications which were produced with the hope of guiding the policy of the Reagan administration and which highlighted 'the crisis of overregulation' (Hinish, Jr 1981: 697)? This project was framed as an assault upon the US 'nanny state' with the professed aim of reducing its size and denuding its regulatory scope. Yet Mirowski and others would have us believe that all this is a mere smokescreen for behind-closed-door discussions between the neoliberal fundamentalists and policy makers.

The final problem with the 'double truth' type of argument is it is able to explain virtually all policy developments during the neoliberal era as manifestations of the neoliberal thought collective conspiracy – including policies which quarantine people from markets and thus contradict the spirit of neoliberal prescriptions. It is not clear, for example, why the persistence of some universalist institutions – such as the NHS in Britain – which is a feature of the neoliberal era, is not attributable to the far-sighted manipulations of the neoliberal collective in trying to establish the legitimacy of the neoliberal project by leaving intact popular pre-neoliberal institutions, thereby preserving social harmony. To put the objection another way, it is not clear by what criteria Mirowski would judge that neoliberal ideas were not influential. Which institutions are neoliberal and which not? According to the 'double truth' concept, everything could be attributable to the neoliberal thought collective and neoliberalism is everywhere.

One can readily see how this weakness of the double-truth argument speaks to a key element of Hayek's normative theories. Ultimately, Hayek's view of the proper role of the state is ambiguous. It is not at all clear, from Hayek's published work, what he thought the proper size or scope of the state should be. Indeed, for Hayek, these were highly flexible variables. Hayek's ideas were thus amenable to appropriation to justify a range of state types and state activities. This renders somewhat problematic the idea that Hayek's views on the state were responsible, for example, for the neoliberalism of the Pinochet regime in Chile. While Hayek's writings could certainly be selectively appropriated and used as justification, the notion that Hayek's ideas were responsible for the Pinochet regime's economic policies is problematic if only because Hayek's ideas are plural and ambiguous and could plausibly justify all sorts of contradictory types of state and regime (and helps explain Hayek's own justification of the Pinochet regime (see Mirowski 2009: 446)). Beyond the few specific policy proposals put forward by Hayek, Hayek's normative agenda is thus not amenable to having its direct causal influence tested. Rather, as will be examined in more detail in Chapter 7, ambiguities, flexibilities, lacunae and inconsistencies in Hayek's work point to the broader ideological nature of neoliberal doctrine – at once adaptable and malleable, yet also coherent and forceful. At root it was a doctrine that played to the interests of owners and managers of capital. And the ambiguity of the role of the state allowed neoliberal doctrine to be deployed to justify a variety of different arrangements of the institution with the monopoly over the means of violence necessary to enforce the prerogatives of capital that were privileged by the foundational heart of neoliberal doctrine.

Therefore, the argument that neoliberal ideas in essence entailed the advocacy, in private, of the imposition of state-led market rule, and that this drove the neoliberal policy agenda, seems implausible. Although the double-truth concept does capture certain important aspects of the neoliberal thought collective – namely that there are contradictions within neoliberal thought regarding the role of the state and that there was plurality and argument among the neoliberal thought collective behind closed doors, while they often demonstrated considerable solidarity in public – these are much more useful in understanding the ideological aspect of neoliberal ideas, discussed in Chapter 7, than in demonstrating the strong causative role of neoliberal ideas in the roll-out of neoliberal policy. While neoliberal doctrines are certainly able to be deployed selectively to justify neoliberal policy regimes, even when such regimes were a long way from the small state ideal, it would be wrong to assume that they therefore acted as blueprints that guided such changes. On the one hand, it is clear that the broad thrust of neoliberal fundamentalist discourse was for a smaller state, with less regulation. On the other hand, those aspects of fundamentalist neoliberal discourse that allowed for a broader range of state functions in implementing neoliberalism, such as the intellectual work of Hayek, offered, as Keynes noted, little guidance as to where to draw the line between acceptable and unacceptable state regulation, size and scope.

Transmission Mechanisms from the Neoliberal Movement to Policy Makers

Having demonstrated the weak correlations that exist at anything other than a very broad level of generalisation between the normative prescriptions of neoliberal theorists and the actual policy practices of neoliberal states, it is now worth turning attention to the second condition that needs to be satisfied for the idealist thesis of neoliberal policy change to be considered plausible: the existence of mechanisms enabling the transmission of neoliberal ideas from their originators to policy makers, and the activation of such mechanisms.

A key assumption of ideas-centred accounts of the rise of neoliberalism is that, during the 1970s–1990s, policy makers became captured by the ideas of fundamentalist neoliberals and this explains the neoliberal trend of policy across the capitalist world. Therefore, in evaluating the idealist proposition that fundamentalist neoliberal ideas drove the neoliberal policy transformation, we must determine whether there were identifiable channels of influence from the neoliberal movement to policy makers that were responsible for the implementation of neoliberal policy.

It is relatively easy to identify potential transmission mechanisms from neoliberal intellectuals and think tanks to policy makers. The literature on the rise of think tanks and the new right provides many examples, whether it be tutelage of policy makers by key neoliberal intellectuals, involvement of policy makers in neoliberal forums, policy makers hosting visits by neoliberal intellectuals, or active involvement of fundamentalist neoliberals in policy networks. Typically, in idealist accounts, the existence of potential transmission mechanisms is assumed to be sufficient to deduce the operation of causation. That is, in such accounts, rather than demonstrating the existence of ideational causation, it is often enough to identify potential transmission mechanisms for ideational causation to be assumed to exist. However, as Stone (1996: 683) cautions in the case of Britain:

> Even if leaders such as Margaret Thatcher were known to consult think-tank documents or that the Fabians and IPPR have the ear of Tony Blair, it is a quite different thing to say that think-tank policy recommendations become policy-decisions.

The assumption by ideas-centred theorists and commentators that the existence of causation can be inferred from the presence of potential mechanisms for the transmission of neoliberal ideas usually takes either one of two forms. The first is to identify, describe and analyse the highly organised nature of the neoliberal thought collective and, from this, simply infer that, given the broad correlation between neoliberal theory and practice, the former drove the latter. The second is to identify organisational or personal links between neoliberal intellectuals or think tanks and neoliberal policy makers and then to assume that these links enabled the neoliberals to influence policy makers. Typically there is a presumption that ideas drive policy, but not its demonstration. As Ganev (2005: 364) argues, to move beyond assumptions about the forces driving neoliberalism, to a more plausible, evidence-based account: '[idealists] have to explain why the ideas in question mattered so much and to specify the mechanisms whereby these ideas shaped both policy making and policy implementation'.

Useful warnings against simple stories of ideational causation are, interestingly, provided by some of the leading pioneers of two recent research programmes that have put ideational approaches back on the intellectual agenda of the social sciences more broadly: constructivism and performativity. While the constructivist tradition has been deservedly criticised for a tendency to 'overemphasise' (Marsh 2009: 680) ideas as the determinant of political change, it does nonetheless offer useful self-reflections on the difficulties of demonstrating ideational causation. Vivien Schmidt (2011: 55), for example, warns of shortcomings in the family of ideational approaches to which those examined here belong: 'The most popular theories of ideational change, those that focus on paradigm shifts, are arguably the most problematic; they fail to specify closely enough the process of ideational change, that is, how old ideas fail and new ideas come to the fore', and that 'establishing causality with respect to ideas and discourse can be problematic … the question of causality is an empirical one of showing when ideas and discourse matter and when they don't' (ibid.: 61–2). This problem of causation is also recognised by Donald MacKenzie, a pioneer of performativity studies, the focus of which is the creation, or 'performance' by economic ideas of the world they describe. He argues the causative power of ideas is impossible to prove. Correlation does not imply causation 'because the change could have taken place for reasons other than the effects of the use of the theory or model' (MacKenzie 2006: 21).

Such observations suggest avenues for scrutinising the assumptions underpinning ideational accounts of the rise of neoliberalism. First, correlations between normative ideas prescribing particular policies, and actual changes to policy are necessary, but not sufficient, conditions to demonstrate ideational causation. The possibility that 'the change could have taken place for reasons other than the effects of the use of the theory or model' must be considered. Second, where correlations between normative prescription and policy practices can be established, it is then necessary to specify 'the process of ideational change' – what mechanisms for transferring ideas to policy makers existed, and were these activated? Moreover, if fundamentalist neoliberal ideas were influential, it is important to specify how such ideas mattered (Mehta 2011: 25).

Therefore, if the ideational thesis of neoliberal policy change is to be plausible, it is not sufficient simply to demonstrate that there were close personal and institutional links between the neoliberal movement and policy makers. It must be demonstrated that such linkages resulted in policy makers being influenced by the neoliberal movement in such a way that they changed their policy preferences and agendas to mirror those being advocated by the neoliberal movement. However, as was noted earlier, theses of neoliberal ideational causation typically take for granted and assume rather than demonstrate the existence of such influence. This leads such ideational arguments to miss the incomplete nature of the linkages and transmission mechanisms between the neoliberal movement and policy makers in the neoliberal era.

The relationship between Milton Friedman and successive administrations in the USA provides a case in point. As an adviser to Presidents Nixon and Reagan (Cato Institute n.d.), there is clearly a mechanism by which Friedman was potentially able to exert significant influence over both presidents and their administrations more generally. Indeed, idealist accounts of neoliberalism typically assume that such close relationships translated into direct policy influence. However, it is relatively easy to find examples that paint a contrary picture and closer scrutiny of the evidence suggests that the reality was much less clear cut than idealist arguments would suggest. For example, Nixon chose to implement extensive price controls within the US economy, contrary to the wishes of Friedman (Friedman 2000: 245–6). Indeed, Friedman (2000: 244) describes Nixon as 'the most socialist of the presidents of the United States in the 20th century'. It was not until the presidency of Democrat Jimmy Carter that the process of internal economic deregulation began, with the deregulation of the airline industry (Yergin and Stanislaw 1998: 344–5), yet Friedman was not a confidant of, nor adviser to, Carter. With respect to the Reagan presidency, it is certainly true that Reagan was known for his small government rhetoric. Indeed, his policy discourse mirrored in many respects that of the neoliberal think tanks and he implemented an extensive programme of deregulation while Friedman was his adviser (Friedman 2000: 248). However government deficits expanded under Reagan's watch (Heclo 2008: 559) and protectionist measures were extended (Richman 1998) both contrary to the small government and free trade ideals of Friedman. This led Friedman to accuse the Reagan administration, publicly in his *Newsweek* columns, of 'hypocrisy' and 'schizophrenia'. As Peck (2010: 115) notes, even though Friedman would later write that 'no other president in my lifetime [came] close to Reagan in adherence to clearly specified principles dedicated to promoting and maintaining a free society', Friedman also 'expected so much of the Reagan administration, only to be disappointed' (ibid.).

Moreover, although the Federal Reserve between 1979 and 1982, in shifting its policy orientation to targeting the money supply, came to be associated with the doctrine of monetarism as expounded by Milton Friedman, the actual influence of Friedman upon this shift seems minor, at best. While Konings (2011: 132) is certainly correct to argue that the monetarism of the Federal Reserve 'never functioned in textbook fashion', to the extent that the Fed Reserve did become monetarist during this period, this was primarily the result of the Fed Reserve chairman, Paul Volcker, as well as other board and staff members pursuing a pragmatic monetary policy strategy, the goal of which was to dramatically lower inflation (Konings 2011: 134; Krippner 2011: 116–17). Volcker had a rocky relationship with Friedman who was critical of the Fed chair (Silber 2012: 231). He was wary of Friedman's fundamentalist doctrines, believing them to be unsuited to the realities of policy making, stating 'my own support for the use of monetary "targets" does not start from a "monetarist" perspective' (ibid.: 163).

What does this tell us about the influence of fundamentalist neoliberal ideas over policy? At the very least it demonstrates that the reality of policy making is much more complex and uneven than the fairly simple, linear, and 'uni dimensional' (Marsh 1995) accounts of ideational causation seem to assume. Moreover, it suggests that it is difficult to sustain the argument that fundamentalist neoliberal ideas and intellectuals drove the neoliberal policy transformation. This bears out the findings of several detailed studies of think tank influence. Hames and Feasey (1994: 229) for example question whether activists from the neoliberal think tanks in the USA, who were institutionally incorporated at various levels into the Reagan administration, actually used these positions to pursue radical neoliberal policies:

> The vast majority of the senior appointees [to the Reagan administration] came from the policy celebrities hired by the think tanks in the 1970s. It is unclear to what extent such individuals took with them the agenda of their home think tank or whether, instead, they took their own particular views and expertise on the individual area they were appointed in. (Hames and Feasey 1994: 229)

Turner makes a similar claim about neoliberal intellectuals in positions of political power more generally: 'Whilst neo-liberal intellectuals were attempting to reconstruct policy agendas to create a new "liberal" utopia, neo-liberal politicians on the New Right were less willing to implement such extreme measures' (Turner 2008: 217).

Many echo Stone's conclusion that: 'despite anecdotal accounts, there is very little evidence that think-tanks have direct impact on the policy and legislative processes' (Stone 1996: 683). Hames and Feasey, for example, in their analysis of the relationship between think tanks and the Reagan and Thatcher governments found that: 'if influence means providing specific examples of public policy than can solely or even predominately be shown as the responsibility of the think tanks, then wild claims for think tank influence should be muted' (Hames and Feasey 1994: 227). They argue that 'In the final analysis few observers could deny that the role of think tanks in the policy construction of both Reagan and Thatcher was modest' (p. 228) and that 'the number of public policies and laws that can be placed at the door of think tanks is so small. There is virtually no example of any legislation on either side of the Atlantic that was entirely and uniquely due to one individual think tank' (p. 232). Denham and Garnett's analysis of the relationship between neoliberal think tanks and the Thatcher government confirms this perspective. They contend that, although close relationships were evident between neoliberal think tanks and the Thatcher government, there is little evidence that the think tanks drove the neoliberal transformation of British policy during the late 1970s and 1980s: 'the record of the New Right groups in the 1980s is ... disappointing, given the opportunities for access which apparently existed' (Denham and Garnett 1996: 52). They go on to argue that: 'many of their ideas got no further than the pamphlet stage. Education vouchers, negative income tax and prohibition of strikes in essential public services were all endorsed by the "think tanks", but were rejected by responsible ministers' (p. 53).

There is thus evidence to suggest that the existence of close personal and institutional linkages between neoliberal intellectuals and policy makers does not explain the neoliberal turn in policy making, even in the case of the governments of Reagan and Thatcher who made little secret of their affinities with the leading lights of the fundamentalist neoliberal movement and its think tanks. However, in assessing the idealist thesis of neoliberal policy change, it should also be investigated whether there were examples of governments which implemented agendas of neoliberal policy change, but which had little contact with, or antipathy to, the fundamentalist neoliberal movement, its intellectuals and its think tanks. The existence of such examples would constitute more evidence against the idealist thesis of neoliberal policy change as it would mean that the crucial transmission mechanism for neoliberal ideas from think tank to policy maker did not exist.

One such example is to be found during the period from 1983 to 1996 in Australia when successive Labor governments implemented a far-reaching neoliberal transformation of the state and economy. During this period major public utilities were privatised or corporatised, company tax and the top marginal income tax rates were reduced, marketisation was extended into key areas of public welfare provision, the currency was floated in 1983 and the central bank moved towards a policy of inflation targeting, and an extensive programme of deregulation was implemented touching most industries within the economy. As Pierson (2002: 184) notes, 'all of this helped to establish the reputation of the ALP under Hawke and Keating as the first neoliberal Labour government' – indeed they were among the first neoliberal governments globally, existing contemporaneously with the better-known regimes of Reagan and Thatcher.

However, unlike the Thatcher and Reagan regimes, senior figures in the Labor government and Labor Party were publically hostile towards the think tanks, and often cast them in vitriolic terms through the media. For example, Prime Minister Hawke labelled one of the more prominent fundamentalist neoliberal groups, the H R Nicholls Society, 'troglodytes and lunatics' (Taylor and Hewett 1986: 1). Senior Government Minister John Dawkins described the 'new right' (essentially a synonym for the neoliberal think tanks) as 'treasonous' (Hywood and Taylor 1986: 4). Labor National President and Special Minister for State, Mick Young, implored the party to put aside its differences and unite against the common enemy in the form of the 'new right' (Taylor 1986: 1). Young claimed the new right stood for 'busting the unions and busting the welfare net' (Steketee 1986: 1) that is, if the neoliberal agenda of the think tanks was implemented it would destroy those egalitarian institutions at the core of Labor's commitments.

Former Labor MP, Stephen Martin (2003), recalls that:

> at different times ministers in the parliament would refer to comments made by people associated with those different [neoliberal] organisations and use it to make political points about where they were wrong. And in debates you would often hear MPs refer to individuals associated with those organisations and declare where they thought the organisations and their philosophies were wrong.[1]

Such public hostility is hardly surprising. The fundamentalist neoliberal groups in Australia made no secret that one of their central aims was to undermine the power of trade unions and dismantle the institutions which gave them legitimacy, most important of which was the industrial relations arbitration system. Such claims were a direct threat to the material foundations of the Labor party which governed at a Federal level during this period. Trade unions provided a significant proportion of Party funds, and the history of the two institutions were intertwined. This meant that the fundamentalist neoliberal think tanks were only able to gain limited traction for their ideas among government ministers a handful of whom were sympathetic and retained close relationships with the think tanks.

However the lack of access by the think tanks to key decision makers extended beyond elected members of Parliament. Several key senior bureaucrats and advisers of the time argue that the neoliberal think tanks played a marginal role, at best, in the policy development and execution of the public service under Labor. Senior bureaucrat under successive Labor Governments, Michael Keating, for example, argues that the neoliberal think tanks 'had little influence. I doubt that most politicians in the Labor Government had ever read them and I doubt many senior bureaucrats ever read them'.[2] Ross Garnaut, former economic adviser to Labor Prime Minister Bob Hawke, says of the neoliberal think tanks: 'They weren't very central to the story [of economic change]'.[3]

All of this is further evidence which undermines the plausibility of the assumption that it was the influence of fundamentalist neoliberal intellectuals and ideas that it was primarily responsible for the neoliberal policy transformation in capitalist economies from the 1970s onwards. On the one hand, some of the early steps down the neoliberal policy path by an ostensibly social democratic government in the 1980s and 1990s, seems to have been undertaken without the existence of identifiable channels for the fundamentalist neoliberals to wield significant influence over policy makers. On the other hand, where potential channels of influence existed, for example during the Reagan administration, it would seem these were often not able to be used to shape policies according to the normative prescriptions of the fundamentalist neoliberal vision of how states and economies should be organised, except in a very general sense. Even when fundamentalist neoliberal activists were in positions of potential policy influence, they did not always implement the policy prescriptions of the fundamentalist neoliberal movement. That is, fundamentalist neoliberals did not always act strictly according to their fundamentalist neoliberal ideas. Moreover, policy makers often did not act on the advice of fundamentalist neoliberals when that advice was to implement the blueprint of fundamentalist neoliberalism.

This should, perhaps, not be surprising, given the character of fundamentalist neoliberal discourse. Particularly with respect to the output of think tanks, and the public arguments put by Milton Friedman, the fundamentalist neoliberals tended to be uncompromising in their advocacy of a utopian form of economic organisation which was, in many respects, radically different from what prevailed at the time. Because of this, it was largely unsuited to the realities of policy making in capitalist states. Denham and Garnett (1996: 53) argue that:

> the disappointment of the free-market zealots points to a surprising failure of their own: a tendency to overlook the pressures of public office, which prevent the full-blooded pursuit of ideological purity. Given that 'think tank' enthusiasm for economic liberal measures was so narrowly shared, one cannot wonder that the Prime Minister was initially reluctant to follow their ideas very closely.

Desai makes a similar point:

it is important to note also that from the think-tanks' own perspective, there were significant slips and shortfalls between their ambitions and their eventual role in Thatcherism and the Thatcher governments ... within Mrs Thatcher's first few years in office it became clear that their theories and proposals were far from the overriding consideration before the government: that political and electoral convenience remained very important – too much so for the taste of the more zealous members of the think-tanks. (Desai 1999: 60)

Marsh points to the Thatcher government's 'strategic political judgements about electoral prospects' (Marsh 1995: 607) which led it, more often than not to 'pragmatic rather than ideological' (p. 606) approaches to policy. This accords with the observations of some policy makers regarding the influence of ideas and think tanks. Robert Reich (in Davidson 2010: 25–6), for example, claims:

To many critics, the last two decades of the twentieth century were the age of a manic 'neo-liberalism' imposed by ideological fanatics on a reluctant world. This picture is false. The change in politics was, with very few exceptions, introduced by pragmatic politicians in response to experience.

Meanwhile, Eric Roll (in Kandiah and Seldon 1996: 193–4) reinforces the general anti-idealist perspective:

When you are sitting in the Treasury, whether you are the Chancellor or a junior minister, or whether you are the Permanent Secretary or the adviser, the problems do not present themselves day in day out as a choice between, let us say, Hayek or Keynes. They present themselves in quite specific decisions that have to be taken fairly quickly ... You have to deal with these realities, which cannot be dealt with or resolved just on the basis of broad principles.

The evidence presented here suggests that neoliberal changes, to deploy MacKenzie's phrasing, 'could have taken place for reasons other than the effects of the use of the [fundamentalist neoliberal] theory or model'. However, it also gives consideration as to whether fundamentalist neoliberal ideas did, in fact, play a significant role in the neoliberal transformation of states and economies, even if their direct influence over the formulation of policy was limited.

WHAT WAS THE ROLE OF NEOLIBERAL IDEAS IN THE RISE OF NEOLIBERALISM?

It need not be inferred from the previous discussion that neoliberal intellectuals played *no* role in the implementation of deregulation, privatisation and marketisation. Indeed, it seems plausible to suggest that fundamentalist neoliberal ideas had a significant causal influence over policy in *some* cases. Even those studies of think tanks that cast doubt upon the claims that neoliberal think tanks drove the neoliberal policy revolution argue that examples of direct causation from neoliberal ideas to neoliberal policies, do exist. However, the argument that has been developed here is that, for the most part, this did not occur according to the template for change advocated by neoliberal think tanks. Indeed, the influence of fundamentalist neoliberal ideas is much more complex and variegated than what is suggested by the idealist thesis.

Useful 'ways in' to an appreciation of the complex and variegated role of neoliberal ideas are offered by studies of the role of ideas in constructing the earlier 'Keynesian' era of economic regulation. Rather than assume the world became a mirror of Keynes' prescriptions, several studies (Hall 1989b; Jones 1989) point to the 'multiple roles that ideas play in the political world' (Hall 1989a: 363). They also show that ideas are interpreted in a range of different ways and that policy makers sometimes act other than the way prescribed by the supposed dominant economic policy paradigm. Such conceptual tools allow analyses to move beyond narrow assumptions about causation and give a more nuanced account of the role of fundamentalist neoliberal ideas in processes of neoliberal transformation.

Moreover, some concepts drawn from the idealist literature are of use in teasing out the role of fundamentalist neoliberal ideas. For example, the work of Blyth, while in many respects conforming to the assumptions that are critiqued in this chapter by arguing that ideas act as 'blueprints' for institutional change (Blyth 2002: 258–9), also develops a rather different approach to the role of ideas by arguing that ideas can act as 'weapons' (ibid.) in processes of political economic transformation. For Blyth, ideas used as weapons can 'delegitimate' alternative viewpoints and 'contest existing institutions'. Similarly, while Campbell's claim that ideas wield direct influence as 'programs' – 'technical and professional ideas that specify cause-and-effect relationships and prescribe a precise course of policy action' (Campbell 2001: 167) – is only weakly supported by the argument developed here, his proposition that ideas act as 'frames', seems rather more promising. For Campbell, '[i]deas provide actors with symbols and concepts with which to frame solutions to policy problems in normatively acceptable terms' (p. 175).

Neoliberal think tanks deployed their discursive arsenal as weapons against those advocating restrictions to business prerogatives and those opposed to neoliberal measures more generally. They also provided a language and set of concepts with which supporters of neoliberalism could frame debates and arguments in ways that justified and lent legitimacy to processes of neoliberal change. Fundamentalist neoliberal ideas provided a broad framework for the trajectory of change – greater reliance upon the private sector for the delivery of services and greater deregulation – rather than a more specific winding back of the state. That these were relatively coherent internally and were supported with reference to principles such as individual freedom and economic efficiency, and opposed to entrenched special interests, meant they could be used by neoliberal governments to justify and legitimate their policy agendas. Denham and Garnett (1996: 52), for example, argue that the neoliberal think tanks provided 'intellectual legitimacy for the Thatcher governments' in Britain, while Harvey (2005: 19) puts a similar view, albeit from a different theoretical perspective: '[t]he theoretical utopianism of the neoliberal argument has, I conclude, primarily worked as a system of justification and legitimation for whatever needed to be done to achieve this goal [of restoring class power]'.

In other cases the effect was to radicalise political debate, pushing the boundaries and the centre of such debate further to the right (see Béland and Waddan 2000; Reese 2005). Relatively good access to the news media and the use of 'emotionally powerful' (Reese 2005: 151) discourse helped to open up a new terrain of political debate about the proper role of the state in the economy. Béland and Wadden suggest the logic of this process 'is to push proposals that are *now* considered too radical by most Americans, but which may begin to undermine confidence in Social Security and create a *future environment* for the passage of more conservative legislation' (2000: 205). Neoliberal think tanks and fundamentalist intellectuals therefore 'had a dramatic effect on what constitutes the politically imaginable' (Hames and Feasey 1994: 234).

Others have suggested that the think tanks played an important role in cohering a neoliberal movement, even if the influence of their normative visions on policy was more limited. They helped to provide momentum for neoliberal ideas within the Right (Denham and Garnett 1998: 34), as well as training a 'new cadre' (Smith 1991: 206) of neoliberal activists.

Environmental policy illustrates these points. As Beder (2000) has shown, in response to the successes of the environment movement across the advanced capitalist economies, neoliberal think tanks began to mobilise against environmentally protective regulations that restricted capitalist freedoms. To this end, three broad tactics were deployed by think tanks. First, neoliberal think tanks mobilised conceptual tools developed by neoclassical economists in order to justify the use of market mechanisms and the creation of private property rights over the nature as the best way of ensuring environmental protection (Beder 2001: 130). As Beder (2001: 130–31) argues:

> The market solutions being advocated by neoliberal think tanks provide corporations and private firms with an alternative to restrictive legislation and the rhetoric to make the argument against that legislation in terms that are not obviously self-interested.

This assisted and complemented the process whereby 'corporate and economic elites have actively and successfully promoted certain federal environmental policies to create new long-term opportunities for profit-making' (Gonzalez 2001: 115). Second, neoliberal think tanks demonised environmental groups, attempting to undermine their legitimacy with policy makers and the broader public. Environmentalists were cast 'as "radicals" who distort evidence and exaggerate problems' (Jacques et al. 2008: 353) and who were motivated by anti-Western agendas. Indicative of this discourse is the Heritage Foundation's claim that environmentalists posed 'the single greatest threat to the American economy' (quoted in Beder 2000: 96). The third tactic deployed by neoliberal think tanks was to cast doubt on the seriousness of environmental degradation, thus undermining the need for widespread policy change, in what some have accurately labelled 'the organisation of denial' (Jacques et al. 2008).

However, to focus exclusively upon ideas as the key explanatory variable for the neoliberal policy transformation runs the risk of 'los[ing] sight of the significance of institutional and wider structural variables which inevitably shape agency and institutional change processes' (Bell 2011: 884). The influence of neoliberal ideas should be understood as contingent upon contextual circumstances in which they were deployed. It seems plausible to suggest that fundamentalist neoliberal ideas often became diffused, diluted, selectively appropriated and mixed with other ideas and agendas so that while they were certainly influential, they were not the driving force behind the neoliberal revolution. Similarly, while Mirowski's 'double truth' argument was critiqued earlier for its overly-simplistic account of the influence of the neoliberal thought collective, he is nonetheless surely correct to question 'whether most people who subscribe to something like neoliberalism actually understand it to be constituted as a coherent doctrine with a spelled-out roster of propositions, or instead treat their notions as disparate implications of other beliefs' (Mirowski 2013: 34).

Fundamentalist neoliberal intellectuals and think tanks 'were one of a number of sources for political ideas' (Hames and Feasey 1994: 227). Less radical neoliberal ideas circulated through forums other than the think tanks or from the mouths or pens of neoliberal fundamentalists. Furthermore, given evidence against the direct transfer of ideas from neoliberal think tanks and fundamentalists to policy makers, it seems reasonable to contend that neoliberal policies in practice were often implemented not according to some grand neoliberal meta-blueprint, but rather as piecemeal, experimental and pragmatic (albeit, as discussed in later chapters, such pragmatism was often shaped by class relations) responses to political and economic circumstances. In this regard, the study of the development of an 'Anglo-liberal growth model' by Hay and Smith (2013) is illuminating. They argue that while it is possible to retrospectively detect the emergence of coherent policies and institutions underpinning a regime of economic growth in the Anglophone capitalist economies in the neoliberal era, 'there is also a danger of assuming too clear and conscious a conception among policy makers of the "growth model" that, in effect, they were constructing' (Hay and Smith 2013: 291). 'We do not see policy makers as animated by a vision of the growth model they were building', they argue, rather, it 'was certainly stumbled upon serendipitously' (ibid.). This too suggests that other factors were important in driving change, because they provided the context in which neoliberal ideas were useful. The discrepancies between the normative visions of the neoliberal think tanks and state policies suggests the presence of strongly constraining institutional environments that mediated fundamentalist neoliberal ideas. Furthermore, the role of business interests in providing financial support to the neoliberal think tanks is a relevant factor in explaining their longevity. The social relations of production between capital and labour and changing economic circumstances also help explain the context in which neoliberal ideas came to prominence. As others have argued, the role of ideas can only properly be grasped when considered in the context of the institutions and power relations within which they are enmeshed – when ideas are considered as dialectically related (Marsh 2009: 679; Bell 2011: 884) to both institutions and interests. This will be explored further in Chapter 7.

CONCLUSION

This chapter has critiqued the idealist assumption that the rise of neoliberalism in practice was due to policy makers coming under the influence of the ideas of fundamentalist neoliberal intellectuals and think tanks. It has been shown that, beyond very broad-level correlations between ideas and policies, the idealist assumption is lacking in supporting evidence. Furthermore, contrary evidence has been presented which undermines the plausibility of the idealist assumption as an explanatory framework for neoliberal policy change. In contrast to the idealist thesis it has been suggested that fundamentalist ideas were important in the neoliberal policy revolution, but that they did not directly cause it. Fundamentalist neoliberal ideas provided economic and philosophical justification and legitimation for neoliberal agendas, but they were not the reason policy makers turned to neoliberal solutions.

Recognising this more limited role of neoliberal ideas in the neoliberal policy transformation prompts consideration of what did drive the neoliberal policy revolution, if not neoliberal ideas. This will be discussed in the next chapter which will also consider the reason for the discrepancies between neoliberalism in theory and practice. Such issues matter for reasons other than mere intellectual curiosity. Indeed, they are important for understanding the dynamics of the present economic crisis and the future prospects for neoliberalism, as well as the prospects for alternatives to it. For, if the rise of neoliberalism was driven by more than ideas, so too are alternative ideas to neoliberalism not likely to be sufficient for the winding back of neoliberal policy practices. This issue takes on an urgent character in the context of the current global economic crisis when the very future of neoliberalism appears to be in question.

NOTES

1. Stephen Martin, interview the author.
2. Michael Keating, interview with the author.
3. Ross Garnaut, interview with the author.

4.   Always embedded neoliberalism

INTRODUCTION

This chapter outlines the framework for an alternative understanding of neoliberalism to that offered by idealist approaches. Previous chapters demonstrated that 'actually existing neoliberalism' is not simply a mirror of the normative prescriptions of fundamentalist neoliberal theorists, nor is it primarily a product of the influence of those ideas. This prompts consideration of the need for a more satisfactory understanding than that provided by the ideas-centred account, as well as the reasons for the discrepancy between neoliberal theory and practice, and the factors which drove the rise of neoliberalism.

The chapter first explains why there has always been a discrepancy between neoliberal theory and practice. Using insights from Marxist and Institutional political economy as well as drawing upon historical examples, it is argued that the state has been central to the formation and expanded reproduction of capitalism throughout its history. The growth of the state under neoliberalism simply continues a long-term trend evident at least since the nineteenth century. Because the state plays a central role in the reproduction of capitalism, it was always unlikely that neoberalism in practice would ever achieve the normative goal of the withering away of the state as envisioned by neoliberal theorists.

Second, the concept of 'always embedded neoliberalism' is developed to provide a useful framework for analysing neoliberalism in practice. This concept is drawn from Fred Block's (2003) concept of the 'always embedded market', by which is meant that markets always depend upon social support structures in order to function. Thus, they are always embedded in social relations, but such embedding takes different forms in different historical periods and geographical and political contexts. Similarly, actually existing neoliberalism has been 'always embedded' in social support structures, albeit the precise nature of these have varied by country and have developed unevenly over time. It is argued that the social structures in which neoliberalism is embedded can be usefully understood as class relations, institutions and ideology. The dependence of neoliberalism upon these social support structures explains both the discrepancy between neoliberal theory and practice as well the apparent durability of neoliberalism in the face of the global financial crisis.

THE STATE AS A PERENNIAL FEATURE OF THE CAPITALIST ECONOMY

Many narratives of the history of capitalism posit the existence of a golden age of *laissez-faire* during the nineteenth century, characterised by a minimal state and free markets, which subsequent ages have marked a departure from as states came increasingly to interfere in autonomous market processes. Such an oversimplistic reading of history typically also views the neoliberal era as something of a return to this *laissez-faire* pattern of small states and free markets.

However, as with the neoliberal era, where more detailed investigation reveals the centrality of the state to this period of supposed free market ascendancy, so too does a closer examination of the *laissez-faire* period reveal that an active state was far from absent and played a crucial role. When Polanyi ([1944] 2001: 147) wrote that the '*laissez-faire* economy was the product of deliberate state action … *Laissez-faire* was planned', he was referring to the burgeoning of new roles undertaken by the state that were crucial to the expansion of capitalist economic processes. As Polanyi also argued, '[t]he road to the free market was opened and kept open by an enormous increase in continuous, centrally organised and controlled interventionism' (p. 146).

Indeed, states have been central to the development and spread of capitalism throughout its history. A key part of this process by which the state facilitated the development of capitalism was the ongoing phenomenon of 'enclosure', whereby land previously characterised by common communal usage rights and regulated by custom and tradition was effectively privatised (Patriquin 2004: 208–9). One way in which states assisted this process was through the creation of private property rights over land. In England, for example, private property rights over land were codified through application of common law by the courts and in the eighteenth and nineteenth centuries through Acts of Parliament (Wood 2002: 109, 127–8; Patriquin 2004: 204–9). The British state also alienated land for private use abroad by claiming legal right to land used by indigenous populations and distributing it among private land holders and granting them property rights over it (Wood 2003: 89–101). More directly coercive means were also employed, for example the suppression of dissent against enclosure and the assertion of common or customary rights such as the British state's use of force against the 'Diggers' at St

George's Hill in 1649 (Hill 1987: 107–13; De Angelis 1999). Such direct coercion was also used abroad by the British state in violently suppressing resistance to land dispossession by indigenous populations (Wood 2003: 89–101). On the one hand this process, which Marx (1990: 873–940) referred to as 'primitive accumulation', was crucial in converting land into a commodity that could be priced and traded. On the other hand it was also important to the development of capitalism by dispossessing people from their land, thus leaving them without their means of livelihood and creating a new and growing class of people who would become dependent for their survival on selling their labour power for wages.

Other acts and actions by the state also helped to enforce the norms of wage labour thereby contributing greatly to the development of capitalism. Workhouses, anti-vagrancy and anti-begging regulations associated with the Poor Laws helped ensure that unemployment was an even nastier and more brutal form of existence than would otherwise be the case and helped to enforce waged work as the only means of survival for the propertyless class (Piven and Cloward 1972: 3–41). The hand of the state was also apparent within the sphere of production, providing on the one hand for social protections contributing to the sustainability of wage labour, such as through the *Factory Acts* (Hobsbawm 1981: 123–5; Marx 1990: 389–411), but on the other helping to enforce the prerogatives of management by denying workers the rights of self-organisation through trade unions via, for example, the *Combination Acts* (Thompson 1982: 546–65).

Firms benefited in other ways too from the strong hand of the state. From the 1400s European states used charters to facilitate the establishment of companies with monopoly trading rights to extend the imperial reach of the chartering state, using violence if necessary. From the late 1800s, states again facilitated the institutional form of capital through the development of limited liability regulations (Rafferty 2001: 154–5). Early capitalist manufacturers benefited from the state-facilitated access to raw materials, such as cotton, through the slave trade, and the decimation of the Indian cotton industry by British colonial administrators, thus eliminating a competitor to British cotton production and creating a new market for the same (Wood 2003: 106). Moreover, tariff protections were common within the leading capitalist powers throughout the nineteenth century, even during the so-called *laissez-faire* period (Nye 1991).

None of this is to downplay the 'legal and organisational differentiation between state and economy' (Panitch and Gindin 2012: 3) that is one of the distinguishing features of capitalism as compared with the preceding feudal societies in which pertained a 'unity of economic and political powers' (Wood 2002: 177–81). Indeed, it is this differentiation that gives rise to the appearance of states and markets and separate and antithetical spheres of human activity. However, the brief historical survey just presented bears out Polanyi's ([1944] 2001: 145) argument that 'free markets could never have come into being merely by allowing things to take their course', and that such measures contributed to a long-term expansion in the economic size of capitalist states. This is clearly the opposite of what is assumed by those who see states and markets as separate and antithetical spheres of human activity and who see state involvement with the economy as a form of interference. Active states have been normal parts of the capitalist economy throughout its history. Indeed they have been central to the development of capitalism and, as will be argued later, they are necessary for its expanded reproduction. This suggests that the fundamentalist neoliberal view of the proper role of the state is out of step with the historical record, and therefore that it was always unlikely that neoliberalism in practice would resemble the normative prescriptions of such intellectuals. To understand the role of the capitalist state in the neoliberal era requires an understanding of its broader, longer-term dynamics, which in turn requires an understanding of the social relations at the heart of the capitalist system.

THE ALWAYS EMBEDDED ECONOMY

Previous chapters outlined how the idealist view which understands neoliberalism as a process driven by, and mirroring, fundamentalist normative visions of intellectuals like Friedman, Friedrich von Hayek, and the think tanks which proselytised their ideas. It was argued that the dominant idealist view of neoliberalism leads many to understand the neoliberal era as one in which economic processes have become ever more distant from social processes: as an era in which the economy has become disembedded from society. As has been shown, however, such idealist assumptions are poor guides to understanding actually existing neoliberalism and the processes by which neoliberal transformations of states and economies occurred. Nonetheless, if we are to arrive at a more satisfactory understanding of neoliberalism and the processes driving it, it must be grounded in an appreciation of the broader dynamics of capitalist economies and their social embeddedness. The necessary dependence of capitalist economies on social relations, processes and institutions must be teased out if we are to clear away unhelpful abstractions and lay the foundations for a more clear-sighted examination of neoliberalism. Coming to terms with this requires, in the first instance at least, a detour away from examining concrete neoliberal forms, and into the realm of political economic theory, in order to return with appropriate conceptual tools for analysing actually existing neoliberalism.

The concept of the socially embedded economy is derived from the work of Karl Polanyi. In his best-known publication, *The Great Transformation* ([1944] 2001), Polanyi described the transition from feudalism to capitalism – or, what he called a 'market economy'. Polanyi is often thought to have argued that this transition from feudalism to capitalism entailed the separation of the economy from its social foundations, its disembedding from the structures that gave it coherence under feudalism. Such a process of disembedding was disastrous for society as it became subjected to the economic logic of the 'self-regulating market'. This common account assumes that economies can be either embedded in, or disembedded from, society, and that the degree of institutionalised social protection reflects the degree of embeddedness. Gemici (2008: 25) calls this the concept of 'embeddedness as a historical variable'.

There is certainly some support for this position in Polanyi's work. For example, Polanyi ([1944] 2001: 71) writes that 'never before our own time were markets more than accessories of life'. He goes on to argue that 'a self-regulating market demands nothing less than the institutional separation of society into an economic and political sphere' (p. 74). One can readily see how this concept of embeddedness/disembeddness has been appropriated in idealist understandings of neoliberalism, and deployed to describe neoliberalism as a process whereby the economy becomes disembedded from society, much as the *laissez-faire* system of the nineteenth century allegedly entailed a similar process of separating economic from the social.

However, as Block (2003) has argued, while Polanyi's work can be read in this way, another, more satisfying understanding of embeddedness can be inferred from *The Great Transformation*. Block argues that, during the writing of *The Great Transformation*, Polanyi began to move towards a conception of the economy as being 'always embedded' in social institutions and processes. However, because of the time constraints he imposed upon himself in order to publish the book before what seemed to be looming as the end of World War Two, Polanyi was unable to formalise this conceptual shift and his book thus reflected 'contradictions and conflicts' with respect to the embeddedness concept (Block 2003: 276). Block (ibid.) argues that 'Polanyi glimpsed the idea of the always embedded market economy, but he was not able to give that idea a name or develop it theoretically because it represented too great a divergence from his initial starting point'.

The concept of the 'always embedded market economy' was expressed much more clearly by Polanyi (1957) in his later essay 'The Economy as Instituted Process' in which he argued that the 'substantive meaning of economic' (by which he essentially meant the conception of the economy as a system of material provisioning) is superior to the 'formal meaning of economic' (by which he meant the study of choices made under conditions of scarcity, as conceived by neoclassical economics) because the substantive definition of the economic was universally applicable, whereas the formal definition was only relevant to understanding a 'market economy', and even then it provided only a partial representation of it. According to Polanyi, the substantive definition of 'economic' enables the recognition that human provisioning has been organised according to different logics – reciprocity, redistribution and exchange – in different places and at different times in history. Social institutions are always necessary to provide regularity and stability to these economic logics. Thus Polanyi (1957: 250) argues that '[t]he human economy, then, is embedded and enmeshed in institutions, economic and noneconomic'.

Block (2003: 276) argues that this concept of 'the always embedded market economy', which Polanyi was able to articulate in later work, also 'provides the most powerful and enduring way to make sense of Polanyi's core arguments in *The Great Transformation*'. However, its utility goes beyond a coherent reading of *The Great Transformation*. Indeed, for the purposes of this analysis, the extent to which the concept of the always embedded economy matches Polanyi's ideas is not really the point. Numerous credible alternative interpretations of Polanyi's work exist. Rather than an exercise in Polanyi-ology, the development of the concept of the always embedded economy is useful in so far as it illuminates key elements of actually existing capitalist economies and, more particularly, their neoliberal variant. While some argue that the 'always embedded economy' concept is a 'commonplace' idea (Dale 2010: 201), such an evaluation ignores how far removed this concept is from mainstream understandings of the economy–society relationship which persist today just as they did in Polanyi's time. Relative to orthodox approaches, it is thus a radical concept.

Such a conception of embeddedness is akin to what Gemici (2008: 25) describes as 'embeddedness as a methodological principle'. The strength of this methodological conception of embeddedness is that it recognises that markets and economic processes more generally are socially constructed. As Gemici (2008: 26–7) writes, it 'invites the researcher to look for the social processes that structure and shape economic life' and is therefore opposed to the artificial separation of the economic and social spheres of human activity. This conception of embeddedness recognises

that 'the emergence of markets was almost always deliberately engin-
eered by the state' (Chang 2002: 547). Indeed, it invites the conclusion at
the heart of the institutionalist tradition of political economy, that 'the
market is itself an institution' (Hodgson 2007: 2), rather than conceiving
of the market as simply a collection of atomised individuals. Pushing the
argument further, it is clear from this understanding of the socially
embedded economy that '[r]egulation is a necessary condition for the
functioning of the market, not only a compromise between economic
imperatives and social values' (Levi-Faur 2005: 19).

If the economy is 'always embedded' in social institutions and
processes, then it should not be surprising that the normative neoliberal
ideal of free markets has not been realised in practice. Indeed, the
'always embedded market economy' concept prompts recognition that
neoliberalism is a utopian project, in that it posits not merely 'the best
place' (from the point of view of its advocates) but also 'no such place'.
As Brenner and Theodore (2002: 353) argue, 'neoliberal doctrine represents states and markets as if they were diametrically opposed principles
of social organization, rather than recognizing the politically constructed
character of all economic relations'. Therefore 'actually existing neoliberalism' was always likely to differ from the normative prescriptions of
its proselytisers.

On this view, those who understand neoliberalism in practice in terms
of its normative commitments to free markets, a retreat of the state or a
process of disembedding, have also mischaracterised it. For, just as
capitalism, or the market economy, is 'always embedded', so are historically specific manifestations of capitalism, such as 'actually existing
neoliberalism', always embedded. It is useful therefore to speak of
'always embedded neoliberalism', and it becomes necessary to understand the ensemble of ideational, institutional and class-based configurations in which neoliberalism is embedded.

CAPITALIST SOCIAL RELATIONS

In order to tease out the dynamics of always embedded neoliberalism, it
is necessary to understand the specific social processes and structures
within which neoliberalism, and capitalist economies more generally, are
embedded. This, in turn, enables an understanding of state–economy
relations which explains not only the observable durability of the state,
but also its behaviour in the neoliberal era. What follow then is a 'back to
basics' examination of the key social (class) relations that underpin
capitalist economies and which give them their unique dynamism and

contradictions. The nature of capitalist states and ideologies will then be located within these distinct social relations, before turning to a more explicit consideration of how an understanding of these structures is crucial for appreciating the development of always embedded neo-liberalism.

In a broad sense, the capitalist economy can be understood as embedded within the social relations of production, which are crucial in 'shaping both the market and the state' (Radice 2010: 35). Capitalism is a historically specific form of economic organisation based upon particular relations between economic agents. This is one of the key insights of the Marxist approach to political economy. While Marx is often portrayed as privileging the 'economic' over the 'social' in his understanding of capitalism, a closer reading of Marx's work demonstrates this portrayal is far from accurate. In a well-known passage from *A Contribution to the Critique of Political Economy*, Marx (1970: 20–21) argued that:

> In the social production of their existence, men inevitably enter into definite relations, which are independent of their will, namely relations of production appropriate to a given stage in the development of their material forces of production. The totality of these relations of production constitutes the economic structure of society, the real foundation, on which arises a legal and political superstructure and to which correspond definite forms of social consciousness. The mode of production of material life conditions the general process of social, political and intellectual life.

This has often been interpreted as simply meaning that capitalist economic processes determine social processes: laws, politics, culture and so on. However, in this passage Marx is actually pointing to the socially constituted nature of the economy. The economic base, or mode of production mentioned by Marx, is constituted by both the forces and relations of production. This latter phenomenon, as Wright (2005: 9) argues, means 'the people that participate in production have different kinds of rights and powers over the use of the inputs and over the results of their use'. Marx's point is that the capitalist economy is constituted by class relations. Exclusive ownership and control of the means of production is concentrated in the hands of a small group, or class, of capitalists. This class owns the outputs of production, which are sold for profit. Because members of this class are in competition with each other, the process of production can only be reproduced if the owners of the means of production are able to produce outputs of greater value than the inputs and sell these in markets for a profit, or cease production. In a capitalist economy this can only occur because another group, or class, of people, who do not own productive property, are compelled by these circumstances to sell their capacity to work, or labour power, to those who do own the means of production, and purchase what they collectively produce. Such relationships, Marx argues, are at the heart of capitalism and help to explain its central dynamics.

Fusing this with Polanyi's insights about embeddedness, the capitalist economy should be understood as embedded within a specific set of social, or class, relations. Such class relations condition not only the nature of work in a capitalist economy, but also shape the nature of economic and political processes more broadly. These features are captured by Wright (2005: 28–30) who argues the Marxist theory of class has several strengths that set it apart from other approaches to class analysis which are worth briefly exploring in turn.

First, Wright argues that the Marxist class analysis provides a theory 'linking exchange and production' (Wright 2005: 28). The social relations that define one's class position simultaneously define the ways one participates in exchange relations. Marx argues that because wage labourers are defined by their alienation from the means of direct production, they are reliant for their subsistence on the purchase of commodities through markets from those to whom they sell their labour-power in production (see, for example, Marx, 1992: 119). So, the situation of 'market dependence' (Wood 2002: 2) that is characteristic of capitalist societies is inscribed in the nature of that system's basic class relations between labour and capital. Moreover, the fact that capitalists need to sell commodities to the people who produce them, while simultaneously having an incentive to depress their real remuneration, means that the perennial problem of effective demand emerges directly from the class relation at the heart of capitalism. This dynamic found expression in the neoliberal era as workers' real wages across the advanced capitalist countries either stagnated or grew very slowly, but demand was maintained via the extension of credit to working class households – facilitated by neoliberal processes of financial deregulation. Concurrently, more spheres of social life were brought into the market sphere through privatisation, deregulation and marketisation, which, particularly in the global South, also often meant independent producers losing access to their means of livelihood – especially in the form of productive land – this forcing them into waged labour and market dependence.

The second strength of Marxist class analysis identified by Wright is it 'understands conflict as generated by inherent properties of [class] ... relations rather than simply contingent factors' (Wright 2005: 28). In order to realise a profit, owners are required to exploit wage labourers – 'like all other buyers he [the owner of capital] tries to extract the maximum possible benefit from the use-value of his commodity' (Marx 1990: 342). However, outside the sphere of immediate production, writes Marx, the worker 'belongs to himself' (Marx 1990: 717) and therefore workers bring to the sphere of production interests other than those of the capitalist. Conflict between labour and capital over priorities within the sphere of production is inevitable. This helps explain the particular dynamics of class conflict in the neoliberal era whereby capital has sought to increase profits by increasing the exploitation of workers. This has occurred through real wage suppression and work intensification, enabled, in part, by labour market deregulation and the increase in managerial prerogatives within the sphere of production.

Marx's theory of class, according to Wright (2005: 29), is also a theory of power relations. Workers are afforded a degree of power to resist exploitation and thereby enforce their priorities upon capital. This is because capital is dependent upon wage labour for the production of surplus value: it is 'the capitalist's most indispensible means of production' (Marx 1990: 718). But workers are also dependent upon the exchange of their labour power for wages, therefore binding workers to capital by 'invisible threads' (ibid.: 719). This makes it costly, but not impossible, for workers to withhold their labour power as a form of resistance to capitalist priorities. This helps explain the changing pattern of power rleations between capital and labour in the neoliberal era. Open class conflict has been a feature of the neoliberal era, as labour has resisted capital's attempts to force the costs of restructuring on them. Partly as an outcome of such struggles, however, the ability of organised labour to resist has been weakened and, in some cases, made more costly during the neoliberal era.

The fourth strength of Marxist class theory, according to Wright (2005: 29), is it 'contains the rudiments of what might be termed an endogenous theory of the formation of consent'. This follows closely from the previous point. Because capitalists are dependent upon the cooperation of those from whom they extract labour effort, they cannot rely purely upon coercive methods of exploitation. Inevitably, they must also rely upon strategies that generate consent among workers. For Wright, this helps explain not only firm-level strategies, but also the development of broader ideological norms which justify exploitation to the exploited. As discussed in Chapter 7, while neoliberalism has been deeply unpopular, because of its exploitative character and disruptive effects upon people's everyday lives, it is important to recognise the extent to which consent to neoliberal governance has been generated. As market dependence has been extended, those elements of neoliberal doctrine that frame social relationships as relationships between individuals transacting in markets, have greater resonance with people's lived experience, and provide a legitimating discourse for such changes. Moreover, certain sections of the working class derived material benefits from the neoliberal era, while the persistence of some universalist social institutions helped to blunt the harder edges of the neoliberal policy regime, thus contributing to its legitimacy.

The fifth strength of Marxist class theory, according to Wright (2005: 30), is it contains 'concepts for historical and comparative analysis'. For Marx, the different class relations that prevail within each historical period determine that period's essential character:

> What distinguishes the various economic formations of society – the distinction between for example a society based on slave-labour and a society based on wage-labour – is the form in which this surplus labour is in each case extorted from the immediate producer, the worker. (Marx 1990: 325)

As Wright (2005: 30) notes, this insight provides 'a powerful road map for comparative research' as it identifies the variable from which stem many of a society's systemic features. With respect to neoliberalism, this suggests that it is important ground an understanding in the core dynamics of capitalism, but also to appreciate the extent to which neoliberalism is a product of historically specific institutional transformations. Neoliberalism needs to be understood as distinct from that which preceded it, even as there are continuities with the previous 'Keynesian' era. Such a perspective also provides a lens through which to evaluate the extent to which neoliberalism has been transcended in the wake of the global economic crisis, and the dynamics that continue to re-shape it. These principles are crucial for an understanding of neoliberalism. As a moment within the history of capitalist social relations, neoliberalism is shaped by the forces and contradictions that provide the capitalist system with its dynamism. However, as a historically specific moment within the development of capitalism, neoliberalism has unique features that set it apart from other capitalist eras.

THE CAPITALIST TYPE OF STATE

The recognition that capitalist economies are embedded within a particular set of class relations also points toward a more satisfactory conception of the state than that which underpins most of the dominant idealist interpretations of neoliberalism. Indeed, it helps to explain why states have been perennial and expanding features of the capitalist economy throughout its history, and therefore why the state did not wither away with the advent of neoliberalism.

Although capitalist economies are constituted by the specific relations of production between capital and labour as described previously, these class relations, in and of themselves, are not sufficient conditions for their own reproduction – by which is meant 'the processes which permit what exists to go on existing' (Aglietta 2000: 12). The reproduction of capitalist social relations, and of capital accumulation more generally, is, as Jessop (2002: 18) notes, 'improbable' without reference to something at least partially outside of them. Two problems are apparent. First, the capital relation requires mediation for its reproduction. Without such mediation class conflict can become socially destructive and threaten the foundations of the capitalist economy. Second, many of the preconditions for capital accumulation are not produced within the capital relation itself, and therefore need to be secured by other means. Crucial inputs including labour power, money, land and knowledge are not produced within the capital relation. Neither are the rules and standards that are necessary for the 'regularization' (Jessop and Sum 2006: 4) of capital accumulation over time. Therefore, logically, and functionally, something else is required for the expanded reproduction of these social relations. Historically, it is the 'capitalist type of state' (Jessop 2002: 37–42) that has facilitated the reproduction of the capital relation and the capitalist economy more broadly.

Mediation of the capital relation is required because of its inherently conflict-ridden nature. While such conflict is inherent, it is also potentially destructive. This dynamic is evident in Marx's detailed examination of the actions of the state in ensuring the reproduction of labour-power by setting limits on the length of the working day, thereby reducing the physical burden of work on labourers. Marx (1990: 718) notes 'the maintenance and reproduction of the working class remains a necessary condition for the reproduction of capital'. Engels (1985: 208) argues:

> in order that ... classes with conflicting economic interests, shall not consume themselves and society in fruitless struggle, it became necessary to have a power seemingly standing above society that would moderate the conflict and keep it within the bounds of 'order'; and this power, arisen out of society but placing itself above it and alienating itself more and more from it, is the state.

Historically, states have developed institutions and regulations for moderating class conflict, including arbitration courts, labour relations boards and legislation providing frameworks for the conduct of negotiations over the employment relationship. While these sometimes afford a degree of protection to labour, as well as recognising and legitimating their collective representative bodies in the form of trade unions, just as important a part of the state's historic role in mediating class conflict has been the limitation and coercion of organised labour. While 'market coercion' – the imperative to work for wages in order to survive, alongside the threat of unemployment – can be crucial in disciplining workers to labour under conditions set out by managers and owners, it is not always sufficient. It is for this reason that Wood (2002: 178) argues that '[t]he economic imperatives of capitalism are always in need of support by extra-economic powers of regulation and coercion'. This helps to explain the perennial presence of the state in the regulation of the firm – for example, as in the case of the *Combination Acts* – to limit the ability of labourers to resist work, form unions, take industrial action as well as to suppress the actions of organised labour through violence or law. Not that states are the only source of violence or coercion against workers. As Clarke (1991: 166) points out, it is a myth that the state has an absolute monopoly on the use of violence. Firms have historically employed a range of violent extra-economic strategies to discipline recalcitrant workers – such as the use of strike-breaking vigilantes, paramilitary forces, private investigators and security guards. However the state is in the unique position of being able to codify, universalise and claim political authority to undertake such coercive measures.

A further reason for the perennial presence of the state in capitalist economies is the capitalist economy's inability to produce the inputs necessary for its own reproduction. As an institution not constrained by the need to produce for profit, the state plays a crucial role in producing and securing such inputs. Several theorists in the Marxist and Polanyian traditions have pointed to this problem, which is captured by O'Connor (1998: 23):

> neither human labour power nor external nature nor infrastructures including their space/time dimensions are produced capitalistically, although capital treats these conditions of production as if they are commodities or commodity capital. Precisely because they are not produced and reproduced capitalistically, yet are bought and sold and utilised as if they were commodities, the conditions of supply (quantity and quality, place and time) must be regulated by the state or capitals acting as if they are state.

Marx, for example, viewed labour power – the only commodity that can itself produce value – as the most important input to the production process. Labour power, however, is not produced by firms in profit-oriented production processes, but socially (Jessop 2002: 14). Polanyi ([1944] 2001: 75) made a similar point, arguing that labour (like land and money) is a fictitious commodity – while it shares some characteristics of 'genuine commodities' (it has a price and is sold on markets), it is 'not produced for sale'. The state therefore has an important role in 'making workers' (Peck 1996: 23–45). This occurs, for example, through the provision of education, training, housing and healthcare, as well integrating workers into labour markets by, for example, making unemployment an unattractive option (such as the crowding of the unemployed into workhouses under the Poor Laws) and enabling people to get to work through provision of transportation networks. As Marx recognised (1990: 718), 'the maintenance and reproduction of the working class remains a necessary condition for the reproduction of capital', yet because capital alone is unable to secure such reproduction, the state plays an important role in ensuring the reproduction of labour-power by quarantining it from the full force of markets and capitalist imperatives by, for example, setting limits on the length of the working day, thereby reducing the physical burden of work on labourers. Thus social protections are functional not only to the mediation of class conflict, but also to securing the reproduction of labour power.

Similarly, land is a 'fictitious' commodity' that exists naturally (Polanyi [1944] 2001: 71–80), yet forms the terrain upon which production occurs and is the source of many raw materials crucial for production. 'Land', as Polanyi (p. 75) explains, 'is only another name for nature, which is not produced by man'. As with labour, the state plays an important role here in securing the commodity status of land – converting it from a naturally occurring use value into a tradable commodity through the creation of private property rights over land. The aforementioned history of enclosure in England provides an obvious example of this, but it is only one among many recurrent examples of the state acting to secure land, or nature more broadly, as a commodity.

Money is identified as a fictitious commodity by Polanyi. While money is created by for-profit private sector banks through fractional reserve banking and loans, the currencies in which such money is denominated are the creation of states. Indeed, states provide the crucial function of underpinning trust in money as a unit of exchange and store of value – the universal equivalent of all other commodities without which the commodity exchange that is central to capitalism would be unlikely to occur. For the capitalist system to be reproduced requires securing the production and integrity of these inputs of labour, money, land, environmental conditions and raw materials more broadly and the institution that is uniquely placed to do this is the state.

The third reason for the centrality of the state to capitalist economic processes is its provision of other preconditions for markets that are unlikely to be secured by profit-based production alone. Most important among these is the framework of rules that allow for the regularisation and reproduction of profit-based production and market exchange. The process of capital accumulation, and the capital relation itself, do not contain within themselves enforceable rules specifying rights and obligations of economic conduct, nor enforceable sanctions for the transgression of such rules. While private, profit-motivated agents have formed collective institutions to provide such rules (many stock exchanges are examples of this), historically it has been the state that has played an important, evolving and indeed expanding role in the provision and enforcement of such rules. The need for the state to play such a role is in fact recognised by leading neoliberal theorists. Yet neoliberal theorists such as Friedman believe that such a framework of rules can be provided by a minimal state. However, history has demonstrated that the opposite is in fact the case. This is not surprising: as capitalist economies have expanded in both size and complexity, so have state regulations expanded, developing new rules to facilitate the regularisation of new markets and forms of production.

It would be wrong to infer from this, however, that capitalist states are led automatically or inevitably to play the functionally necessary role of reproducing the capital relationship. Nor would it be correct to assume that states simply always act 'in the interests of the capitalist class'. Rather, capitalist states are characterised by contradictory dynamics with respect to their regulation of capitalist social relations and accumulation. On the one hand, states are functional to the reproduction of the capital relationship and capital accumulation, as has already been noted. Moreover state revenue is dependent upon the fortunes of capital accumulation via taxation. Concurrently, by virtue of the centrality of accumulation to the budgets of states and to the welfare of its citizens, the owners of the means of production are able to exercise disproportionate influence over state policy. On the other hand, however, states are, at root, political institutions, and therefore their viability is dependent upon the maintenance of political legitimacy. This is why O'Connor (1973: 6) argues that 'the capitalistic state must try to fulfil two basic and often mutually contradictory functions – *accumulation* and *legitimization*'.

Two conclusions follow from this. First, the state is both a perennial feature of capitalism and one of its essential institutions. Thus, to cast state regulations as 'interferences' is to misunderstand the nature of the state in a capitalist economy. In capitalist economies, states are integrally related to the process of capital accumulation. State involvement in the economy to secure systemic legitimacy and the legitimacy of the state itself is inevitable. Idealist accounts which assume that economies can be disembedded from state support structures, or that markets and states are separate spheres of human activity, or that it is possible for states to wither away under capitalism therefore mischaracterise the nature of capitalist markets and the historical role of states within them.

Second, the trajectory of state development is unknowable *a priori*. It is crucially dependent upon and integrated with processes of capital accumulation. However, such processes are themselves internally contradictory and conflict ridden. While capital accumulation exhibits secular expansive tendencies, its development is also uneven and characterised by both stability and crisis. Moreover, the state also shapes processes of accumulation, which creates feedback loops that in turn condition the nature of the state. However, because the state is also a political institution, its trajectory has a degree of autonomy from processes of accumulation. These distinct but related dynamics mean that while it is useful to speak in general terms about the 'capitalist type of state' as advocated by Jessop (2002: 37–42), it is important to recognise that capitalist states vary temporally and geographically and have path-dependent features which lock in certain logics and inhibit others.

For an understanding of neoliberalism, these perspectives require that attention be given to the centrality of the state to the ongoing political economic transformations of the neoliberal era. They prompt recognition of the integral relationship between state and capitalist social relations, and the ways in which these in turn are shaped by the attempts by state elites to secure the sometimes contradictory aims of capital accumulation and political legitimacy. Moreover, it focuses analysis on the ways in which the perennial dynamics of the capitalist type of state are overlaid and mediated by historically specific and path-dependent institutional developments, which can have their own unique dynamics and contradictions.

CAPITALIST IDEOLOGY AND HEGEMONY

Just as the capitalist type of state needs to be understood as situated within capitalist social relations, so can the production, circulation and deployment of ideas only properly be apprehended within these same social relations. Marx, and Marxist scholarship more generally, have rightly been criticised for their tendency to offer a highly deterministic and reductionist view of the role of ideas within capitalism. Statements like 'the ideas of the ruling class are in every epoch the ruling ideas' (Marx and Engels 1976: 67), give credence to such critiques. Nonetheless, it is possible to derive from Marx, and Marxist scholarship, a more nuanced treatment of the role of ideas which grounds them in the dynamics of capitalist social relations, while still according ideas with contingency and independent force, thus overcoming unsatisfactory deterministic formulations.

The tenor of this book and its critique of ideas-centred accounts of neoliberalism is very much in accord with Marx's (1977: 20–21) argument that '[t]he mode of production of material life conditions the general process of social, political and intellectual life'. However, such an argument need not be read in highly rigid or deterministic fashion to imply, as has so often been the case, that ideas are merely epiphenomena, nor that they simply express class interests. Drawing upon both Marx and Gramsci it is possible to outline a more satisfying alternative conception role of ideas in a capitalist economy.

A recurring theme of Marx's *Capital* is the distinction he draws between essence and appearance and its importance for an understanding of the capitalist economy. The nature of the capitalist economy means that much of people's everyday encounters with it occur at the level of immediate appearances. However, to focus solely upon this level of immediate appearance as constituting the economy is to ignore the underlying essence which structures capitalist economic processes. Marx argues that such a mistake is made by 'bourgeois' economists. They take the focus of economic analysis to be the relationship between commodities and their prices. To do so, however, obscures the social (class) relationships that give rise to commodity production and exchange that is mediated by money. Nonetheless, Marx (1990: 169) suggests that bourgeois economics is not simply born of a desire misrepresent the nature of the capitalist economy:

> The categories of bourgeois economics ... Are forms of thought which are socially valid, and therefore objective, for the relations of production belonging to this historically determined mode of social production, i.e. commodity production.

Marx (1990: 165) outlines his concept of the 'fetishism of the commodity' by which he means the process whereby 'the definite social relation between men ... assumes ... the fantastic form of a relation between things'. Crucially this fetishism of the commodity emerges out of the structure of the capitalist economy. It is normal, Marx is arguing, for people to view the economy in terms of commodities and their prices, because in an economy increasingly mediated by money and markets, this is how people experience economic processes in the normal course of their everyday lives. But when people purchase commodities they do not see or directly experience the labour nor the class relations that brought those commodities into being.

In articulating the theme of essence and appearance and the concept of the fetishism of the commodity, Marx provides the basis for a materialist approach to ideology. 'The mode of production of material life conditions the general process of ... intellectual life' at least in part because the material structure of the economy privileges a particular interpretation of itself. Because people's everyday encounters with the economy through commodity exchange necessarily obscure underlying class relations, intellectual theories of the economy which focus solely or primarily upon this sphere of immediate appearance tend also to ignore the existence of the exploitative class relations and power dynamics that underpin the capitalist economy. Therefore such economic theories including, as we shall discuss in more detail in Chapter 7, neoclassical economics and fundamentalist neoliberal doctrine, offer a naturalisation and justification of capitalism and its dominant class. Moreover, those who hold such views are not engaging in pure fantasy, nor are they mere dupes of ideological state apparatuses. Rather, their view of the world emerges out the material structure of the economy, even as they ignore and obscure key elements of it.

This view of ideology can be further augmented by turning to the prison writings of Antonio Gramsci. One of the great virtues of Gramsci's prison writings is its attempt to supersede the Marxist dichotomy between the economic base and the social and political superstructure. In contrast to this position Gramsci argued that there is a 'reciprocity between the structure and superstructure' (Gramsci 1999: 366), and that:

> The claim, presented as an essential postulate of historical materialism, that every fluctuation in politics and ideology can be presented and expounded as an immediate expression of the structure, must be contested in theory as primitive infantilism, and combated in practice with the authentic testimony of Marx. (p. 407)

Here Gramsci rejects the notion that the economic structure creates, in linear and mechanical fashion, the superstructure. Such views constitute 'primitive infantilism' because they are an overly simplistic rendering of the work of Marx, and not reflective of real social processes. Instead, Gramsci articulates a more dialectical view of the relationship between 'structure and superstructure', and a multi-directional approach to causation. As Morton (2007: 96) argues, '[t]he theoretical innovation Gramsci introduced was that whilst the economic "structure" may set certain limits, it was also acknowledged that so-called "super structural" factors have a degree of independent autonomy'.

Emblematic of this is Gramsci's writing about the role of ideas, where he posited 'a "necessary reciprocity" between the social relations of production and ideas' (Morton 2007: 96). While Gramsci understood ideas to emerge out of concrete social relations, they were complex social phenomena which typically brought together disparate elements, from highly developed theoretical precepts, to 'common sense' notions which he variously describes as the 'philosophy of non-philosophers' and the 'folklore of philosophy' (Gramsci 1999: 419). Moreover, Gramsci clearly saw ideas as shaping people's conduct. He writes of the 'solidity of popular beliefs' (pp. 377, 423–4), and highlights the ways in which beliefs condition people's behaviour – the 'imperative character they have when they produce norms of conduct' (p. 424). Ideas can therefore be thought of as having a materiality in a double sense. On the one hand they emerge out of concrete social relations and historical conditions, while on the other they are a material force that structures people's conduct.

This understanding of ideas was important for Gramsci's investigations of hegemony – 'the supremacy of one group or class over other classes or groups' (Fontana 1993). Gramsci sought to understand how hegemony is achieved through the organisation of both coercion and consent. But for hegemony to move beyond mere domination, prevailing discourses must compliment processes of accumulation as they are experienced by people in their everyday lives, and extra-economic state coercion cannot be the primary form of rule.

Importantly, hegemony cannot simply be deduced from the economic superstructure of any given period. Rather, as Stuart Hall (1988: 53) writes:

> Hegemony is *constructed* through a complex series or process of struggle. It is not given, either in the existing structure of a society or in the given class structure of a mode of production.

Chapter 7 will consider this understanding of ideas, ideology and hegemony in more detail with respect to neoliberalism, with a particular focus upon the extent to which there is an ideological congruence between neoliberal theory and actually existing neoliberal changes to the economy; the extent to which the transformation of discourses, institutions and class relations have combined to produce consent to neoliberalism; as well as the extent to which neoliberal transformations of the economy concurrently foster anti-neoliberal subjectivities.

EMBEDDED NEOLIBERALISM

It has been argued that the capitalist economy is embedded within a particular set of social relations and institutional ensemble, and that the state is a crucial component of the latter. This clearly undermines the legitimacy of accounts that understand states and economies as separate and antithetical social spheres, as well as those idealist explanations of neoliberalism which focus upon processes of disembedding and the withering away of the state. However, it also opens the way for a more fruitful understanding of neoliberalism than that which is offered by the dominant idealist account. Moreover, attention to ideology and hegemony paves the way for a reconsideration of the role of neoliberal ideas in the rise and expanded reproduction of neoliberalism. This, in turn, provides the basis for evaluating the implications for neoliberalism of the current global economic crisis.

Just as the capitalist economy has always been embedded within social relations and institutions, so too has neoliberalism, an historically specific manifestation of the capitalist economy, been always socially embedded. The institutions, norms and social relations within which neoliberalism is embedded have provided a supportive social structure for its development. Nonetheless, this supportive social structure has not been without its internal contradictions, and it is such contradictions, as we shall see, that are crucial to understanding the current crisis. In this sense, embedded neoliberalism is akin to what has been described by various Marxist traditions of scholarship as a social structure of accumulation, a mode of regulation, a regime of accumulation (Jessop 1997) or a historical bloc (Cahill 2008a). The process of neoliberalisation, then, has been one of continual remaking of the socially embedded nature of neoliberalism which, while uneven in its geographic and temporal dimensions, has nonetheless adhered to a broad 'metalogic' (Peck and Tickell 2002).

This is quite distinct from other concepts of embedded neoliberalism that have variously been proposed. Moreover, it overcomes their significant limitations, is consistent with a view of capitalist economies more generally as being 'always embedded', and does not assume a neat coherence between neoliberal ideas and neoliberal policies and economic processes.

Phil Cerny, for example, has put forward a concept of 'embedded neoliberalism' that is conceived primarily in ideational terms. For Cerny, neoliberalism is in the first instance 'a relatively closed doctrine', which during the last three decades has been transformed 'into a hegemonic concept that is seeping into and co-opting the whole spectrum of political life' (Cerny 2008: 3). Cerny (2008: 2) argues that neoliberal discourse 'has become deeply embedded in 21st century institutional behaviour, political processes and understandings of socio-economic "realities"'. For Cerny, then, causal priority is accorded to neoliberal ideas. Neoliberalism as a discourse, or set of ideas, becomes institutionally embedded and normalised, and thus structures the behaviour of policy makers and other elites.

Cerny accords causal priority to neoliberal ideas but encounters problems when accounting for variation in the neoliberal practices, and in explaining why these practices diverged from doctrinal neoliberalism. Cerny (2008: 40) admits such a wide variety of neoliberal ideas and such flexibility within neoliberal discourse that it is not at all clear what neoliberalism might mean. For example, according to Cerny (ibid.), '[n]eoliberalism is increasingly what actors make of it'. He also argues that embedded neoliberalism is mediated by other material factors – interests, institutions and other economic processes (pp. 28–39). However, this prompts the question of what is causally prior in political economic change and how useful is the embedded neoliberalism concept if other (non-ideational) social forces are actually driving such changes? While prompting consideration of the embedded nature of neoliberalism, the analytical utility of Cerny's concept is therefore limited. This is not to dismiss the argument that a neoliberal commonsense has developed among policy makers. Rather it is to recognise that, in order to understand the embedded nature of neoliberalism and the dynamics of neoliberalism, an understanding is required of the relationship between the ideological and other mechanisms through which neoliberalism is embedded.

Bastiaan van Apeldoorn (2009) also offers a concept of embedded neoliberalism as it pertains to the European Union. He views 'embedded neoliberalism' as a 'hegemonic project', undertaken by states, and 'reflecting as well as mediating the interests of social and political forces bound up with transnational European capital' (van Appeldorn 2009: 22). He understands European neoliberalism as embedded to the extent that it is combined with socially protective policies and institutions at the national level. He also identifies a contradiction between, on the one hand, such policies which contribute to the embedded nature of neoliberalism and, on the other hand, the 'disembedding' (p. 24) dynamic at the heart of neoliberalism, which is evident primarily at the supra national European level. This concept of embedded neoliberalism relies upon a particular interpretation of Polanyi – one in which Polanyi supposedly conceived of socially protective economic processes as ones which contributed to a dynamic of social embeddedness, and an antithetical set of liberal economic processes which serve to disembed the economy from its social foundations:

> Drawing on Polanyi, embeddedness here refers to the role of the state in sustaining and reproducing markets by in effect protecting society from the destructive effects of the self-regulating market ... The term 'embedded' in embedded neoliberalism thus refers to what Polanyi called the *principle of social protection.* (van Apeldoorn 2009: 24–5)

The problem with van Apeldoorn's formulation is that it is not clear why only socially protective regulations contribute to embeddedness and not other forms of state regulation of economic activity. Surely these latter regulations are also fundamentally social in nature? The strength of van Apeldoorn's conception, on the other hand, is that it points towards a concept of neoliberalism as constituted by state practices and embedded class relations (van Apeldoorn 2009: 31–8).

While the analytical utility of the conceptions of 'embedded neo-liberalism' as put forward by Cerny and van Apeldoorn are therefore limited, each does nonetheless point towards elements of a more fruitful analysis of neoliberalism. Cerny's conception draws attention to the ways in which neoliberal practices are embedded in 'shared mental model[s]' (Cerny 2008: 2) and the formation of a neoliberal 'common sense' (ibid.) among political and economic elites. On the other hand, van Apeldoorn draws attention to the ways in which neoliberal policy practices are embedded within a distinct configuration of class relations, but also prompts consideration of the existence of contradictions between differ-ent elements of neoliberalism.

If we are to take seriously the concept of the 'always embedded economy', and infer from this that neoliberalism is an inherently socially embedded economic form, then any account of 'embedded neoliberalism' must identify the distinct mechanisms through which neoliberalism is socially embedded, but also resist the temptation to counterpose this against elements of neoliberalism which supposedly entail disembedding of the economy from its social foundations. Cerny and van Apeldoorn each point to some of the mechanisms through which neoliberalism is socially embedded; however, each also misses key dimensions of the social embeddedness of neoliberalism. Moreover, Cerny's ideational approach limits his analysis of neoliberalism to the realm of ideas, and tends to assume too great a coherence between ideas, policy practices, and transformations of the economy. In contrast, by positing the existence of an embedding/disembedding dialectic within neoliberalism, van

Apeldoorn's account misses crucial institutional elements which contribute to the social embedding of neoliberalism, even if at the same time they undermine principles and practices of social protection. In combination, therefore, Cerny and van Apeldoorn identify mechanisms through which neoliberalism is embedded, while each author's conception of the mechanisms they discuss remain analytically limited.

By drawing together these analyses, and paying attention to the critiques that have been developed so far in this chapter, a more complete and analytically useful understanding of neoliberalism is possible. Three major mechanisms can be identified through which neoliberalism is 'always embedded' in society.

First, neoliberalism is embedded through class relations. As Albo (2002: 48) argues, '[n]eoliberalism developed out of an important shift in the balance of class forces and the defeat of the left, and in particular social democracy'. Transformations to the regulatory apparatus of states (through privatisation, deregulation and marketisation) facilitated changes within processes of capital accumulation, which in turn led to: a weakening of the power of organised labour and a strengthening of the power of capital at both the level of the firm and the level of state policy making; a freeing of capital from many of the restraints imposed upon it as a result of the post-World War Two 'class compromise' in many advanced capitalist economies; and an expansion of the sphere of commodification, via deregulation and the opening up of former state-monopolised services to profit-making enterprises.

Such neoliberal changes are self-reinforcing. The strengthening of capital in the employment relationship, alongside the enhancement of its already 'privileged position' (Lindblom 1977: 170–88) in the policy process, help to entrench neoliberal practices at the level of the firm and the state for as long as they are viewed by large owners of capital to be in their interests. Therefore, neoliberal practices are embedded in the transformations within the social (class) relations of production that define neoliberal era.

Second, neoliberalism is embedded institutionally. The most important vehicle for this institutional embedding is the state. As noted, neoliberalism has not resulted in a retreat of the state from the economy, and the state has also been integral to the implementation, reproduction and extension of neoliberalism. As Peck and Tickell argue, while many of the key institutions, alliances and social truths that characterised the post-World War Two capitalist order were dismantled, or 'rolled back' through the process of neoliberalisation, the implementation of neoliberalism entailed the 'roll-out' of new forms of regulation:

> In the course of this shift, the agenda gradually moved from one preoccupied with the active *destruction and discreditation* of Keynesian-welfarist and social-collectivist institutions (broadly defined) to one focused on the purposeful *construction and consolidation* of neoliberalized state forms, modes of governance and regulatory relations. (Peck and Tickell 2002: 384)

New rules and their enforcement were required for ostensibly deregulated markets as well as for markets in which privatised entities operated. Thus market deregulation is better conceived of as 're-regulation' (Anderson 1999), including the institutionalisation of labour market regulations which privilege employers over employees. Moreover, the roll-out of the neoliberal policy regime has included the development of regulations and institutions that predispose states to further neoliberalisation, effectively constitutionalising neoliberalism as has occurred, for example, through the WTO and the European Union.

Third, neoliberalism is embedded ideologically and discursively. Neoliberalism has become the new political 'common sense' (Cerny 2008: 39; Macartney 2011: 25), at least among policy making elites. Although neoliberalism has now become the dominant framework through which social and economic policies are made across the capitalist world, there is an unevenness to this. So, while, as Cerny (2008: 3) argues, neoliberalism has become a 'hegemonic concept' in a policy sense, it is also 'highly internally differentiated ... made up of a range of linked but discrete subcategories and dimensions'. This recognises that while there has been an ideological and policy convergence around a neoliberal core among both conservative and social democratic parties in most advanced capitalist nations, there remains, for example, differentiation between conservative and social democratic forms of neoliberal strategy and discourse.

The socially embedded nature of neoliberalism points to its durability and helps to explain recent policy directions of many governments, particularly in the advanced capitalist economies. That neoliberalism is ideologically embedded means that a generation of policy makers have only known neoliberalism as the common sense frame for conducting and evaluating policy. The institutional embeddedness of neoliberalism affords it enormous inertia. The class embedded nature of neoliberalism means that accumulation strategies of the owners of capital are premised upon the maintenance of neoliberal forms of regulation and, unless a significant shift in the balance of social forces occurs, have significant political power to prosecute these interests.

None of this, however, should be read to suggest that embedded neoliberalism operates as a seamless, monolithic whole. Rather, embedded neoliberalism is deeply contradictory. On the one hand, there is a certain congruence and mutually reinforcing dynamic between the different spheres in which neoliberalism is embedded. Neoliberal state transformations facilitate processes of capital accumulation and transformations within capitalist class relations, the power dynamics of which, in turn, help to lock in further institutional neoliberalisation. Concurrently, neoliberal ideology provides an intellectual and moral framework for justifying neoliberal transformations of states and economies, while such transformations provide the only material context in which such an ideology could possibly become dominant. On the other hand, however, there is no guarantee that transformations within any one 'sphere' within which neoliberal policy norms are embedded, will contribute to neoliberalism's expanded reproduction. For example, while neoliberal ideology offers a view of the world that justifies neoliberal transformations and the concomitant accretion of capitalist class power, such neoliberal transformations have also provided the context for the development of anti-neoliberal discourses and movements. Meanwhile, economic instability, insolvency and the destruction of value unleashed through processes of deregulation have forced states to take extraordinary measures to stabilise neoliberal economies and secure conditions for capital accumulation and political legitimacy.

This leads, as Peck (2010: 25) argues, to a situation of '*roiling* neoliberalism, as a still-dominant but deeply flawed "settlement", increasingly buffeted by crises'. As shall be discussed in Chapter 8, the current global financial crisis is perhaps the greatest example of the inherent contradictions within embedded neoliberalism. On the one hand, neoliberal transformations clearly provided the conditions for the emergence of crisis, which elicited extraordinary policy responses by states, including nationalisations which had hitherto been anathema during the neoliberal era. On the other hand, however, part of the responses by states has been to turn to neoliberal policy norms as a form of crisis management. Therefore, in spite of the proclamations of the death of neoliberalism in the wake of the crisis, it has remained more durable than may have been expected had it been a mere ideational phenomenon. This reflects the particular nature of its social embeddedness established over the previous 40 years, as examined in the following chapters.

CONCLUSION

In this chapter it was argued that the neoliberal policy regime is an inherently socially embedded phenomenon. This is in contrast to the idealist conception of neoliberalism, which tends to view it as entailing a separation, or disembedding of the economy from its social support structures, most particularly the state. To make this argument, the chapter outlined the concept of the 'always embedded economy' drawing on the work of Polanyi and Block. Just as the capitalist economy has been always embedded in social institutions and relations, so too has neoliberalism always been socially embedded. Drawing upon the Marxist tradition, the chapter then examined the class relations in which capitalist economies are embedded, and the ways these shape, but do not fully determine, the dynamics of states and ideologies which, in turn, also serve to embed and shape economic activity. It was proposed that the durability of neoliberalism is most usefully understood by examining the ways in which these dynamics and institutions have interacted to embed the neoliberal policy regime in a historically specific pattern of class relations, institutional logics and ideological norms. The next three chapters provide a detailed examination of each of these three mechanisms through which neoliberalism is embedded. This provides the context for understanding the resilience of neoliberalism, as well as the emergence of crisis and states' responses to it. Moreover, it provides the necessary preconditions for an assessment of the limitations and possibilities of moving beyond neoliberalism.

5. The class embedded nature of neoliberalism

This chapter begins the more detailed examination of the specific mechanisms through which neoliberalism is socially embedded by focusing upon the transformations within class relations that underpinned profits and capital accumulation during the neoliberal era.

The chapter begins by examining the contours of economic performance in the global and advanced capitalist economies under neoliberalism. It takes issue with those Marxist scholars who characterise the era as one of persistent stagnation, long downturn or unresolved crisis. In contrast, it is argued that the economic crisis of the 1970s provided the context and impetus for a state-facilitated neoliberal restructuring of production and finance, resulting in increased rates of profit and GDP growth from their lows of the 1970s. The chapter then examines how this was dependent upon, and in part helped to produce, a transformation of the balance of power within the social relations of production such that the associational power of labour was weakened, capital increased its ability to assert its prerogatives over labour, while labour concurrently became much more integrated into global circuits of finance.

It is argued that, as a consequence of such changes, the neoliberal policy regime became embedded in a pattern of class relations, where capital was able to suppress real wage rises and deploy labour more flexibly within the production process, take advantage of a significant transfer of assets from the public sector to the private sector as well as the enclosure of previously non-commodified areas of life, and enjoy considerable influence over state policy making. The class embedded nature of neoliberalism highlights both the durability of neoliberalism due to the enhanced political power it has afforded to capital as a class, as well as the extent to which capital as a class is reliant upon continuing neoliberalisation for its profitability.

THE NEOLIBERAL ERA: LONG DOWNTURN, OR CAPITALIST EXPANSION?

In order to understand how the profit-making strategies of capital have become dependent upon neoliberalisation, and how the power of capital *vis á vis* labour has been strengthened in the neoliberal era, it is first necessary to examine the economic trajectory of the neoliberal era itself. How were the parameters of the capitalist economy reshaped, and what were the implications?

Perhaps the dominant progressive narrative about economic performance in the neoliberal era is that of economic decline. Several leading progressive scholars have argued that the neoliberal era is characterised by persistent economic stagnation and crisis, evidenced by the failure of rates of profit and GDP growth to 'recover' to the levels achieved during the 'golden age of capitalism'. Emblematic of this perspective is the work of Robert Brenner, to whose analysis an entire edition of *New Left Review*, probably the world's leading left-wing scholarly journal, was devoted in 1998, and later reprinted with a new 'Preface' and 'Afterword' by Verso (Brenner 2006). But Brenner's argument resonated beyond the walls of academia, with his *The Boom and the Bubble: The US in the World Economy* (2002) being described in the *New York Times* as 'The best financial history of the period yet' (Madrick 2002). Brenner's argument was that the period since 1973 is best described as a 'long downturn' (Brenner 2006: xix), characterised by 'persistent stagnation' (Brenner 2002: 7) in the advanced capitalist economies. A similar argument is to be found in David Harvey's (2005) *A Brief History of Neoliberalism*, probably the best-known study of neoliberalism yet to appear (and certainly the most cited, with 5943 citations on Google scholar at 21 May 2013, almost 4000 more citations than the next most cited work). Harvey (2005: 157) argues that neoliberalism, while giving 'the appearance of incredible dynamism' has a 'dismal' (p. 154) record of achieving capital accumulation, and 'has broadly failed to stimulate worldwide growth' (ibid.). The late Chris Harman, leading theoretician of the International Socialist Tendency, painted a similar picture, writing of a 'slowdown in productive accumulation' (Harman 2010: 235) and describing the era as the 'Years of Delusion' (pp. 229–53).

A feature of many interpretations of the neoliberal era as one of economic decline is the use of the long post-World War Two economic boom as the yardstick against which contemporary economic performance is measured. Brenner, for example, defines the neoliberal era as a period of economic downturn and stagnation by showing that many key

economic variables, such as GDP growth and rates of profit, were lower
on average in the advanced capitalist economies in the decades after 1973
as compared with the long boom years (for example, Brenner 2006:
xxvii, 5, 240). Harvey's assessment is also based upon tracing a decline
in decade average rates of GDP growth from the 1960s to the 2000s
(Harvey 2005: 154). Similarly, Harman (2010: 232) notes the 'continuing
low level of the profit rate compared with the "golden age"'. Capitalist
economic performance is judged a failure because of the inability to
'regain its dynamism' (Brenner 2002: 285) of the long boom period,
because of the lack of a 'recovery' of profit rates to the highs of the
golden age (Harman 2010: 232) or failure 'to bring about the restoration
of system-wide economic vitality' (Brenner 2006: xix). Brenner (2002: 4)
casts the alternatives for the world economy as a period of 'long
downturn' or 'a new "long upturn" that will bring unprecedented international prosperity, much as the post-war long boom did from the end of
the 1940s until the early 1970s'. This is presumably why he argues that,
to the extent that there have been economic expansions in the neoliberal
era, they should be discounted for not being 'sustainable' (p. 240).
Alternatively, such economic expansions or booms as have existed are
viewed as the product of 'exogenous' factors (Brenner 2006: 335),
including permissive monetary policy and a burgeoning financial sector
generating speculative profits. Harvey (2005: 159) similarly, argues that
'[t]he main substantive achievement of neoliberalism has been to redistribute, rather than generate, wealth and income', the main vehicle for
which is 'accumulation by dispossession', a recasting of Marx's concept
of primitive accumulation whereby the state forcibly commodified areas
of society previously quarantined from profit-oriented markets through
processes such as privatisation (Harvey 2005: 159–65).

Dominant though such interpretations are among progressive scholars,
they are characterised by several shortcomings which lead them to ignore
crucial elements of economic performance in the neoliberal era. Examination of these shortcomings provides the basis for an alternative narrative
of economic performance under neoliberalism than that of 'persistent
stagnation'. Such a narrative points to processes of neoliberalisation as
facilitating a revival of capital accumulation in the wake of the 1970s
crisis, albeit on different terms to those which prevailed during the
post-World War Two boom.

The first shortcoming of such narratives of economic decline in the
neoliberal era concerns the use of the 'golden age' as the yardstick
against which subsequent economic performance should be measured.
The post-World War Two era was a unique period in the history of
capitalism that delivered unprecedented high and sustained rates of

economic growth in the advanced capitalist economies, and in the capitalist world economy more generally. Indeed, such unprecedented growth is the reason it has often been labelled the 'golden age' of capitalism. This is highlighted by Angus Maddison's (2006: 262) historical data on GDP growth which show that average annual world GDP growth during the golden age (1950–1973) was higher than at any other time in world history. Moreover, the same is true of the Western European economies. Crucially, however, in both of these cases average annual growth in the neoliberal era was higher than at any period prior to the golden age. While GDP growth in the USA during the neoliberal era was a little less than one percentage point lower than its average during the golden age, this was still a higher rate of growth than in the period 1913–1950 which preceded the golden age. This suggests two conclusions. First, 'establishing the post-1945 golden age as the standard … sets the bar too high' (Panitch and Gindin 2005b: 145) and 'the unique quarter century long post-war boom (1949–1973) ought not to be the benchmark against which everything else is deemed a "crisis"' (McNally 2009: 45). Second, when considered in longer-term historical perspective, the economic performance of the neoliberal era is rather more robust than is suggested by proponents of the 'long downturn' thesis.

A further problem with characterisations of the neoliberal era as one of stagnation which rely upon detecting an alleged 'failure' of rates of growth or profit to 'recover' to their golden-age highs, is that it is not clear why such an alleged 'failure' should matter. That profit rates in the 1990s, for example, were not as high as profit rates in the 1950s or 1960s could have had little or no bearing on investment decisions during the former period because they are separated by such a long interval of time. As Davidson (2010: 55–6) points out:

> unlike Marxist economists, capitalists do not tend to look back over a forty-year period to compare conditions then with their current situation … The decisive issue is instead whether the rate of profit is sufficiently high for them to continue to invest in production and be confident of an acceptable return and between 1982 and 2007/09 this was largely the case.

It seems, therefore, rather arbitrary to take years during the golden age as the point to which profit rates should return if they were to be judged to be healthy. Why not go further back in time? There does not appear to be a sound basis for choosing the golden age except that it helps one to offer evidence for the argument of a falling rate of profit.

The second shortcoming, common to many narratives of economic decline, is their choice of periodisation for their time-series data. Rather than using year-by-year indicators of GDP growth, adherents to the economic decline thesis typically take average rates of GDP growth for the entire golden age and compare this with the entire subsequent period. Alternatively, they take decade average rates of growth and compare them from the 1950s through to the 2000s to show a long-term economic decline (Brenner 2006: 240). However, different periodisations of time-series data produce different narratives of economic performance. For example, inclusion of the 1970s and early 1980s, during which the global capitalist economy was experiencing ongoing crisis, produces a picture of substantially lower average rates of GDP growth than if a later periodisation is taken. As Panitch and Gindin (2005b: 113) note, real GDP growth averaged 3.4 per cent per year in the US economy from 1984 to 2004, only 0.4 percentage points lower than during the golden age of capitalism (1953–1973).

The third shortcoming of many accounts of economic decline in the neoliberal era is their positing of state- or finance-facilitated growth or profits as artificial and exogenous to the capital accumulation process and therefore that these factors should properly be discounted in any assessment of economic performance. Such arguments are ahistorical in their ignorance of actually existing processes of capital accumulation, in which states and finance have always played a central role. Moreover, they suffer from a problem of consistency. If those same arguments (that state- or finance-facilitated growth is somehow an artificial or exogenous interference in processes of capital accumulation and economic growth and should therefore be discounted) were applied to the 'golden age of capitalism', against which the neoliberal era is often measured, then the golden age too would be found wanting as its unprecedentedly high rates of economic growth and profit would be revealed as heavily 'inflated' by growing state and financial sectors of the economy. It is well-known that the decades after World War Two witnessed a significant expansion in the absolute and relative economic size of the state, and that states also expanded the range of economic activities in which they were engaged (Glyn et al. 2000: 61–2). Indeed, it is for these reasons that the golden age is often labelled as the era of the 'Keynesian welfare state'. Less well-known is that financial capital blossomed during this period too, even in the context of 'financial repression'. As Panitch and Gindin point out, '[t]he profits of [US] financial firms grew faster than non-financial profits through the 1950s and 1960s' (2005a: 53), underpinning a 'dramatic expansion of US financial markets' (2012: 119). It is not at all clear why the growth of these sectors during the 'golden age' is not also considered relevant for the evaluation of comparative economic performance by those who adhere to the neoliberalism as economic decline thesis.

The fourth shortcoming in several accounts of the neoliberal era relates to those that frame it as a period of ongoing or unresolved crisis. While it is theoretically possible that the capitalist system could be in a state of crisis for a period of three to four decades, key developments within the neoliberal era suggest that the period of crisis for capitalism was short-lived and confined to the 1970s and early 1980s. Key markers of crisis were on the wane by the 1980s. Rates of industrial disputes were in decline. Rates of profit were rising, and GDP growth was positive. It is certainly true that unemployment remained higher in many countries than during the golden age (although in many countries there was a decline in unemployment from the 1990s) and that real wages stagnated or grew very slowly. While the temptation among progressive scholars is to interpret as a crisis the failure of the neoliberal era to achieve the same levels of growth, profit and employment as during the golden age, to do so denudes the concept of crisis of its analytical utility, for it means that only in exceptional circumstances during the centuries-long history of capitalism, was that system not in crisis. McNally (2009: 45) makes the point well:

> prolonged expansion with rising levels of output, wages and employment in the core-economies is not the capitalist norm; and the absence of all of these is not invariably a 'crisis'. It is utterly misleading to imagine that capital is in crisis every time rates of increase in world or national GDP fall below five or six per cent per annum.

Moreover, as Davidson (2010: 55) argues, it is difficult to understand the significance of the more recent global financial crisis had the period 'not been preceded by a period of growth and expansion' and instead if it had been one of unresolved crisis.

If the economic performance of the neoliberal era is to be assessed, then the account needs to move beyond the unhelpful conceptual frames just identified. When considered in its own right it is clear that a period of expansion in the capitalist economies began from about 1983. According to IMF data (IMF n.d.), real GDP of the world economy expanded from its low of 0.7 per cent in 1982 and grew at an average annual rate of 3.6 per cent until 2008, after which the effects of the GFC brought about a contraction. The lowest point was the period of 2.2 per cent annual growth during 1991–1993. In the G7 economies, the picture is similar, albeit at lower rates of growth than the world economy from the 1990s. After the recession of 1982, the G-7 economies expanded until 2008. During the same period, the USA, which is often taken as indicative of the health of global capitalism, experienced two phases of expansion –

1983–1990 and 1992–2007 – punctuated by a contraction. While rates of growth were, in each case, lower on average than during the post-war boom years, they were hardly indicative of a period of economic stagnation. Therefore, rather than assessing the period as one of near-permanent economic decline, it is necessary instead to understand the qualitative foundations of accumulation and economic reproduction during the neoliberal era.

The next section examines the foundations of this economic expansion in the neoliberal era. The class-based nature of the neoliberal expansion is identified, as a prelude to demonstrating the ways in which neoliberalism has become embedded in a specific set of class relations.

THE FOUNDATIONS OF PROFIT AND GROWTH IN THE NEOLIBERAL ERA

The economic expansion, just described, is explained by several inter-related factors. Crucially, as will be elaborated later in this chapter, these factors should properly be understood in class terms: that is, as contingent upon and constitutive of the class relations between capital and labour. This provides the context for an explanation of the ways by which neoliberalism is embedded in a specific balance of class forces.

A useful measure of the underlying health and dynamism of the capitalist economy is the rate of profit. It is an indicator of the surplus funds available to capitalists for re-investment as well as a guide as to expectations of capitalists about the prospects for future returns. There is little agreement, particularly among Marxists, about how to measure the rate of profit. Reasons for this include the problems of different national accounting figures between different countries, the problem of mapping Marxist value-theoretic categories onto variables that are measured in prices, disagreement as to the status of the various 'counteracting factors' that Marx (1991: 339–48) said mitigated the tendential fall in the rate of profit, and disagreement as to what is being measured – profit before tax, after-tax profits, or after-dividend profits (see Dumenil and Levy 2011: 58–9; Dunn 2011: 536–40). Nonetheless, many Marxist examinations of this phenomenon during the neoliberal era present a similar trajectory for the rate of profit (Moseley 2003: 212; Shaikh 2010: 48–52; Dumenil and Levy 2011: 58, 152, 270). Taking the US economy as the most common case study, these examinations show that there was a decline in the rate of profit from its high in the mid–late 1960s to its low point on the early 1980s, before it began to rise again and stabilise, albeit at a lower average rate than during the 'golden age' (of course, there were yearly fluctuations around these longer-term trends). This is consistent with the picture already described of an economic expansion beginning from around 1983.

The key to the rise in the rate of profit during this period was the slowing of real wage increases. As Glyn (2006: 116) shows, 'real wages have grown very slowly in the OECD countries since 1979, an extraordinary turnaround from the 3–5% growth rates of the 1960s' (see also Glyn 2006: 6). In the USA average real wages grew by about 0.5 per cent per year from 1979, and about 1 per cent per year in Europe and Japan. From 1980, in the USA, real wages grew slower than the historical trend relative to productivity (Shaikh 2010: 49–50). This meant that even modest productivity growth was able to significantly outstrip real wage rises, thus delivering increased rates of profit to capital. Moreover, as Shaikh (2010: 52) notes, the rate of profit of enterprise (essentially the rate of profit, less the 'opportunity cost' of interest, where an inverse relationship holds between rates of interest and rates of profit of enterprise) in the USA declined more precipitously than the rate of profit up to 1982, partly due to significant increases in interest rates during the period of stagflation. Thereafter, there was a steep increase in the rate of profit of enterprise, suggesting the combined effect of the suppression of real wage increases, and the steady decline in interest rates. Thus wages, productivity and monetary policy underpinned the improving sentiment of capitalists with respect to profits.

This of course prompts consideration of why the suppression of wages did not lead to a crisis of effective demand due to the inability of workers to purchase what they produced. The three chief factors that averted such a crisis and contributed to GDP growth were debt-financed consumption, private investment in capital formation and government expenditure. Their contribution was uneven across the neoliberal era, both temporally and geographically, and rates of increase of private investment (and government expenditure), mostly stayed below those enjoyed during the golden age of capitalism (Dumenil and Levy 2011: 151–2).

Underpinning this were two profound transformations of the global economy – a new global organisation of production, and an expansion of global finance (for a discussion, see Glyn 2006: 50–103; McNally 2011: 40–60) – each, at least in part, facilitated by the neoliberal transformations of the economy discussed in Chapter 2. While the global reorganisation of manufacturing production was well under way by the 1960s, this was accelerated by the economic crisis and states' responses to it. The reduction of tariff protections in the advanced capitalist countries put extra pressure on those manufacturing capitals located in the advanced

capitalist countries to lower costs or increase productivity. The rapid
increase in interest rates in the late 1970s and early 1980s created further
pressure. These factors, combined with the 'intensified competition' and
ongoing 'excess capacity' (Brenner 2006) that had been building in the
global manufacturing sector since the latter years of the golden age to
force a 'shake out' of capital in the manufacturing sector of the advanced
capitalist countries and create a window for the growth of lower-waged
manufacturing production in developing economies, particularly in Asia.
The surpluses generated from such low-waged production provided some
of the foundations of the sustained demand in the advanced capitalist
economies (especially the USA) as they were recycled, through international circuits of credit, to households in core economies to fund
domestic consumption (including consumption of the imported manufac-
tured goods from the aforementioned low-wage economies) and to fund
US government deficits in the 2000s all of which underpinned effective
demand in the global economy (Dieter 2005: 55–73; Gowan 2009: 24–6;
Bellofiore et al. 2010: 125–6).

   The second key factor underpinning demand was the transformation of
global finance. The deregulation of finance from the 1970s enabled the
creation of new financial instruments and, combined with low interest
rates in the later neoliberal period, facilitated greater access to credit for
working class households, particularly in the US (Konings 2011: 145–7).
As Glyn (2006: 54) notes: '[r]emoval of such restrictions (financial
deregulation) generated aggressive competition for customers and much
easier access to credit. The result was greater access to borrowing and
periodic boosts to household spending, particularly in the USA and UK'.
This consumption was financed partly by Asian banks and governments
looking for outlets for the surpluses generated by their expanding
manufacturing sectors. But it was also facilitated by corporations based
in the core economies looking for outlets for the retained earnings from
their profits that would yield higher rates of return than investment in
fixed capital and wealthy households, their share of global wealth
boosted by growing inequality, seeking interest bearing assets (McNally
2009: 60–61). No doubt the explosion of the finance sector of the
economy also provided the funds for the development of new technologies (through venture capitalists, for example), thus contributing to
investment expenditure, even if this also led to enormous waste and
losses (such as the overvaluing of information technology start-up
companies and the subsequent dot-com bubble). Moreover, as Panitch
and Gindin (2005b: 119) suggest, the growth of finance created new
disciplines for firms to produce more efficiently, thus also possibly

contributing indirectly to investment in fixed capital expenditure in the neoliberal era.

NEOLIBERALISM AS A CLASS-BASED SYSTEM OF ACCUMULATION

Having discussed the economic foundations of the economic expansion of the neoliberal era, its class dimensions can now be identified. Many writers, particularly those writing from within a Marxist conceptual framework, have described neoliberalism as a class-based project (Albo 2002; Dumenil and Levy 2004, 2011; Harvey 2005; Davidson 2010). The precise meaning of this varies by author, with different interpretations of 'class' informing the different conceptualisations of the neoliberal era, such as defining class as a set of elites, as a set of institutions, as given by distributional shares and as a particular set of social relations. The following account draws upon the concept of class as a specific set of social relations, as outlined in Chapter 4. Changes within these social relations find expression in changes to the institutional, structural and associational power of labour and capital, in the distributional shares going to each, in the way that the labour process is organised, and to the role of money and credit in the circuit of accumulation. These different expressions of changes within capitalist social relations partly map onto the different understandings of class deployed by key Marxist writers about neoliberalism.

While it is important not to imbue these changes with 'a strategic coherence they never possessed' (Davidson 2010: 16), each of these was part of the outcome of responses to the crisis of profitability of the 1970s by capital, labour and states. In the broadest sense, these neoliberal changes were all direct responses by capital and states to the basic causes of the economic crisis: falling rates of profit and the breakdown of the Bretton Woods system. Capitalism was reshaped in the interests of the owners of productive property and finance, and this facilitated a new era of capital accumulation and the expanded reproduction of the capitalist system.

However, such changes also partly arose out of some of the symptoms of the crisis. While the 1960s and 1970s are often remembered as periods of radical student protest, what is less well-remembered is the upsurge in labour militancy during these years. Indeed, the period from the late 1960s through to the early 1980s was one of intense and quite visible class conflict across the major capitalist economies (Glyn 2006: 5; Winslow 2010: 2–3). It was particularly pronounced in the heartland of capitalism, described by Aaron Brenner (2010: xi) as 'one of the largest strike waves in US history, during which workers twice set records for the number of strikes in a single year'. The primary cause of this militant upsurge by labour was attempts by capital to suppress wages and intensify work in response to the declining rate of profit they were experiencing at the time (R. Brenner 2010: 70). The situation of full employment no doubt strengthened labour's position, at least in the early years of the moblisation.

Not only was there an upsurge in labour militancy, such militancy often also found expression through wildcat strikes and other unorthodox tactics including sabotage. As such, the 'rebellion from below' (A. Brenner 2010) during this period represented a profound challenge to capital and the state, and in the USA prompted similarly militant responses from these social forces:

> Though the level and intensity of workplace agitation never reached the peaks of unrest achieved in 1877, 1919, the 1930s, or 1945, workers' bellicosity was great enough to provoke military intervention on several occasions and presidential action numerous times. It inspired dozens of anti-labor injunctions, thousands of arrests, numerous calls for antistrike legislation, and ever more systematic and coordinated efforts on the part of corporate managers to organise against the labor movement. (A. Brenner 2010: xi)

If the labour movement of the time was militant, it was also radical in its orientation. This was true across the core capitalist economies. No doubt this was partly influenced by the broader radical political mobilisations of the time (Winslow 2010: 4). However, the labour movement also led the push for more radical political economic policy programmes. In Europe, for example, social democratic parties in the major capitalist countries developed programmes of extensive nationalisation and for the curtailment of the prerogatives of private sector capital. These included the British Labour Party's 1973 policy to nationalise one third of manufacturing production, the French Socialists' proposal to extend national ownership from 11 per cent to 22 per cent of industry, and the 1976 Meidner plan of the Swedish Social Democrats for the gradual extension of worker ownership of the economy's largest corporations through the compulsory issuance of shares dedicated to funds controlled by wage earners (Glyn 2006: 18–21). As Glyn argues (2006: 8): 'It is hard, 30 years or so later, to appreciate the sense of alarm engendered by the industrial strife and distributional conflict of the late 1960s and 1970s'.

Neoliberalism emerged out of this period of naked class conflict. On the one hand it was a response to the radicalism of the time, to the

demands for greater democracy, to the loss of the authority of management within the sphere of production, and of state elites within society
more generally, as well as to the working class victories that had now
become 'barriers to accumulation' (Panitch and Gindin 2012: 15). On the
other hand, it was also an outcome of this period of intense class conflict.
Ultimately the period must be judged as a defeat for labour as, despite its
many victories, labour was unable to impose a favourable settlement
upon capital. Indeed, actually existing neoliberalism was largely a
settlement to the crisis of the late 1960s and 1970s, to the crisis of
profitability, and to the broader economic and social crises, and on terms
determined largely by and favourable to, capital.

It is certainly true that neoliberalism emerged unevenly, and that one of
the keys to this unevenness was the relative strength of labour between
different national economies. In the 1980s and early 1990s, for example,
it was the global South and the Anglophone advanced capitalist economies, where the strength of organised labour was most weakened, that
neoliberalisation became strongest. In contrast 'The persistent power of
labor [in Western Europe] provided the key political force that held off
the neo-liberalization that took place in the Anglo-Saxon countries in
those years' (A. Brenner 2010: xvii; see also Glyn 2006: 127). However,
it is also the case that labour was unable to put in place durable
institutions capable of insulating itself against the neoliberal tide. Indeed,
in some cases, labour movement organisations were complicit in ushering
in neoliberal measures. For example, in Britain the Trades Union
Congress supported the Labour Government's wage suppression policy in
the late 1970s up to the 'Winter of Discontent' of 1978–89 (Kerr 1981:
6). Similarly, in Australia, but over a much longer period, the Australian
Council of Trade Unions was a party to the Prices and Incomes Accord
with successive Labor governments from 1983 to 1996 which led to real
wage stagnation, a decline in industrial militancy, and the co-opting of
the trade union leadership into the broader neoliberal agenda being
implemented by the Labor government (Cahill 2008b: 325–9). In the
USA, the leadership of many large unions engaged in concession
bargaining with employers throughout the 1980s and 1990s which both
denuded working conditions and facilitated the introduction of lean
production (Moody 2012: 12).

Moreover, once neoliberalism had become dominant logic of policy
making in the USA its global roll-out gained enormous momentum
(Panitch and Gindin 2012: 14). As Davidson (2010: 37) argues:

> Once the neoliberal order had been established in the USA and imposed on
> the transnational economic institutions which it controls, the model acquired a

cumulative force: in the developed world, the need to compete with the USA compelled other states to try to adopt the organisational forms which seemed to have given that economy its advantage; in the Global South states accepted conditions which restructured their economies in neoliberal ways in order to obtain access to loans and aid.

Thus, neoliberalism emerged directly out of the economic crisis and resulting class conflict of the 1970s. It is now worth examining in detail how transformations to capital accumulation which underpinned economic performance in the neoliberal era were dependent upon key transformations within capitalist social relations of production, which in turn were facilitated by the neoliberal transformations of the state.

The Changing Balance of Class Forces

Perhaps the most important development underpinning patterns of capital accumulation and economic performance in the neoliberal era is the changed balance of class forces brought about by the weakening of labour and the strengthening of capital. Several factors contributed to this changed balance of class forces, some of which had the weakening of labour as their immediate goal, some of which led only incidentally to the weakening of labour.

As discussed in Chapter 2, labour market deregulation was a key feature of the neoliberal era. It was implemented across the advanced capitalist economies and, particularly through structural adjustment programmes, in developing economies as well. Labour market deregulation entails developments such as according management greater flexibility and discretion over the deployment and dismissal of labour within the production process. This makes it much easier for managers to force the costs of restructuring, or of changes to market conditions, onto labour through, for example, dismissal, reducing or increasing hours, and job broadening through understaffing. The deregulation of employment conditions also enables the rise of precarious forms of employment, such as casualisation, which also helps to reduce labour costs. A further element of labour market deregulation is the placing of restrictions upon trade unions, inhibiting their ability to organise, take industrial action, recruit members or engage in 'pattern bargaining' (Blanchflower 2006: 3). This weakens the capacity of organised labour to resist the further neoliberalisation of industrial relations, and can contribute to a more quiescent culture within trade unions. Moreover, labour market deregulation can entail the removal or weakening of rules and institutions that privileged unions. This removes important institutional supports that had historically strengthened the bargaining position of trade unions. Such changes work in concert with restrictive regulations to weaken the capacity of trade unions to resist neoliberalisation and to weaken their ability to enforce the interests of labour upon managers.

Another important component underpinning the changing balance of class forces in the neoliberal era was direct attacks upon organised labour by states, or by capital supported by states. Although less universal in implementation than labour market deregulation, its effects were felt across national economies. Those attacked often were not the biggest unions, but they were sometimes iconic, historically powerful and progressive unions. In any case the attacks by government sent a message to other unions about the consequences of resistance to neoliberal priorities. Those cases mentioned in Chapter 2 were but the highest profile of many disputes during the period in which states employed militant tactics against trade unions directly, or supported the use of such tactics by capital against labour.

Alongside these attacks were compromises by labour movement leaders that unintentionally helped weaken the associational power of labour as a class. These include examples mentioned earlier in the chapter such as the Accord in Australia, and concession bargaining by unions. As Moody (2012: 6–7) notes, the effects across the USA of the concessions agreed to by the UAW leadership in the Chrysler dispute in 1979 were more profound than those arising from the PATCO dispute:

> [f]rom that time on, one union after another agreed to wage-cuts and freezes as well as changes in working conditions, almost always without a fight. This essentially political choice would lay the basis for further retreat. The surrender of 1979 led to a dramatic collapse in almost every major form of trade-union activity across the US economy. This collapse began even before the 1980–1982 recession took hold, and well before Ronald Reagan fired 15,000 air-traffic controllers when their union, PATCO, struck in August 1981. Between 1979 and 1983, union-membership in the private sector fell by 26 per cent.

The labour movement leadership's responsibility for the weakening of organised labour is also evidenced by the many union amalgamations and mergers which 'tended to reduce the urgency of new organising for many unions' (Moody 2012: 15) and brought about a demobilisation as radical and activist-oriented unions were subsumed into larger union structures that were inherently less militant. This is not to ignore the many successful struggles by labour against neoliberalism, both at the industrial and political level. Rather, it is simply to highlight that, as Glyn

(2006: 127) argues, 'it seems impossible to depict all of this as signaling anything other than a major retreat for labour'.

All of these changes occurred alongside the development of greater political organisation and coherence among the capitalist class (Phillips-Fein 2009; Hacker and Pierson 2010: 175–7). This, in conjunction with the declining organisational strength of labour, boosted the already 'privileged position' (Lindblom 1977: 170–88) of business within capitalist states. It meant that there was a diminished counterveiling force against the interests of business. As Hacker and Pierson (2010: 179–80) argue, '[s]trong labor unions are closely associated with low levels of inequality and more generous social programs … The decline of organized labor has greatly diminished the pressure on policymakers to sustain or refurbish commitments to social provision made in the middle decades of the last century'. Indeed, as noted earlier, there appears to be an inverse correlation between extent of neoliberalisation, and strength of organised labour. The changing balance of class forces from the 1970s onwards therefore facilitated a roll-out of neoliberalism, not only with respect to industrial relations, but to social and economic policy more broadly.

Sectoral and Geographic Reorganisation

Deregulation of finance and trade contributed to a global reorganisation of production (albeit this trend was already evident prior to the 1970s) and it was this, as much as the crisis, that states were responding to via deregulation. The greater cost pressure placed upon manufacturing capital in many advanced capitalist countries caused a 'shakeout' of less efficient producers in this sector. This led to widespread redundancies in areas of trade union strength. Not only did this affect union membership density at the level of national economies, it had a more severe and localised impact upon trade union capacity in regions reliant upon manufacturing employment where levels of unionisation had been high.

The global reorganisation of production had three main elements, each of which contributed to a revitalisation of capital accumulation. First, although there was a slowdown in private investment growth in the core capitalist economies during the neoliberal era, some of the investment that did occur was in the roll-out of new, more efficient capital goods such as computerised and robotic production systems (O'Connor 2010: 699; McNally 2009: 47) that required fewer workers to operate. Second, work processes were organised according to the template of what has broadly been referred to as 'lean production' (McNally 2009: 46; Moody 2012: 12–13), which involved work intensification and job broadening to increase productivity. Third, manufacturing production was relocated to lower-cost areas. Such relocations occurred within the core capitalist countries – such as the relocation of manufacturing capital to 'the low-wage, non-union South' in the USA (Moody 2012: 8; see also Panitch and Gindin 2012: 16) – as well as globally, as capital formation and FDI rapidly increased in low-waged developing economies, particularly in Asia (McNally 2009: 50–51; O'Connor 2010: 699). Fourth, there continued in the advanced capitalist economies an increase in the employment and output shares of the services sector of the economy, and a decline in those of manufacturing.

Another important feature of the global reorganisation of production was privatisation and industry deregulation. It carved out a new arena for profit-making activities by commodifying state- or commonly-owned, assets. This, combined with deregulation which allowed the establishment or expansion of private competitors to markets traditionally dominated by the state sector, 'allowed companies to expand markets into sectors from which they were previously excluded and established conditions for international mergers and acquisitions which state-ownership tended to deter' (Davidson 2010: 39). David Harvey has called this part of the process 'accumulation by dispossession', recasting Marx's notion of 'primitive accumulation' to something that, in Harvey's view, those outside of Marxist scholarship can more readily comprehend and identify with. While to describe privatisation as 'dispossession' gives an inaccurate sense of property relations pertaining to state-owned assets (that is, the extent to which such assets were owned by the people was only ever minimal and indirect at best) the concept does capture something of the loss of potential control and accountability over such assets that privatisation brought about. Moreover, while Harvey is clearly wrong when he argues that accumulation by dispossession outstripped capital accumulation as a major source of private wealth in the neoliberal era (see Dunn 2009), his concept does highlight the massive transfer of social wealth to capital that processes of privatisation achieved (see Glyn 2006). Harvey thus demonstrates a continuity in the process of primitive accumulation between the historical events described by Marx that provided the preconditions for the emergence of capitalism, and the neoliberal era. As in the early capitalist period, too, primitive accumulation under neoliberalism had a twofold benefit to capital – it provided a new sphere for capital accumulation by commodifying previously non-commodified or partially commodified sources of wealth, and it extended the reach of market dependence into sections of the population previously able to subsist outside of the wage-labour system.

For labour, the results were negative in three main ways. First, the massive increase in market dependence facilitated by primitive accumulation, particularly in developing nations such as China, 'have swelled the ranks both of the employed global working class and the global reserve army of labour' (McNally 2009: 52). While potentially boosting the structural power of labour on the one hand, it weakened it on the other. Second, the process of privatisation often entailed significant job-shedding in areas of union strength. Typically, opening up of markets through deregulation led to the development of industries with lower rates of unionisation than prior to privatisation. Third, the transfer of large-scale corporations from the state to the private sector weakened the ability of labour to use such democratic control as existed over those assets to mitigate neoliberal restructuring, or quarantine working class living standards from market fluctuations. As Fine (2010: 98) argues, 'the presence and interests of organised labour in social reproduction have also been considerably weakened through depoliticisation, privatisation and so on'.

Changing Distributional Shares

Changing distributional shares of national income also point to the class-based nature of neoliberalism. Two trends indicate this quite clearly. The first is the share of total income as split between wages and profits. Labour's share of national income declined on average across the OECD from the 1970s throughout the neoliberal era. This decline was from a high of 75 per cent in 1975 to about 66 per cent in 2005 (Glyn 2006: 190–91), and it occurred alongside a concomitant rise in the profit share of GDP across the advanced capitalist economies in the neoliberal era (ibid.: 7). As Glyn (2006: 190–91) notes, this 'may not sound dramatic – but it represents an increase of more than one third share of income is accruing to capital'. These trends are primarily explained by the ability of capital to enforce its prerogative upon labour, and to increase profits at labour's expense (as explained earlier in this chapter).

The second, and related, trend is that of growing income inequality. Within the advanced capitalist economies, this has been a pronounced feature of Anglophone nations, particularly the USA, during the neoliberal era (Piketty and Saez 2006; Hacker and Pierson 2010: 155–68). In these economies, the share of national income going to the top 1 per cent has increased during the neoliberal era, while that accruing to the top 10 per cent has remained relatively steady, with a decline in the share of income going to the bottom 90 per cent. As Piketty and Saez (2006: 202) explain, this increase in the income share of the top 1 per cent is almost totally explained by an increase in labour income to this group – that is, the salaries and bonuses of CEOs and managers. As Dumenil and Levy (2010: 48–52) note, this helps contextualise the steady share of wages in the USA during the neoliberal era, as the wages share of national income actually exhibits a steady decline since 1975 when the labour incomes of the top 5–10 per cent are excluded.

Thus the neoliberal era has been one characterised by increasingly unequal rewards and compensations, especially in those economies where neoliberal transformations have been most extensive, the result of which has been the owners and controllers of capital benefiting disproportionately at the expense of the working class more generally.

Changing Roles for Money and Finance

Transformations to the ways in which states regulated money and finance also facilitated transformations within capitalist social relations that were fundamental to the nature of capital accumulation in the neoliberal period.

One element of this was the reorientation of monetary policy towards inflation targeting and away from the goal of full employment in many states. This entailed the acceptance, and normalisation, of a higher rate of unemployment than had typically prevailed during the post-war boom years. Intellectually, this was justified by the concept of the 'natural rate of unemployment' – that demand-side policies, such as monetary or fiscal stimulus, except in the extraordinary circumstances of demand-deficient unemployment, would only serve to raise inflation and could not lower unemployment (Mitchell 2000: 50–51). According to the theory, unemployment could be reduced if monetary policy provided a stable climate for private sector investment, and if labour market and other rigidities were removed through deregulation (see Friedman 1968: 9). Economically, a high rate of unemployment was functional to inflation targeting, as it inhibited workers' ability to achieve wage rises, thus narrowing the likelihood that wages would put pressure on inflation. The class implications of this are clear: as Panitch and Gindin (2012: 14) note: 'Breaking the inflationary spiral [of the 1970s] involved, above all, disciplining labor'. There was to be a permanently large reserve army of labour putting downward pressure upon wage claims and undermining the confidence of labour to press for increased wages and conditions, and increasing the power of management to substitute recalcitrant for unemployed labour. As O'Connor (2010: 698) argues:

The rise in unemployment was important in that it loosened labor markets, undermined the power of unions and threatened worker gains. By reestablishing and expanding the reserve army of labour joblessness and the fear of joblessness became key instruments in the struggle to raise profitability.

The second, and related, change to states' regulation of money and finance that facilitated significant transformations within capitalist social relations was financial deregulation. It removed restrictions upon the ability of firms to use finance as a vehicle for profit and facilitated the burgeoning of new financial instruments. Financial deregulation, and associated changes, also helped to make access to credit for working class households much easier (Konings 2011: 146–7, 154–5). In the USA, as Konings (2011: 155) notes, working class households, 'simultaneously faced with stagnant wages and the ample availability of credit liquidity, increasingly treated access to credit as a source of income to cover basic cost-of-living expenses'. This, combined with the increasing marketisation of areas of social policy and public provision, had the effect of integrating working class households much more into circuits of finance capital, often in ways they only dimly perceived, if at all (see Bryan and Rafferty 2010). In this sense, finance should be understood not merely as 'a framework of institutions, interlocked in a complex network' (Dumenil and Levy 2001: 579), as Marxist theorists have traditionally understood it, but as a fundamental feature of capitalist social relations. Moreover, the phenomenon of financialisation should properly refer, not only to the increase in financial sector profits as a share of total profits (Krippner 2011: 33), important though this is, but also to 'that set of transformations through which *relations between capitals and between capital and wage-labour have been increasingly financialised* – that is, increasingly embedded in interest-paying financial transactions' (McNally 2009: 56). The class dimension of this is highlighted by Lapavitsas (2009: 132): 'In financialised capitalism, the ordinary conditions of existence of working people have come increasingly within the purview of the financial system'.

On the one hand this meant that workers were exposed through their integration into financial markets to the vicissitudes of such markets. For many, the material implications of this only became apparent after the onset of the global financial crisis. On the other hand, these new income streams for capital became crucial to the expanded reproduction of the capitalist system as a whole, and were important in underpinning profits in the mid to late neoliberal era.

THE CLASS EMBEDDED NATURE OF NEOLIBERALISM

Not only is neoliberalism a class-based project, whose key parameters have been shaped by class struggle and reflect, broadly, the interests of capital at the expense of labour, neoliberalism has also become embedded within a reshaped pattern of class relations which emerged at least partly out of naked class conflict between capital and labour from the 1970s onwards. This class embedded nature of neoliberalism lends it enormous inertia and durability. Neoliberalism has become embedded in a specific set of class relations as the profit-making strategies of the capitalist class came to be dependent upon the maintenance or extension of neoliberal forms of regulation. Capital, for example, is dependent upon the ability to deploy labour flexibly within the production process in order to achieve acceptable rates of return. Finance capital requires new avenues for profitable investment, and is dependent upon ongoing privatisations and public–private partnerships to provide some such new spheres (and some major law and accounting firms specialise in advising on and deriving windfall fees from such ventures). Operators in marketised areas of service provision are generally dependent upon government subsidies, whether in the form of direct transfers or regulations privileging their access to clients. Employers have come to rely upon a macroeconomic approach that prioritises low inflation at the expense of full employment. All of this means that capital has an interest in neoliberalism. Moreover, capital is in a strong position to secure this interest because of its own political power, and the weakened power of organised labour as a potential counterveiling political force.

Chapter 4 highlighted how Marx's theory of class is also a theory of power. By focusing on transformations within capitalist class relations, the present chapter has drawn out concurrent shifts within the balance of power between capital and labour in the neoliberal era. The power of capital to enforce its prerogatives has been strengthened within the workplace, while the political power of capital to shape the trajectory of state policy has also been bolstered. Both of these power shifts are crucial to an understanding of the expanded reproduction of neoliberalism.

However, as intimated in the previous chapter, the embedded nature of neoliberal policy norms has not simply been functional to their expanded reproduction, it is also deeply contradictory. The inherent problem of securing effective demand in a capitalist economy was resolved through the greater availability of credit afforded to working class households, even as real unit labour costs were lowered through wage suppression. Concurrently, the financial sector of the economy boomed alongside relatively low levels of fixed capital investment. However, this made the entire system of accumulation vulnerable to 'financial contagion' and, in 2007, it ensured that a crisis within one section of the home loan market in the USA would reverberate throughout the global economy, causing a major slump. A further dimension of the contradictions inherent within the class embedded nature of neoliberalism is evident in the growing power of capital, and the increasing market dependence brought about by the expansion of the field of commodification that has contributed to the revitalisation of capital accumulation in the wake of the economic crisis of the 1970s. While functional to the restoration of conditions for capital accumulation, the increasing power of capital has brought with it problems of legitimacy. Growing concern about the power of big business was evidenced prior to the onset of the global financial crisis by the rise of the global justice/anti-globalisation movement, and since the onset of the crisis it has been manifest in numerous movements against neoliberal austerity in the global North and South. Similarly, the extension of market dependence through primitive accumulation has created a social base for opposition to neoliberalism as it has destroyed traditional livelihoods, just as devalorisation in the global North has created resentment against neoliberal globalisation.

CONCLUSION

This chapter has outlined the ways in which, since the 1970s, the neoliberal policy regime has become embedded within a transformed set of class relations that have bolstered the power of capital, and diminished the power of labour. The chapter argued that the roll-out of the neoliberal policy regime facilitated a reorganisation, and revitalisation of capital accumulation globally. As a result, the neoliberal era has witnessed patterns of accumulation with different parameters to those of the 'golden age of capitalism'. While rates of growth and profit were, on average, lower than during the post-World War Two boom years, and unemployment higher, for capital the neoliberal era was nonetheless a truly 'golden age' (Panitch and Gindin 2012: 16). This was achieved by dismantling institutions and social relations that, by the 1970s, had become barriers to accumulation. Most particularly, it entailed weakening the power of organised labour, legally expanding the scope of capital to enforce its prerogatives within the workplace, expanding the sphere of commodification and removing barriers to the global circulation of finance and production of value. It was argued that capital has thus become dependent for its future profitability upon the maintenance and expanded reproduction of the neoliberal policy regime, as well as being afforded considerable ability to defend the neoliberal policy regime due to the balance of class forces being recalibrated in its favour. Although not without contradictions, the class embedded nature of neoliberalism has thus contributed significantly to its durability and inertia. The next chapter will examine ways in which neoliberalism has become institutionally embedded, most particularly through a series of rules and regulations which mandate that states privilege neoliberal policy norms. This process of institutionally embedding neoliberalism has, in part, been facilitated by the change in the balance of class forces outlined in the present chapter and has often exacerbated such changes by further privileging capital in the delivery of social services and in access to state policy making.

6. Institutionally embedded neoliberalism

It has already been demonstrated that the state has been a central player during the neoliberal era. Rather than being retrenched, or withering away, states constructed a new institutional architecture as part of the 'roll-out' of new neoliberal forms of regulation, even as they 'rolled back' older forms of socially protective regulations. Thus 'actually existing neoliberalism' is quite different from the image of neoliberalism presented by those wedded to idealist modes of thinking.

Chapter 4 argued that neoliberal practices have become embedded in a range of social processes – institutions, class relations and ideological norms – and that these contribute to its expanded reproduction and lend it significant durability. This chapter elaborates upon the ways in which neoliberal practices have become institutionally embedded. By this is meant the development of institutional frameworks that predispose states to neoliberal policy practices. Two broad institutional frameworks that contribute to institutionally embedded neoliberalism are examined. The first is the regulatory bias towards neoliberalism through formal rules that privilege neoliberal policy practices, including various forms of competition policy as well as new rules governing the conduct of monetary and fiscal policy. The second is the privileging of neoliberal policy practices by international lending agencies, most notably the International Monetary Fund (IMF) and the World Bank, which states are mandated to follow as a condition of receiving loans in times of budgetary distress. In each of these cases, neoliberal practices are institutionally embedded by quarantining such practices from popular deliberation. Thus, a process of de-democratisation is at the heart of the socially embedded nature of neoliberalism and is central to its reproduction and durability. Moreover, the institutionally embedded nature of neoliberalism facilitates and reinforces the embedding of neoliberalism within capitalist class relations.

THE STRUCTURAL BIAS TOWARDS NEOLIBERALISM

Writing of the constraints imposed upon the ability of member states to conduct autonomous fiscal and monetary policies by the European Union (EU), van Appledorn (2009: 26) observes that 'policy making is structurally biased towards policies of neoliberal restructuring'. This prompts recognition that the roll-out of neoliberalism has entailed more than just the construction of new institutions to regulate markets in which corporations have been granted greater freedoms or in which newly privatised entities now operate. Rather, it has also entailed the enactment of new regulations that commit states to neoliberal forms of governance. These are 'structurally biased' towards neoliberalism because they provide a framework of rules and obligations that privilege and commit states to neoliberal forms of regulation and response. While the fiscal and monetary policy constraints of the European Union provide a clear example of this, the structural bias extends beyond the sphere of European macroeconomic management. It is embodied in various forms of competition policy, in the EU and beyond, and in the articles of the World Trade Organisation (WTO) as well as numerous free trade agreements, all of which commit states to neoliberal forms of governance. Not only does this highlight that actually existing neoliberalism is underpinned by much more than fundamentalist neoliberal ideas, it also suggests that a shift in the ideological adherence of policy makers away from neoliberal norms is far from a sufficient condition to bring about a shift away from neoliberal forms of state regulation.

Indeed, as several authors have observed, the structural bias towards neoliberal policies gives them a constitutional element (Gill 2001; Nicol 2010). The neoliberal bias is institutionally embedded in such a way as to make neoliberal policy norms part of the rules, principles and precedents by which nation-states are governed, thus effectively constitutionalising neoliberalism. Nicol (2010: 46) therefore calls such measures a 'constitutional law protection of neoliberal capitalism', which draws attention to the ways in which such regulations limit the policy freedom of states to move in non-neoliberal directions, irrespective of the ideology or policy preferences of state elites.

The following section will detail key examples of institutionally embedded neoliberalism which underpin the structural bias towards, and constitutional nature of, neoliberal policy norms, before turning to a consideration of the de-democratising tendencies inherent within such structures and the ways in which they reinforce the class embedded nature of neoliberalism, privileging not just neoliberal forms of policy, but the interests of the owners and controllers of capital as well.

The constitutionalisation of neoliberalism occurs at both the national and supranational levels. At the supranational level neoliberalism has been institutionally embedded and constitutionalised via states joining or making legally binding commitments to supranational economic institutions including the IMF, World Bank, WTO, European Union, EU and various multilateral trade agreements such as the North American Free Trade Agreement (NAFTA). The mechanism by which neoliberalism becomes embedded through these institutions varies, with the former two institutions – the IMF and World Bank – providing a less durable form of institutionally embedded neoliberalism than the latter agreements, treaties and supranational governance bodies.

The contrast between the IMF and the WTO provides a good example of this differential durability. Both have their origins in the post-World War Two era, as key institutions for regulating the international political economy during this period. Moreover, both were later transformed into institutions which facilitated the expanded reproduction of neoliberalism. However, differences in the membership, applicability and enforcement of the rules of each organisation are at the heart of differences in the ways in which each contributes to the expanded reproduction of neo-liberalism.

The IMF facilitates the institutional embedding of neoliberalism through the conditions attached to the loans it brokers for nation-states. That this supranational organisation requires states to implement a range of neoliberal institutional transformations as a condition of access to finance means that, in such states, neoliberalism becomes state policy irrespective of the ideological disposition of state elites. Thus, neoliberal policy norms are institutionally embedded within the conditional lending rules of the IMF.

Founded in 1944 at the Bretton Woods conference, the IMF was central to the international fixed exchange rate regime that prevailed in the post-World War Two period. The IMF was able to support the stabilisation of currencies around their par value (Peet 2009: 76). Membership was based on subscription, with the level of subscription determining the share of votes controlled and the level of subscription in turn set by, and in favour of, the dominant powers at the end of World War Two. Thus the USA had the largest share of votes at approximately 17 per cent, and this allowed the USA, and the other major capitalist states, to exert significant influence over the policy of the IMF (Chorev and Babb 2009: 465–6).

The rationale for the continued existence of the IMF was threatened by the collapse of the Bretton Woods system of fixed exchange rates in the 1970s (Chorev and Babb 2009: 468; Peet 2009: 79). However, the crisis of the global capitalist system offered it a new lease of life. The third world debt crisis of the 1980s turned out to be a catalyst for the neoliberal transformation of the IMF. The US state led the brokerage of private sector funds through the IMF to prevent the default of indebted states, but attached a new set of neoliberal conditionalities to the loan packages (Chorev and Babb 2009: 468). This was the 'Baker Plan', which required 'the privatisation of burdensome and inefficient public enterprises', the liberalisation of capital markets, 'growth oriented tax reform' and trade liberalisation (ibid.: 468–9). It marked the birth of structural adjustment programmes being a condition for the receipt of funds from the IMF, which worked closely with the World Bank on this.

The IMF was now a key institution refashioning the economies of the global South along neoliberal lines. Importantly, however, the expansion of neoliberalism through the IMF occurs only through its conditional lending programme. This is highly limited in applicability. Only those experiencing crisis would apply for funds, and only if they are unable to source the funds themselves through the private sector. This is most commonly limited to states in the global South (although there are a few notable exceptions, such as Britain in the 1970s and, more recently, Greece during the global financial crisis). So, while neoliberal norms are embedded in the conditional lending practices of the IMF, and while this has led to the dramatic neoliberalisation of many states and economies, the global reach of such practices is actually circumscribed by the conditions under which states are likely to turn to the IMF for financial assistance (Chorev and Babb 2009: 472–5).

A rather different way of embedding neoliberalism takes place through institutions like the WTO, the European Union and various multilateral trade agreements. In these cases, in becoming a member of such organisations, or a signatory to such trade agreements, states open their national economies and forms of economic regulation to being reshaped according to the neoliberal principles that structure such institutions. This makes the neoliberal norms promulgated through such institutions much more universal in their reach and applicability (Chorev and Babb 2009: 473).

The WTO is perhaps the most obvious example of this form of institutionally embedded neoliberalism. Its origins are in the General Agreement on Tariffs and Trade (GATT) of 1947 (Chorev and Babb 2009: 466). The GATT committed members to reducing tariffs and other barriers to trade, and thus has continuities with the neoliberal era. However, it was in the 1990s that it was transformed more fully into a vehicle for neoliberalisation. The WTO emerged out of the Uruguay Round of GATT in 1994. These negotiations extended the jurisdiction of the body into new areas and tightened enforcement rules (Chorev and Babb 2009: 470–71). The purview of the WTO was extended to services and intellectual property (Chorev and Babb 2009: 470–71). It limits the ability of governments to implement socially protective regulations in several ways. First, the Most Favoured Nation provision requires all WTO member states to be given equally favourable treatment – if a favourable concession is given to the products originating in one country by another, then it must be extended to all (Kelsey 2008: 28, 30; Peet 2009: 187). Second, the National Treatment provision requires states to extend the same favourable conditions to foreign corporations trading within their borders as they do to domestic corporations (Kelsey 2008: 28). Third, the Agreement on Trade Related Aspects of International Property Rights (TRIPS), limits the ability of states to facilitate the provision of cheap generic medicines and pharmaceuticals because it enforces the private property rights of multinational pharmaceutical companies over the patents for such products (Peet 2009: 223–6).

Unlike the IMF, where membership does not carry the obligation of adhering to a strict neoliberal logic, and where only those in financial distress sought its services, the 'single undertaking rule' of the WTO is a mandatory commitment of all members to all WTO rules (Chorev and Babb 2009: 471). States are able to bring cases against those who defect from such rules, with the possibility of sanctions for non-compliance. This means that WTO members sign up to adherence to a broad neoliberal framework of rules. Neoliberalism then is, in effect, constitutionalised and underpins the rules to which states must adhere.

A less obvious example of constitutionalised neoliberalism is the European Union and its 'economic constitution'. The EU has been praised for its distinct 'social model' because it is thought by many to provide the institutional underpinnings for a 'social market economy' based on the enlightened extension of social protections to all within its purview (Hermann 2007: 61). However, while it is certainly true that the institutional architecture of the EU contains numerous commitments to the protection and extension of social rights, some of which are inherently social democratic in nature, much more durable and binding is its privileging of neoliberal norms.

The neoliberal components of the European Union that have received most attention and recognition are those relating to fiscal and monetary policy. However, perhaps the more pernicious and far-reaching mode by which neoliberalism has become embedded in the institutional architecture of the EU and its member states is through the process of 'legal integration' (Scharpf 2010). Essentially, the nature of and precedents established by the European Court of Justice (ECJ) mandate the incremental neoliberalisation of the regulatory frameworks of the EU's member states, irrespective of the ideological disposition of the governments of such states.

This is particularly true with respect to competition policy, which was embedded in the precursor institutions to the EU (Buch-Hansen and Wigger 2010: 28). However, whereas European competition provisions – such as those embodied in the European Coal and Steel Community Treaty and the Treaty of Rome – were both limited in scope and weakly enforced (Buch-Hansen and Wigger 2010: 28–32), developments since the 1980s have seen them extended in reach to cover a broad range of economic and social policy areas, and with much more binding applicability.

While there are numerous instances of neoliberal regulations being enacted at the EU level, the principal means by which neoliberalism has become institutionally embedded within Europe is juridical. The particular set of treaties which underpinned the European Union, and their interpretation by the European Court of Justice (ECJ), gives neoliberalism both inertia and momentum. It allows for the expanded reproduction of neoliberal regulations, almost irrespective of the ideological disposition of member state governments, or of the European Parliament itself. As Scharpf (2010: 216) argues, decisions taken by the ECJ in the 1960s 'interpreted the commitments that member states had undertaken in the Treaty of Rome not merely as obligations under international law but as a directly effective legal order from which individuals could derive subjective rights against states ... [and] asserted the supremacy of this European legal order over the law of member states', which effectively established a legal framework which bound member states to the decisions of the Court. The subsequent *Dassonville* ruling in 1974 effectively embedded neoliberalism in the Constitution of Europe by declaring that 'any national rules and practices affecting trade could now be construed as nontariff barriers to trade' (Scharpf 2010: 217). This extended the range of social protections within European member states that could effectively be considered unconstitutional by the ECJ because they did not adhere to neoliberal norms. Since then, the bias towards neoliberalism has been extended to make it more difficult to exclude private capital from the delivery of services and infrastructure previously monopolised or dominated by governments (Scharpf 2010: 220). Moreover, the 'principle of mutual recognition' which emerged from the *Cassis* decision (1980) whereby 'regarding those areas and products for which the European Union had not introduced specific European wide regulations, member states were obliged to accept products and services that are legally produced and marketed in one of the other member states' (Hermann 2007: 71), means that a process of competitive deregulation has been institutionalised within the EU. Each of these measures, as Bugaric (2013: 29) argues, 'systematically biases EU policy making in a neoliberal direction ... The neoliberal foundations of the single market and the EMU have imposed real and significant institutional constraints for progressive policy making'.

Within and beyond Europe, many states have implemented policies that further constitutionalise neoliberalism. Through various forms of competition policy states have structured key arenas of regulation according to neoliberal norms, and have established neoliberal norms as the benchmark against which state policy is evaluated and its legitimacy determined. Australia, which has pioneered the widespread roll-out of competition policy, provides a good example. In 1995 the *Competition Policy Reform Act* was passed by the Australian Parliament. It entrenched a series of neoliberal practices at all levels of government in Australia. Chief among these are competitive neutrality and private sector access to public service provision. The former mandates that government enterprises 'should not enjoy any net competitive advantage simply as a result of their public sector ownership' (quoted in King 1997: 271). This means that such enterprises should not receive subsidies or favourable treatments that are not enjoyed by the private sector, and that there should be a preference for corporatisation (ibid.). The latter measure mandates market deregulation and structural separation of government-owned enterprises in order to allow for-profit private sector firms to enter markets previously monopolised by the state. As McDonald (2007: 355) notes, this legislation 'marked a radical, profound and audacious shift in policy formulation ... the imperatives of competition became entrenched in *all policy* across Australia'. All levels of government were required to review their existing laws against the principles of National Competition Policy by the year 2000, and every ten years thereafter (King 1997: 281). By 2007 'almost 2000 pre-existing legislative Acts [had] been reviewed to ensure they comply with competition principles' (McDonald 2007: 350). The result was that neoliberal norms became entrenched as a central logic of the Australian state, binding policy makers and bureaucrats irrespective of their particular ideological worldviews. Similar processes can be found in competition policy regimes across the world.

In the sphere of monetary policy, neoliberal norms have been institutionally embedded through commitments to inflation targeting and central bank independence. While such approaches are by no means universal (Epstein (2007: 3), for example, lists only 23 countries to have adopted inflation targeting by 2006), according to Saad-Filho (2007) they form, alongside floating exchange rates, a 'new monetary policy consensus' which constitutes the globally 'dominant monetary policy paradigms' of 'mature neoliberalism'. Such approaches have become constitutionalised via the ascendance of rules-based approaches over discretionary approaches to monetary policy (Mann 2010: 8). For those states which have adopted such approaches, there is little scope for pursuing demand-side full employment policies. As Saad-Filho (2007) argues:

> the insulation of monetary policy from public scrutiny and political control can thwart the coordination of policies that is essential for the success of *any* significant government initiative. It is much harder to deliver the outcomes chosen by the electorate if the government can count on only one set of (fiscal) instruments, while monetary and exchange rate policy may be pursuing entirely different targets that may even compromise the achievement of other socially desirable objectives.

Perhaps the clearest expression of this is in the European Monetary Union (EMU). The goal of the EMU, as codified in the Maastricht Treaty, is price stability. This treaty also codified the independence of the European Central Bank. Alongside this are restrictions upon the fiscal policy autonomy of member-states, whereby they are required to keep deficits and surpluses within +/–3 per cent of GDP, with public debt not to exceed 60 per cent of GDP. The EMU is 'an institutionally embedded and technocratically regulated economic liberalism, founded on law' (Bonefeld 2005: 93–4), which has the effect of '"locking in" political commitments to orthodox market-monetarist fiscal and monetary policies that are perceived to increase government credibility in the eyes of financial market players' (Gill 2001: 47–8).

None of this analysis should be interpreted as suggesting that embedded neoliberal policy norms are ineluctable. There are numerous strategies deployed by states to evade or lessen their constitutional responsibilities to adhere to neoliberal frameworks. Typically, multilateral agreements or national competition policies contain public interest or similar provisions which lessen, somewhat, the scope of applicability of neoliberal rules. Such measures do give states some room for flexibility with respect to the implementation of, and adherence to, constitutionalised neoliberal policy norms. For example, the General Agreement on Trade in Services (GATS), which forms the legal foundation of the WTO, provides exemptions for certain 'services supplied in the exercise of governmental authority' (Article I.3(b)), but only, as Kelsey (2008: 34) points out, 'where they are supplied on a non-commercial and non-competitive basis'. Article XIV lays out several General Exceptions: 'to protect public morals or to maintain public order', and; 'to protect human, animal or plant life or health' (Kelsey 2008: 35) and Article XIII outlines a range of security exceptions which recognise 'the ultimate authority of states to take measures they deem necessary in their essential security interest, and effectively withhold that action from WTO review' (ibid.: 36). Nonetheless, the scope for states to evade their neoliberal obligations is significantly constrained. Moreover, such public interest clauses do little to diminish the momentum and inertia afforded to neoliberal norms through such constitutionalising forces.

INSTITUTIONALLY EMBEDDED NEOLIBERALISM ENFORCES THE SOCIAL RELATIONS OF NEOLIBERALISM

Institutionally embedded neoliberalism strengthens the power of capital by amplifying the other neoliberal disciplines that operate upon state elites, including the disciplines of international financial markets. This occurs in several distinct ways.

First, the constitutional privileging of private sector capital in the delivery of public services facilitates the expansion of private for-profit institutions with a direct interest in the maintenance and expansion of such neoliberal norms. The profit-making strategies of an increasing number of firms become geared to neoliberal arrangements which organise the delivery of public services by private providers. This includes the use of for-profit corporations to provide regulation itself. The rise of industry self-regulation has been a notable feature of the neoliberal era (Haufler 2001). Whole sectors of national economies are regulated by codes, with varying degrees of enforceability, which are developed and overseen variously by a combination of industry groups, NGOs and the state. Moreover, in the neoliberal era, norms developed by private sector bodies, such as credit ratings agencies and multinational accounting firms, have increasingly become embedded within the regulatory apparatuses of states. As Braithwaite (2008: 25) highlights, 'many states simply forfeit domains of regulation to global corporations that have superior technical capability and greater numbers of technically competent people on the ground'. This can make such arrangements incredibly resistant to retrenchment, as organised employer interests will mobilise to prevent such an occurrence. This can lead to the phenomenon known as 'policy drift', which occurs when the effects of public policies changed substantially due to shifts in the surrounding economic or social context and then, *despite the recognition of alternatives*, policymakers failed to update policies *due to pressure from intense minority interests or political actors exploiting veto points in the political process.* (Hacker and Pierson 2010: 170)

Second, as Kelsey (2008: 4) writes of the GATS, the aim of constitutionalised neoliberalism 'is to discipline the regulatory choices available to governments'. This occurs not only through binding governments to particular modes of governing, but also through exposing governments much more to market disciplines. For example, by constitutionalising neoliberal approaches to financial regulation, governments are much more exposed, and sensitive, to the freer movement of capital across borders, and the information signals sent about governments by ratings agencies and other large capitals. Similarly, by constitutionalising neoliberal approaches to monetary policy, governments effectively allow a significant component of macroeconomic policy to be determined by rules-based responses to changing market conditions. Each of these phenomena narrow the scope that states have for conducting macroeconomic policy.

Third, many of the measures prescribed through constitutionalised neoliberalism weaken the power of organised labour and bolster the relative strength of capital. Take monetary policy for example. Inflation targeting regimes of monetary policy almost inevitably go hand in hand with a substantially higher average rate of unemployment than prevailed during the post-World War Two boom years (as discussed in Chapter 5). The maintenance of such a significant reserve army of labour is of course justified through an acceptance of the concept of the 'natural', or 'non-accelerating inflation', rate of unemployment. However, the maintenance of the industrial reserve army also assists the achievement of inflation targets as it helps to keep wage rises in check by diminishing the bargaining power of labour. Moreover, the logic of inflation targeting is to tighten the monetary screws when inflation gets close to or goes beyond the targeted band, thus contracting demand and often raising unemployment. A cyclical pattern can thus be produced where unemployment fluctuates around its 'natural rate'. This helps entrench labour movement weakness as an institutionalised feature of the neoliberal era.

All of this has implications for the ability of the vast bulk of humanity to exercise democratic influence over the economy. The differentiation of the 'economic' and the 'political' under capitalism (discussed in Chapter 4) means that:

[t]he essence of the capitalist 'economy' is that a very wide range of human activities, which in other times and places were subject to the state or to

communal regulation of various kinds, have been transferred to the economic domain. In that ever expanding domain, human beings are governed not only by the hierarchies of the workplace but also by the compulsions of the market, the relentless requirements of profit maximisation and constant capital accumulation, none of which are subject to democratic freedom or accountability. (Wood 2012: 317)

Capitalism places certain limitations upon the extent of the democratisation of economic relations, and the dynamics described in this chapter represent an attenuation of democracy (Gill 2001: 59). However, it should not be inferred from this that neoliberalism is inherently undemocratic. As Ayers and Saad Filho (2013: 16) note, 'most neoliberal economies are democratic in the limited sense ... Most non-democratic countries are not neoliberal and ... Most transitions to democracy in the last 30 years whether from military dictatorship, single party rule, autocracy or Soviet style socialism, have been coeval with transitions to neoliberalism'. Nonetheless, each of the ways by which neoliberal policy norms are institutionally embedded contribute directly to a de-democratisation of the economy, effectively quarantining the implementation and expanded reproduction of neoliberal norms from processes of democratic deliberation.

As Stephen Gill (2002: 48) argues, the 'central objective of new constitutionalism is to prevent future governments from undoing commitments to a disciplinary neoliberal pattern of accumulation'. In so doing, such arrangements make governments and economic policies 'less responsive to popular-democratic forces and processes' (Gill 2001: 47). This is evident, for example, in the trend towards both rules-based monetary policy, such as inflation targeting, and central bank independence which result in the 'insulation of monetary policy from public debate' (Saad-Filho 2007). European monetary union arrangements have, for example, as Scharpf (2013) points out, 'removed crucial instruments of macroeconomic management from the control of democratically accountable governments'. In such ways, the de-democratising processes that are inherent features of the roll-out of new neoliberal institutional forms also help to entrench neoliberal policy norms as the guiding logic of state policy, thus contributing to their fundamentally institutionally embedded nature, as well as institutionalising what is effectively a policy choice about the way economic resources will be distributed that favours capital.

CONCLUSION

This chapter has illustrated some of the ways by which neoliberalism has become institutionally embedded in a transformed set of state regulations. Whereas previous chapters outlined some of ways in which the state was integral to the roll-out of neoliberalism and, contrary to the idealist thesis, that processes of privatisation and deregulation went hand in hand with the development of new state institutions and regulations, this chapter has focused attention on a particular set of regulations that commit states to further neoliberalisation. It was argued that this effectively constitutionalises neoliberalism, and makes it less a policy choice of state elites and more a logic of state. Part of the constitutionalisation of neoliberal policies is the quarantining of neoliberalism from democratic deliberation, as it becomes inscribed in the rules to which state elites are accountable. Not only does such institutional embedding further strengthen the power of capital, thus complementing the embeddedness of the neoliberal policy regime in a set of class relations which privilege capital, it also gives added durability to neoliberalism, making it highly resistant to change.

7. Ideologically embedded neoliberalism

Having examined the ways in which the neoliberal policy regime is embedded institutionally, as well as within a reshaped set of class relations, this chapter considers the ways that neoliberalism has become embedded in a pervasive ideological framework. It is argued that neoliberalism has become the 'common sense' policy approach among political elites in most advanced capitalist states. The chapter first identifies how neoliberalism supplanted the older post-World War Two policy consensus in many capitalist democracies. The neoliberal policy convergence among the major conservative and social democratic parties is examined, as is the rise to dominance of neoliberal policy frames among bureaucratic elites who shape and implement state policies.

The chapter then examines the relationship between neoliberal theory and practice. If there are discrepancies between neoliberalism's representation of the world, and the trajectory of the capitalist political economy, particularly with respect to the size and scope of the state, how can neoliberalism have become dominant? Have policy elites simply been hoodwinked by an irrational ideology, or is there a more compelling and complex story to be told? This chapter argues that, in order to understand the pervasiveness of neoliberal ideas among political and economic elites, neoliberal ideas must be read ideologically – as a discourse which at once obscures, but which also offers a partial representation of, reality, privileging capitalist class interests.

The chapter then considers the extent to which neoliberal ideological and discursive frames have gained traction outside of elite circles, within and global population more generally. Has neoliberalism become hegemonic, or is it simply a project pursued by elites that lacks a social support base? This chapter examines the paradox that while resistance to neoliberalism has been ongoing, and while neoliberal policies have often experienced low public approval ratings, neoliberal practices have proved highly resistant to change.

NEOLIBERALISM AS ELITE IDEOLOGY

Chapter 2 illustrated the extent of neoliberalisation across the capitalist world since the 1970s. As numerous scholars have shown, part of this process of neoliberalisation has been a convergence of state policy practices and major party platforms around neoliberalism (Fourcade-Gourinchas and Babb 2002; Shields 2007; Belloc and Nicita 2011; Mudge 2011; Horsfall 2013). For example, Mudge's (2011: 365) survey of the policy platforms of major parties across 51 countries (OECD, central and eastern Europe and Israel) from the 1970s until 2004 found that '[m]ainstream parties neoliberalised their programs across the Western world after the 1970s'. Such parties:

> increasingly emphasised that the state's responsibilities were primarily market supporting, with punitive intervention when necessary: education, work, and the law and order rather than welfare protections. Parties also increasingly described the means by which the state should act in market centric ways. (Mudge 2011: 358)

To note there has been convergence is not to say that all capitalist states have become identical. Conversely, the mere presence of differentiation among states is not evidence against neoliberal convergence, as some have suggested (Haupt 2010). Rather, this is more satisfactorily explained by the uneven process of neoliberalisation that is significantly conditioned by the inherited institutional architecture of any given nation-state (Fourcade-Gourinchas and Babb 2002). It is in this sense that it is proper to speak of the uneven geographical development of neoliberalism and of variegated neoliberalism (Brenner et al. 2010; Macartney 2011). While the timing and articulation with inherited institutions and social relations varies by country, the neoliberal processes of privatisation, deregulation, marketisation, corporatisation and those pertaining to macroeconomic policy have become the dominant framework for policy making across capitalist states globally (Gamble 2009). Neoliberalism is not only dominant within political parties and among members of Parliament, but also within bureaucracies, including the supranational lending organisations that have been so important in the expanded reproduction of neoliberalism (Pusey 1991; Chwieroth 2007).

In Chapters 2 and 3 it was shown that neoliberal normative theories were not the key driving force for the neoliberal transformation of states and economies. However, while neoliberal ideas did not cause the neoliberal policy revolution, they have played an important role in its expanded reproduction. Indeed, the foundational principles of neoliberal theory provide an important discursive framework that guides thinking about the desirable course, nature and scope of policy making in capitalist economies, particularly among political elites.

This discursive frame provides an economic and philosophical justification for neoliberal policies, casting the neoliberal policy revolution as a rational and almost inevitable response to the logic of market forces, as well as casting alternatives to neoliberalism as unrealistic and/or romantic and opponents of neoliberalism as motivated by ideology or narrow self-interest. Within this discursive frame:

> The market is equivalenced as the sphere of economic freedom, while the state is signified as the embodiment of illusory, and ultimately coercive, political freedom. The notion of a self-contained individual subject is privileged, ontologically and epistemologically, while invocations of a collective subject (the 'social', the 'public good', and so on) are regarded with suspicion. The market is valorized as the means of individualized ends, while the misplaced – however well intentioned – politics of social purpose or collective ends is equivalenced with rationalistic, statist fallacies. This neoliberal identity is then skilfully equivalenced, rhetorically, with the identity of the common man/woman (as opposed to a more accurate identification with the powerful elites that have most to gain from the expansion of market freedoms), while statism or socialism is equivalenced with the identity of elitist, unrepresentative, and 'know all' intellectuals. (Phelan 2007: 33–4)

The internal logic of neoliberal theory allows it to act as a highly malleable discourse for justifying actually existing neoliberalism. Much like the neoclassical economics with which it shares conceptual roots, neoliberal theory is unfalsifiable from the point of view of its adherents. As Varoufakis (1998: 341) notes neoclassical 'theories are so structured that no observation can contradict them', since the predictions of neoclassical theory are embedded in its axiomatic assumptions. This is also true of neoliberal theory, which means that the following conclusion reached by Foley (2004: 341) about neoclassical economics, also applies to neoliberalism: '[n]o accumulation of its empirical anomalies or demonstration of its logical inadequacies will somehow magically dispel [its] power'. As noted in Chapter 3, neoliberal theory has an ambiguous stance with respect to the proper role of the state – something that is particularly evident in the work of Hayek. Both of these features allow phenomena that appear to contradict neoliberalism's foundational principles or predicted effects, to be explained away as the product of exogenous interferences, incorrect application of the theory, or as being justified, given the unique set of prevailing circumstances. This type of reasoning is described by Dean (2008: 56) with respect to 'free trade':

According to the fantasy of free trade, everybody wins. If someone loses, then, this simply indicates that trade was not free. Someone cheated, didn't play by the rules. Someone had secret information, the benefits of insider knowledge or advantages of an unfair monopoly.

None of this is to suggest that those for whom this neoliberal discursive frame constitutes part of their common sense conception of the world have necessarily read, imbibed nor fully understood the key canonical texts of neoliberal theory. Indeed, it is not necessary for someone to have read any of the works of Hayek, Friedman, Buchanan or Becker for them nonetheless to interpret the economy and economic policy through the neoliberal discursive frame. Rather such frames are circulated through neoliberal think tanks, significant sections of the mainstream media as well as being privileged by the institutional architecture through which neoliberal policy practices are embedded, as discussed in Chapter 6. Moreover, to the extent that the work of Hayek, Friedman and other key neoliberal intellectuals is specifically drawn upon, it is often cherry picked or selectively appropriated so as to support one's favoured policy option or historical narrative.

In Chapter 4 it was argued that a central flaw of neoliberal theory is its misrepresentation of the nature and role of states and markets in capitalist economies. This stems from its more fundamental rejection of class as an explanatory category. Despite this, however, the neoliberal discursive frame is, at least to a certain extent, materially grounded. That is to say, it does correspond to certain important political economic transformations during the neoliberal era. The processes that are signified by neoliberal discourse are not complete fantasies, even as neoliberal discourse simultaneously obscures these transformations in ways that both buttress and mask the power and interests of the capitalist class which has been the main beneficiary of such changes.

To understand this it is useful to recall Marx's concepts of essence and appearance that were discussed in Chapter 4. The political economic changes to which neoliberal discursive frames correspond are those located within the realm of immediate appearances. They represent one level at which people encounter actually existing neoliberalism. For example, the neoliberal era has seen the extension of the scope of commodification: the range of activities for which engaging in markets is compulsory. This is consonant with the neoliberal discursive frame which takes as its basic unit of analysis individuals in market relationships. The upshot of commodifying processes is, as Foley (2004: 339–40) explains, to '[impose] an inherently quantitative aspect on human activity' and leads to the 'imperative to calculate from a definite point of view, self-interest'. This is because commodification subjects social use values to market exchanges. In one sense then, the neoliberal model of the self-interested, calculating individual is more relevant now than ever before as ever more aspects of social life become commodified and people become more market dependent.

Similarly, in a purely formal sense, individual economic freedoms have been extended through neoliberalisation. People are formally free to engage in a whole host of transactions which were previously not possible, or from which they were previously excluded. For example, under neoliberal policy regimes, people may be formally free to negotiate individual employment contracts, or to choose a private health provider or a private electricity provider. This is clearly in line with the normative proposition of neoliberal theory that individual economic freedoms should be expanded.

Moreover, as argued in Chapters 5 and 6, the policy options available to states are constrained, at least to a significant degree, to a repertoire of broadly neoliberal tools, thus adding resonance to the neoliberal world-view. As Gamble (2009: 4) argues:

> neoliberalism is more than just an ideological cloak for the interests of the powerful. Its ascendancy also accurately reflects in important respects the way in which the modern world is ordered ... [neoliberalism] in part reflects and justifies the fundamental structures that underpin and circumscribe that marketplace ... it also reflects ... that there are certain characteristics of modern society, such as the extended division of labour, individual property rights, competition and free exchange, that have to be accepted as givens rather than choices.

The world that has emerged during the neoliberal era is thus, at a certain level of analysis, functional and congruent with neoliberal discursive frames.

Nevertheless, while neoliberal discursive frames correspond, at one level of analysis, to the transformations wrought under actually existing neoliberalism they simultaneously miss, and indeed obscure, the more fundamental transformations within the social relations that constitute the neoliberal phase of capitalist history. Neoliberal discourse 'represents the relations of modern capitalist society one-sidedly' (Foley 2004: 340) by ignoring issues of power and compulsion and focusing instead on freedom and voluntarism in market exchanges. For example, market exchanges, while formally free, are also underpinned by asymmetrical power relations. Whether it be decisions about what to produce, or on what terms labour power will be hired, the institutionalised form of capital generally occupies a privileged position. Similarly, while market exchanges are formally voluntary, the extension of such exchanges to more and more areas of social life generally arises from people losing access to non-market forms of provisioning, thereby leading to market relations becoming essentially compulsory. Moreover, while formally free to choose, people's actual ability to exercise such market choices is significantly dependent upon their location within the unequal distribution of economic resources that is a feature of actually existing neoliberalism, thus excluding some from access to commodified goods and services. When read as an ideology, then, we may conclude with Lebowitz (2004) that '[i]n the end, the simple message of neoclassical economics (and the neoliberal policy it supports) is, *Let capital be free!*' Neoliberal ideas thus form the basis of an ideology that both explains and misrepresents the world as it is, and as it could be. This ideology has a materiality (Gramsci 1999: 424; Stephen 2011: 216) in so far as it constrains the range of policy options deemed to be legitimate (Avsar 2011: 137), and in so far as it deems alternatives to neoliberalism to be unrealistic or undesirable.

The malleability of this ideology is, in part, demonstrated by the way in which it has become the guiding framework of parties from different sides of the political spectrum. As noted earlier, the neoliberal policy convergence across the capitalist world has been 'bipartisan' (Belloc and Nicita 2011: 123). While neoliberalism is often associated primarily with conservative governments, with iconic leaders such as Thatcher, Reagan and Pinochet, in fact both conservative and social democratic governments and parties have embraced and implemented neoliberalism. Indeed, some social democratic governments, alongside those conservative regimes already mentioned, were at the forefront of pioneering neoliberal transformations of the state, such as the Australian Labor Party (Lavelle 2005). Neoliberal practices have even become central to some of those social democratic governments ostensibly defined in opposition to neoliberalism, such as the Workers Party of Brazil (Petras and Veltmeyer 2003), leading some to speak of a left-wing neoliberalism (Mudge 2011; Saad Filho 2013). For social democratic parties, this has meant jettisoning some of their historical commitments to socialism, restraints upon capital or state ownership of industry. But it has also entailed the grafting of neoliberal discursive frames onto the historical language of social democracy: egalitarianism, fairness and a commitment to the working class. This was certainly the strategy pursued by self-styled 'third way' parties including Britain's New Labour, and the German and Swedish Social Democratic parties. Despite such discursive gymnastics, however, third way parties '[f]ar from breaking with the neoliberal policies of the new right ... [have] continued and, in certain ways, radicalised them' (Callinicos 2001: 121).

While one may certainly agree with Mudge (2011: 358) that, in the process of neoliberalisation, 'the parties that changed most dramatically were on the centre-left', it is also important to note the internal transformations that occurred within traditional Conservative parties. After all, at least in many advanced capitalist countries, Conservative parties were part of the broad bipartisan consensus about economic management during the post-World War Two era. That is to say, they embodied in practice the very collectivism that was so despised by Hayek and other fundamentalist neoliberals. Moreover, the key tenets of trad-itional Conservative ideology are, at least in some important respects, antithetical to neoliberalism. Where neoliberalism gives primacy to individual liberty, conservatives value social order, and the institutions and deep-seated traditions which underpin it, such as the patriarchal family. Where neoliberals propose radical reform, conservatives are wary of rapid social transformations and political blueprints for change. While such contradictions are very real, they were overcome, or allayed, in practice by a combination of political subordination of anti-neoliberal Conservative elements within the major Conservative parties, and discur-sive unification of Conservative and neoliberal rhetoric. With respect to discursive unification, for example, there has developed an argument within Conservative parties and among neoliberal and Conservative intellectuals that the institutions most valued by conservatives, such as the patriarchal family, are best served through neoliberal policies of privatising the provision of welfare – or getting the state off the backs of families and devolving welfare provision to those who are in the best position to respond to the needs of such families, whether that be in the form of for-profit welfare providers or not-for-profit charity groups. This discursive unification is also evident in statements by key neoliberal politicians and intellectuals which conflate individuals and families as the basic unit of analysis – such as Margaret Thatcher's (1987) famous statement 'who is society? There is no such thing! There are individual men and women and there are families', or Milton Friedman's (2002: 12) slippage between the use of individuals and families as his basic unit of analysis in *Capitalism and Freedom*.

The foregoing discussion suggests that since the 1970s there has been a process of ideological transformation that has taken place alongside the neoliberal transformation of states and economies. As discussed in Chapter 1, the ideas-centred understanding of neoliberalism, so dominant among its progressive critics, assumes this process is best explained by political elites coming under the influence of neoliberal doctrine, which caused them to shift their policy preferences in favour of neoliberalism. However, closer scrutiny of such claims in Chapters 2 and 3 demonstrated that such a chain of events was highly unlikely in practice.

In contrast, a more plausible interpretation can be offered if we recall the key features in the development of embedded neoliberalism, and the key dynamics of the capitalist state. In Chapter 4 it was argued, drawing upon the work of James O'Connor, that the capitalist state is governed by the twin, sometimes contradictory, imperatives to secure conditions for capital accumulation and simultaneously also to secure conditions for political legitimacy. The economic crisis that beset the global capitalist economy in the 1970s was a signal that prevailing institutions, social relations and policy responses that had, during the post-World War Two era, served to regularise processes of capital accumulation, had now become dysfunctional with this goal.

What would become of the policy regime of neoliberalism was, increasingly, the dominant response by states to the need to secure accumulation in this crisis situation. No doubt, there are examples of this occurring because a particular politician was committed to the fundamentalist doctrines of Hayek and/or Friedman and pursued their normative agenda as a blueprint, or because a fundamentalist neoliberal intellectual came to be in a position of policy influence and used that position successfully to push their normative agenda. On the whole, however, as suggested in Chapter 3, the reality was much more complex. Policy makers turned to actually existing neoliberalism for a variety of reasons. In part, it was because particular sections of capital advocated privatisation and marketisation as a way of opening up the state to profitable activities, or deregulation, in order to free businesses from restrictions imposed during the post-World War Two era and/or to further subordinate labour within the production process (see Cahill 2002; Hacker and Pierson 2010: 174–82). In part it was seen as a pragmatic response to a set of circumstances that was beyond the experience of most policy makers. Clearly actually existing neoliberalism was constructed by policy makers across the political spectrum with varying degrees of knowledge and awareness of fundamentalist neoliberal doctrines. Such neoliberal doctrines, as argued in Chapter 3, did not provide, for the most part, detailed blueprints or programmes which policy makers diligently followed. Rather, to the extent that they are influential it was, and continues to be, as discursive and conceptual frames – frames that justify neoliberal policies in economic and ethical terms; frames for thinking through policy alternatives; and frames for demonising opposition. Crucially, it is the inherent malleability of neoliberal doctrine, combined with the ways in which it both obfuscates and correlates with the observable reality that is the key to this ideological function.

This is quite distinct from the ideas-centred argument that neoliberal doctrine was swallowed whole by policy makers. It is distinct from the assumption that policy makers were either hoodwinked by neoliberal doctrine, or became disciples of Hayek. It is quite different to the argument that a small but powerful cabal of fundamentalist neoliberal intellectuals managed to insinuate themselves within key policy networks and thereby shape the course of history.

Neoliberal ideas are not the primary force responsible for the rise of the neoliberal policy regime. Rather, they are part of a complex of forces that gave rise to neoliberalism. Nonetheless, as actually existing neoliberalism has been rolled out, neoliberalism, as a set of ideological discursive frames, has become the basis of a policy 'common sense' or 'rationality' (Beeson and Firth 1998) among political elites across the capitalist world. The practices of neoliberalism have become the default approach to policy across the capitalist world and neoliberal theories operate as justifications for such policies, as well as ways of explaining observed reality. To be sure, there is an unevenness to these processes, but the result has been to embed neoliberal policy practices in a pervasive ideological structure, just as they have also become embedded institutionally and within a distinct pattern of class relations. However, the success of such a programme in securing political legitimacy is quite another matter, and it is to this issue that the chapter now turns.

NEOLIBERALISM CONTESTED

While neoliberalism has become hegemonic among policy elites, it has been subject to persistent dissent from those who have been exposed to its regulations. Political mobilisation against neoliberalism is of two types. The first is mobilisation against specific neoliberal policies, proposals or institutions. The second is mobilisation against neoliberalism more generally, particularly in the form of the 'anti-globalisation' movement and the more recent 'occupy' movement.

Although the 'anti-globalisation' movement is probably the most obvious manifestation of organised opposition to neoliberalism, dissent against neoliberalism predates this movement by at least two decades. Whether it be through demonstrations and riots against austerity and structural adjustment programmes in developing economies (146 from 1976 to 1992 according to Walton and Sedden (1994: 39–40)), strikes and worker mobilisations against labour market deregulation, iconic struggles against neoliberal governments such as those discussed in Chapter 5, or a host of other contentious mobilisations against privatisation and deregulation, contestation of neoliberalism contributed to the turbulent history of this era.

When the anti-globalisation movement rocketed into public awareness through the demonstrations against the WTO at Seattle in 1999, most media commentators presented it as a new phenomenon. This, however, was to ignore the way in which this movement emerged out of other struggles against neoliberalism at national and international levels. In addition to those already mentioned, in the mid to late 1990s several important mobilisations against supranational neoliberal agreements and institutions, such as the successful anti-MAI campaign, the protests surrounding the 50th anniversary of the Bretton Woods institutions, and the Zapatista uprising in Mexico and other mobilisations against NAFTA (Starr 2000: 45–53; Bleiker 2002: 191–2; Johnston and Laxer 2003: 39; Ayers 2004: 14–17), increasingly brought anti-neoliberal activists from developing and developed capitalist economies into contact with one another, and helped to cement a 'transnationally-accepted master collective action frame to challenge the prevailing neoliberal orthodoxy' (Ayers 2004: 14). While the movement went by many names – 'anti-globalisation', 'alter globalisation', 'global justice' – it was clearly anti-neoliberal in its orientation.

Two major tactics were used by the movement: protests at the meetings of major supranational institutions associated with neoliberalism, and gatherings of the movement itself, primarily via the World Social Forum. In the former case, the protests at Seattle established a frame for mobilisation against global neoliberalism. Across the world throughout the first decade of the twenty-first century, protests were held outside meetings of the World Trade Organisation, World Economic Forum, International Monetary Fund, World Bank, and the G7 and G8. Typically, these protests 'proceeded in a comparable way: the overwhelming majority of protesters engaged in a variety of peaceful and nonviolent forms of protest, while a small minority committed acts of violence. At times, as in Seattle, Molotov cocktails and battles with riot police led to looting and the destruction of property' (Bleiker 2002: 202). The World Social Forum, in contrast, provides a space for the 'exchange and diffusion of ideas and tactics' (Byrd and Jasny 2010: 357) among movement activists. Meeting between 2003 and 2005 in Porto Alegre, Brazil, and thereafter 'deregionalising' to Europe, Asia and Africa, its ambition was 'to create a vast, interlocking network of activists that would be "horizontal", democratic and participatory' (Tormey 2004: 151) in contrast to the neoliberal institutions to which the movement was opposed.

Dissent against neoliberalism has been an almost inevitable product of the process of neoliberalisation. Trade unions, for example, have mobilised against neoliberal polices, intended to weaken their organisational capacity. Moreover, in seeking to expand the sphere of commodification, neoliberalism constitutes a disruption, sometimes violently so, to people's livelihoods, which has led to protests and mobilisations, for example by peasants dispossessed of their livelihood as a result of land commodification. In addition, by exposing people more fully to market imperatives, neoliberal measures remove or denude some of the socially protective institutions which cushioned people from market fluctuations, once again leading to protests and political mobilisations against neoliberalism. Walton and Seddon (1994: 52–3) suggest that these factors have led to anti-neoliberal protests because they generate a 'sense of injustice grounded in the moral economy of the poor'. Thus neoliberalism creates its own opposition.

It is important to assess the impact of this organised dissent in order to determine whether, and to what extent, it has undermined the durability and socially embedded character of neoliberalism. Mobilisations against neoliberalism have certainly achieved some success. There are many cases of neoliberal policies and proposals being wound back or defeated by popular mobilisations. Then there are the rarer cases where non-neoliberal public institutions have been built from anti-neoliberal political struggles, most obviously in Latin America, especially in Venezuela and Bolivia. A further index of the success of anti-neoliberal mobilisations is, as Peck (2010: 25) argues, that '[t]he anticipation of robust resistance or popular backlashes ... effectively defines no go areas, or zones of softly-softly incursion, for would-be market reformers'. Nonetheless, and perversely, to the extent that such 'defensive' (Almeida 2007) anti-neoliberal mobilisations result in such non-decisions, they may also have the effect of bolstering the legitimacy of neoliberalism more broadly – as the preservation of universalist institutions through non-decisions can make living under neoliberalism more bearable for the vast bulk of the populace. Conversely, the roll-out of neoliberal programmes more generally has continued, despite popular resistance.

The record of the global justice movement is even more modest. Its most significant measurable success was the scuttling of the proposed MAI, prior to the Seattle protests of 1999 (Johnston and Laxer 2003). Since the movement first burst onto the public stage at Seattle, however, its victories have been both less measurable and more limited. For example, the movement might legitimately claim limited victories in forcing the early conclusion of negotiations at some of the supranational forums that were the sites of protests, or that the rise of the global justice movement 'provided the moderate, reform oriented NGOs with unprecedented access to the inner sanctum of the IMF and World Bank' (Bleiker 2002: 196). It is probably also fair to conclude that '[t]he images of radical contestation circulated by the media, though usually preoccupied with petty vandalism or with sniggering references to "anti-globalist protesters", serve to open to contestability elements of the "neoliberal consensus"' (Stephen 2011: 218).

Notwithstanding these victories, as Bleiker (2002: 196) argues, '[s]tructural adjustment programs are still intact and neoliberalism remains the *modus operandi*, and the underlying ideology, of global economic governance'. Predominantly, the reasons for such limited success stem from immanent limitations of the movement itself. Both subjective and material factors are relevant here. The chief subjective factor that limited the potential of the movement to achieve concrete political economic change is the movement's lack of a coherent alternative political economic vision. While the diverse activist base of the movement, which brought together individuals and groups with a range of ideological positions, was a strength in so far as it gave the movement a relatively broad social base, it made an agreed normative agenda difficult. As Ayers (2004: 23) notes, 'while the anti-neoliberal "injustice frame" performed reasonably well in crafting a transnationally shared diagnosis of neoliberalism's faults, movement activists were having more difficulty undertaking prognostic framing'. This was not helped by the generally libertarian ethos that pervaded the movement, whereby diversity of ideological position was legitimated as an end in itself. In this sense Ross (2002: 298) is correct to argue that '[b]ecause tactics are off-limits, to be chosen by individuals or small groups, there is little opportunity to engage in discussion about what actions will be most likely to achieve goals, or even to define what those goals are'. At a subjective level, a further problem with sections of the movement was the implicit acceptance of the terms of political economic analysis as defined through neoliberal ideology, such as 'the ubiquitous perception of globalisation as being the opening up of free markets throughout the world, in trade and capital' (Thomas 2007: 49). Worse, some more moderate elements of the movement also seemed to 'accept the neoliberal rhetoric of trade and capital liberalisation under appropriate conditions' (ibid.: 55), as expressed, for example, in the 'perverse desire within the [movement] to open up LDC markets to foreign capital and trade' (ibid.: 53).

At a more material level, the specific tactics employed by the movement limited its potential to affect political economic change. On the one hand, the almost exclusively event-focused nature of the movement (that is, protests outside the meetings of supranational organisations, or gatherings of movement activists at the World Social Forum) meant that the material foundations of neoliberal policy regimes – the specific state policies of privatisation, deregulation, marketisation and approaches to monetary policy, as well as transformations within capitalist social relations of production and processes of capital accumulation – were left untouched. On the other hand, the belief by significant sections of the movement that the development of democratic and non-hierarchical forms of organisation within the movement constituted, in and of themselves, a direct challenge to neoliberalism and a sufficient condition for its destruction, also led to a strategic trajectory that left neoliberal institutions intact. In this sense the following description of the autonomist tendency within the anti-globalisation movement (although not meant as a criticism by its authors) is quite damning: '[u]nlike the New Left, contemporary autonomous movements reject the seizure of power as a strategy just as surely as they reject the elusive politics of mass struggle; instead they work towards a "revolution of everyday life"' (Starr and Adams 2010: 29). Thus dissent against neoliberalism has been ongoing, but its success in halting or dismantling neoliberalism has been rather modest.

LIVING WITH NEOLIBERALISM

From the late 1970s, and into the 1980s, an interesting debate took place within the British intellectual Left about the nature of Thatcherism (see Bruff 2014). It was sparked by a series of articles written by Stuart Hall and Martin Jacques which, by engaging with Gramsci's notion of hegemony, attempted to understand both the rise of Thatcherism and the seemingly increasingly impotent responses to this by the Left (Hall 1983, 1988; Hall and Jacques 1983). Hall and Jacques argued that Thatcherism was a hegemonic project: an attempt to restructure British capitalism and a concomitant attempt to recast 'common sense' in ways that complimented such restructuring.

Of course, as a distinct moment in history, Thatcherism has passed. Nonetheless, the questions asked and the issues investigated by Hall and Jacques remain relevant for understanding the durability of neoliberalism. So far this chapter has argued that neoliberal policy norms are hegemonic at the level of political elites, and yet generate their own opposition within the population more broadly. This prompts consideration of whether, and to what extent, neoliberal policy norms have been internalised outside of elite circles. We know that opposition to neoliberalism has been ongoing, but how representative is such opposition of broader public sentiments? Have neoliberal policy norms been imposed on unwilling populations, or has the experience of neoliberalism created new complementary subjectivities and generated support for neoliberalism, just as it has generated opposition? In short, to what extent has neoliberalism become hegemonic? Answering this question helps explain the durability of neoliberalism.

To the extent that data is available, it suggests that support for neoliberal policies decreased over the course of the neoliberal era. That is, the experience of neoliberalism tended to make neoliberal policies less popular. Moreover, only rarely have neoliberal policies of privatisation, deregulation and marketisation been popular, or enjoyed majority support within national polities.

Levien and Paret (2012), for example, use data from the World Values Survey to test public attitudes toward neoliberalism from 1990 to 2001 over 20 countries from the global North, the global South and the former Communist bloc. Using questions asking whether private or government ownership of business should be increased and whether individuals or governments should take more responsibility in social and economic provisioning as indicative of attitudes towards neoliberalism, they found that 'the desire for public ownership and social protection was increasing precisely as governments pursued policies moving in the opposite direction' (p. 9). Anti-neoliberal sentiment was more prevalent in the global South and among lower socio-economic groups, and lowest in the global North (pp. 12, 16). This is perhaps explained by the more violent and disruptive processes of primitive accumulation integral to the neoliberal transformations of the global South. This broad picture is borne out by numerous other studies of public opinion towards neoliberalism (Kelley and Sikora 2002; Checchi et al. 2009; Cohen et al. 2011; Denisova et al. 2012). Moreover, there seems to be strong support for universalist welfare institutions in both emerging and developed capitalist economies (Park 2010).

A detailed picture of sentiment towards neoliberalism in the global North is given by the Australian Survey of Social Attitudes. The survey showed that in 2003, after two decades of neoliberalisation, there was strong opposition to private ownership of major utilities (Pusey and Turnbull 2005). This was the period of Australia's major privatisation wave at both state and national levels. Support for private ownership of

Telstra, the telecommunications provider that had been partially privatised in 1997, fell from 39 per cent in 1987 to 9 per cent in 2003.
Similarly, support for the privatisation of Australia Post, the state-owned
mail service, fell from 32 per cent in 1987 to just 5 per cent in 2003.
While this does not indicate outright opposition to all forms of privatisation (47 per cent favour a mix of public and privately owned utilities)
support for full public ownership of services was still much higher at 40
per cent than support for only privately owned service provision, at 13
per cent (Pusey and Turnbull 2005: 164–7). Government is preferred to
private provision of most welfare services too. The same survey reveals
overwhelming support for public provision of education and healthcare,
with smaller majorities also favouring public over private provision of
services for jobseekers, care of the elderly and disabled (Wilson et al.
2005: 116).

In contrast, Prasad (2012) identifies what she views as the 'popular
origins of neoliberalism' in pro-tax cut sentiment within the US elector-
ate which provided the social basis for Ronald Reagan's cuts to marginal
income tax rates, a key part of the neoliberal agenda in the USA. While
Prasad's argument that this undermines class-based explanations of the
rise of neoliberalism is clearly contested by the evidence presented in the
rest of this book, she does draw attention to the fact that there was a
social basis, if not a movement, for some elements of the neoliberal
agenda, at least in the 1970s and 1980s. However, by the early years of
the new century, after two decades of neoliberalism, there is evidence of
a growing expressed willingness to forgo tax cuts so as to fund better
quality social services. While, as we have seen, funding cuts to social
services are not necessary components of actually existing neoliberalism
(and indeed, public finding of some services increased during the
neoliberal era, particularly of welfare), such sentiments are clearly at
odds with the neoliberal tendency for cuts to marginal rates of income tax
and for public rather than private provision. In Australia throughout the
1970s and 1980s, for example, there was a marked decline in the
proportion of the population registering a willingness to increase social
spending on welfare services such as healthcare and education at the
expense of income tax cuts, from a high of 73 per cent in 1969 to a low
of 8 per cent in 1990. This figure remained low at 17 per cent throughout
the 1990s before surging again in the 2000s to 48 per cent in 2003. Those
favouring a reduction in income taxes experienced almost the reverse
trajectory (Wilson et al. 2005: 102–6), contributing to the situation
whereby 'Australians were more willing to forgo income to pay for major
welfare state services in 2003 than they had been at any time in the
previous two decades' (ibid.: 104). A similar survey in Israel found

strong support for welfare state institutions and 'a relatively high willingness to pay for the welfare state, although this willingness was lower than the declared justification for welfare state' (Cohen et al. 2011: 632–3).

Nonetheless, when these findings are viewed in the context of public attitudes towards other elements of neoliberalism, the overall view that emerges is much more ambiguous. Surveys conducted in 2002 and 2003 across developing and developed capitalist economies by the Pew Global Attitudes Project found positive views of the effects of global trade, international corporations and supranational institutions including the World Trade Organisation, IMF and World Bank. In most countries, large majorities judged the impact of global trade on their country to be 'very good' or 'somewhat good', while majorities in 33 out of 44 survey nations saw international corporations as having positive effects (Pew Research 2003a, 2003b). While a 2007 survey by the same organisation found declines in such support within developed economies, 'this could not shake the broad acceptance of the key tenets of economic globalisation' (Stephen 2011: 222). Highlighting a contradictory, or 'ambivalent' (ibid.) attitude towards neoliberalism, the Australian Survey of Social Attitudes 2003 found that while 49 per cent of people agreed that 'free trade leads to better products available in Australia', 52 per cent of people nonetheless agreed that 'Australia should use tariffs to protect industry' (Pusey and Turnbull 2005: 169).

Moreover, while most people do not favour privatisation, a flagship neoliberal policy, opinion surveys in some countries suggest this should not necessarily be interpreted as implying support for nationalisation. One survey of 28,000 people across 28 post-Communist countries found strong antipathy towards privatisation, but overall 54 per cent favoured retaining private ownership of such assets (albeit a large proportion of these favoured forcing the owners to pay the full value accrued through acquiring these assets) while 29 per cent favoured nationalisation, and a further 17 per cent favoured nationalisation followed by a more transparent re-privatisation (Denisova et al. 2012: 46). Similarly, antipathy towards key aspects of neoliberalism has not translated into general support for the anti-globalisation movement. The aforementioned Pew Global Attitudes Project found that while there was 'significant minority support for the protesters in several countries', overall 'people generally have a negative view of anti-globalisation protesters' (Stephen 2011: 222).

All of this paints a rather uneven picture of public attitudes towards neoliberalism. Key elements, particularly privatisation, are unpopular, yet elements of global integration and the global institutions whose power has been strengthened through neoliberalisation are viewed relatively favourably. While there is strong support for universalist welfare institutions, only minorities (albeit sometimes large minorities) express support for explicitly anti-neoliberal strategies, such as nationalisation or the activities of the anti-globalisation movement. Pusey and Turnbull's conclusions about attitudes in Australia are appropriate for summing up attitudes to neoliberalism more generally: '[people] live with the contradictions of the market economy – they see benefits in free markets and trade, but are also aware of their drawbacks, and so continue to believe in an active role for government ... The public continues to support the institutions of the past, even as they adjust to the new arrangements' (Pusey and Turnbull 2005: 179).

While this opinion poll data reveals uneven attitudes towards neoliberalism it also suggests that the main precepts of neoliberal ideology have not been imbibed by a majority of the population globally. It remains, however, to investigate how people experience neoliberalism and whether this experience contributes to a neoliberal hegemony, or whether the durability of neoliberalism is simply a product of ideological consensus among political elites, combined with its embeddedness in a set of transformed institutions and class relations.

On this front, Wendy Larner (2000: 12–13) is surely right to argue that:

> While on the one hand neo-liberalism problematizes the state and is concerned to specify its limits through the invocation of individual choice, on the other hand it involves forms of governance that encourage institutions and individuals to conform to the norms of the market ... Neo-liberal strategies of rule ... encourage people to see themselves as individualized and active subjects responsible for enhancing their own well being.

But how successful are such strategies of 'market governance' (ibid.: 12)? As discussed in Chapter 5, a key element of the transformations of capital accumulation under neoliberalism has been an expansion of the scope of commodification, by engaging capital directly in the provision of public services. Alongside this, numerous services provided by the state have been transformed along market lines. Concomitantly, there has been a discursive transformation whereby those who use such services are framed as customers: citizens are reconfigured as consumers. Holborow (2007: 70) is right to argue that '[t]he "customer" metaphor, which encapsulates the market philosophy of neoliberal ideology, is used much more in official documents that it is spontaneously in people's speech'. Nonetheless, this does not mean that people do not act like customers, or do not view themselves in customer-like ways, even if they eschew describing themselves in such terms. Indeed, under such neoliberal arrangements, people are constituted materially as consumers of public services, even if they reject the discursive assignation. When people buy a private education for the children, or when they purchase private health insurance, or pay a private provider for their electricity, they expect 'value for money'. Their right to the service comes not through citizenship but through their ability and willingness to pay. Thus, under neoliberalism, people are increasingly forced to become the individual consumers of social services prized by neoliberal doctrine, even if such consumers simultaneously reject the policy prescriptions of that doctrine.

It also seems plausible to suggest that the marketisation of everyday life so central to neoliberalism also contributes to individuation. Such a phenomenon facilitates the process of 'commodity fetishism' described by Marx (1990: 165) whereby social relations appear as relations between things. Under neoliberalism, people's relationships with others are increasingly mediated through markets and commodities. This masks the social relations that underpin such markets in a double sense: on the one hand people engage in such markets as individuals, while on the other hand the commodities and the prices attached to them in effect become the market, obscuring the web of institutions and class relations that bring such commodities and prices into being.

None of this is to suggest that people have 'swallowed whole' the ideological precepts of neoliberalism. The world is not full of 'Mini-Me' versions of Friedrich Hayek or Milton Friedman, calculating the precise costs and benefits to them of every action and relationship in which they engage (see Vrasti 2011: 4, for a similar point). Rather it is to highlight the ways in which material changes wrought by neoliberalism to people's everyday lives have, at least to a certain extent, facilitated complementary subjectivities.

Moreover, although increases in inequality and real wage suppression in some countries and within some sections of the working class have been key features of the neoliberal era, neoliberalism has also brought about real material benefits. Inequality of earnings in the neoliberal era means that some benefited much more than others. Despite the generally low average real wage growth across the OECD since the late 1970s (Glyn 2006: 116), some sections of labour fared rather well during the neoliberal period. For example, while US real wages were, on average, stagnant during the neoliberal era, those in the top 10 per cent of wage earners saw their wages grow by 27.2 per cent (ibid.: 117).

Additionally, easier access to consumer credit during the neoliberal era allowed sections of the working class to enjoy the gradual cheapening of a host of consumer goods increasingly produced in the low-waged manufacturing economies of the global South. One need not infer from this that people embraced the broad programme of neoliberalisation. Moreover, these need to be set against other increases in the cost of living brought about through neoliberalisation. Nonetheless, at least in the global North, this 'imperial way of living', based upon 'more intensive access to an asymmetrically structured world market' (Brand 2012: 289), may help to explain why many in the core capitalist countries saw material benefits from free trade. This may also help to explain why antipathy towards neoliberalism has been stronger in the global South than in the global North, as well as why the global South has been the site of the most successful and comprehensive roll-backs of neoliberalism. Nonetheless, even in the global South, there is evidence of support for the benefits to Southern consumers of the neoliberal transformations of global trade (Baker and Greene 2011; Stephen 2011).

It would also seem that some people outside of the capitalist class have a material interest in the reproduction of at least some neoliberal policies. Those whose material well-being has come to depend for example on marketised social services, such as private education or private health insurance, but which are nonetheless in receipt of significant state subsidies, are likely to oppose any attempts to wind back government assistance to such marketised services.

For those most marginalised by neoliberal processes of state and economy transformation, and from whence protest against neoliberalism might reasonably be expected to come, a host of measures have constrained the possibilities of organised dissent. Most obviously, and as discussed in Chapter 5, restrictions upon the legal rights of trade unions to organise have limited the ability of workers to contest programmes of neoliberal restructuring – whether it be those directly related to the labour market, or other neoliberal programmes. Active repression by the state, also discussed in Chapter 5, has also played a role here both in the global North and, more often, in the global South. Moreover, those marginalised by processes of neoliberal restructuring have been targeted and managed by both workfare and prisonfare regimes. Workfare regimes have instituted new disciplines that forcibly integrated people into the precarious and low-paid section of the labour market that has burgeoned under neoliberalism. This is achieved through greater state monitoring and surveillance of their activities, through time limits for receipt of welfare payments, through harsher penalties for non-compliance with the requirement to seek and accept whatever waged work is on offer and, in some cases, to undertake unpaid work as well (Peck 2001). As Wacquant (2009: xv) forcefully argues, the rise of prisonfare regimes, most emblematic of which is to be found in the USA, 'responds not to the rise in crime – which remained roughly constant overall before sagging at the end of the (neoliberal) period – but to the dislocations provoked by the social and urban retrenchment of the state and by the imposition of precarious wage labour as a new norm of citizenship for those trapped at the bottom of polarising class structure'. It addresses the problem of marginalisation, social dislocation and rebellion arising from neoliberal restructuring by criminalising and imprisoning the most marginalised sections of the working class. As Wacquant (2012: 76) notes, '[t]he penal state has been rolled out in the countries that have ridden the neoliberal road because it promises to ... [curb] the mounting dislocations caused by the normalisation of social insecurity at the bottom of the class and urban structure'.

In the midst of such insecurity, conservative and populist discourses have become a feature of the neoliberal era. As noted in Chapter 3, while there is a *prima facie* contradiction between neoliberal and conservative thought, this has not prevented the grafting of certain conservative principles onto broader neoliberal doctrine by neoliberal think tanks. The resulting conservative neoliberal synthesis has formed part of the rhetorical arsenal selectively deployed by neoliberal governments and political parties. As Harvey (2005: 85) notes, 'neoliberal states need nationalism of a certain sort to survive', and nationalistic and racist rhetoric has often been deployed by neoliberal governments. Such discourses have focused blame on an imagined 'other' for the insecurities, anxieties and dislocation generated by processes of neoliberal transformation, or have sought to 'reassure in times of great change' (Johnson 2000: 60). This is evident, for example, in Margaret Thatcher's use of nationalistic discourse during the Falklands War to generate electoral support for her otherwise unpopular neoliberal government, or in the Singaporean government's combination of 'neoliberalism in the marketplace with Draconian coercive and authoritarian state power, while invoking moral solidarities based on the nationalist ideals of a beleaguered island state' (Harvey 2005: 86). One can also see this sort of strategy at work in the deployment of anti-Muslim discourse by neoliberal governments in the wake of the September 11, 2001 attacks on the World Trade Centre, as well as the deployment of racist discourse by a range of Western neoliberal governments to demonise refugees and other immigrants from Africa, Asia and the Middle East. Concurrently, processes of neoliberalisation have provided the context for the rise and electoral success of a range of far right parties on the back of racist, nationalistic and explicitly anti-neoliberal platforms such as Pauline Hanson's One Nation Party in Australia, Joerg Haider's Austrian Freedom Party, Jean-Marie Le Pen's Front National in France and the British National Party (Worth 2013: 72–91). In part these have been legitimated by the racist discourses promoted by neoliberal governments, in part also the re-emergence of the far right has encouraged neoliberal governments to move their conservative discourse further to the right, to outflank their electoral opponents. Thus neoliberalism generates its own contradictions and feedback loops and that generate further social tensions. As Harvey (2005: 86) argues, 'what seems like an answer to the contradictions of neoliberalism can all too easily turn into a problem'.

CONCLUSION

This chapter has examined the ways in which the neoliberal policy regime is embedded within a pervasive ideological framework, which in turn contributes to its durability. While a commitment to the key elements of the neoliberal policy regime has become the norm among political and economic elites across the capitalist world, this is far from the case among the population more broadly. Indeed, public opinion surveys show that some of the key planks of neoliberal policy, especially privatisation, are far from popular. In addition, resistance to processes of neoliberalisation have been ongoing since their inception. While the 'anti-globalisation' movement is probably the most recognisable face of such resistance, organised dissent against neoliberalism has been far more widespread than this and, indeed, predates this movement. Such resistance is explained, it was argued in this chapter, by the socially destructive and disruptive effects of the neoliberal policy regime, which thus generates its own opposition. Nonetheless, this should not be taken to mean that neoliberalism has failed to secure a social base. While the weakening of centres of organised opposition to neoliberalism has been a key to its success, at least as important has been the transformation of everyday lives wrought by the neoliberal policy regime, and the way in which this has both transformed subjectivities and opened a space for neoliberal ideology. The expansion of market dependence has led to greater individuation, and generated material benefits for sections of the working class. Moreover, it has provided a context for neoliberal doctrine to develop as an ideology – as a set of highly malleable discursive devices that offer a partial representation of everyday experience, but that simultaneously obscure reality in ways that legitimate neoliberal processes and those who benefit most from them. Thus, we might conclude that neoliberalism is hegemonic, but that this is a contested hegemony, and one that is vulnerable to disruptive changes of policy or broader economic conditions.

8. The global financial crisis and the future of embedded neoliberalism

The word 'crisis' has several meanings. In its most common usage it refers to 'a time of danger or great difficulty'. Certainly, when people talk about the global financial crisis, this is what they almost always mean. And with good reason: the ongoing fallout from the current crisis has been devastating for the working class throughout the capitalist world. Indeed, to describe the current period as 'a time of great danger or difficulty' is, perhaps, an understatement.

However, there is another meaning of crisis – as 'a decisive moment' or 'turning point' – that gives a different inflection to the recent calamitous economic events. Whether consciously or not, it was in this sense that many progressive commentators wrote of the crisis in the early years after the collapse of the sub-prime mortgage market in the USA. Indeed, among the political left there was an air of inevitability about the imminent collapse of neoliberalism.

It has been the purpose of this book to evaluate such claims and to determine whether the onset of the global financial crisis represents a decisive moment or turning point for neoliberalism, or whether it merely signals a time of danger or great difficulty. In other words, whether, rather than constituting a moment of genuine rupture, there has instead merely been a temporary disturbance to the hegemony of neoliberalism. This was done by first examining the common progressive claim that neoliberalism is at a fatal turning point and finding that this claim is based on untenable ideational assumptions. A more useful alternative conception of neoliberalism as fundamentally socially embedded was then put forward, and neoliberalism was shown to have a highly durable character

This chapter continues the investigation by considering the implications of the current global financial crisis for neoliberalism and the prospects for moving beyond it. The chapter begins by examining responses by states to the global financial crisis to assess whether, and to what extent, they constitute a retreat from neoliberalism. It will be argued that the durability found to be a characteristic of embedded neoliberalism remains evident even in the face of the current global economic down-turn. This provides the basis for the consideration of alternatives.

Of course, the future, as Keynes (1937) noted, is subject to radical uncertainty. It is impossible to know precisely how the current crisis will shape the global economy over the next few decades. The best one can do, therefore, is to put forward plausible hypotheses. Such plausibility must come from grounding speculation about the future in the chief material dynamics of the contemporary political economy. There is no *tabula rasa*. The future is constrained by the present, so any exercise in forecasting must begin here.

NEOLIBERALISM AND THE CRISIS

This book opened by questioning the usefulness of the assumptions underpinning many of the pronouncements by progressive intellectuals that the global financial crisis heralded the end of neoliberalism. Having interrogated those assumptions, and offered a more holistic, alternative interpretation of neoliberalism, it now remains to examine the concrete effects of the global financial crisis upon the future prospects of neoliberalism. The first part of this chapter, therefore, considers the responses by states to the global financial crisis, and whether they constitute a retreat from neoliberalism. However, this will be done not by evaluating such responses against the idealist template of neoliberalism understood as a system of small states and free, unregulated markets. Rather, to understand the ways in which the global financial crisis has affected neoliberalism, it is important to keep in mind the discrepancies between actually existing neoliberalism and the normative programmes of neoliberal doctrine, as well as the fundamentally socially embedded character of the neoliberal policy regime.

While idealist commentators were wrong about the constituent features of neoliberalism, they certainly got one thing right in their pronounce-ments of its demise: the global financial crisis was a direct result of the political and economic transformations of the neoliberal era. This was not, however, due to the retreat of regulation in the neoliberal era. Rather it was a product of the inherently contradictory nature of embedded neoliberalism whereby social relations and institutions that were crucial to facilitating capital accumulation ended up undermining the ability of the capitalist economy to reproduce itself.

As is well-known, the immediate catalyst for the global financial crisis was the collapse of the sub-prime mortgage market in the USA in 2007. However, it is by probing how and why the collapse of a relatively obscure market could have catastrophic global consequences that the deeper, underlying neoliberal origins of the crisis come into clearer view. Embedded neoliberalism provided the context for the crisis on several fronts. Decades of neoliberal financial deregulation facilitated the economic and geographical expansion of finance capital. This process of financial globalisation meant that when the sub-prime market collapsed, the resulting contagion spread rapidly, and internationally. Deregulation also facilitated the development of new financial instruments, as well as the bundling-up and securitisation of mortgages and other income streams, which was a key element in the collapse of major financial institutions. As we have seen, however, this process of financial deregulation did not entail a withdrawal of the state from the regulation of finance. Rather, the state remained important in financial markets, including: authorising banks to hold and trade securitised debt; quarantining financial institutions from public scrutiny; and running a permissive monetary policy which facilitated access to finance for working class households. Furthermore, workers had an added incentive to make use of the new avenues available for accessing finance as they strove to maintain their living standards in the face of low real wage growth. As discussed in Chapter 5, this was a key feature of the neoliberal era and a product of institutional transformations such as labour market deregulation, and a shift in the balance of class forces that gave capital greater scope to impose its prerogatives upon labour. On the one hand, this helped sustain demand during the neoliberal era; on the other, however, it led to the greater integration of workers, via their mortgage and credit card repayments, into global circuits of finance. Finally, the growth of lower waged manufacturing outside of the core capitalist countries, facilitated by neoliberal policies of financial deregulation and tariff reductions, allowed Asian-based banks and governments to fund debt-based consumption in the core economies, thus contributing to the short-term viability of 'privatised Keynesianism' (Crouch 2011: 97–124), but also fuelling the conditions that led to the crisis.

Thus, the global financial crisis was certainly a 'crisis in neoliberalism' (Saad Filho 2010). It will be argued here, however, that it has not yet turned into a 'crisis *of* neoliberalism' (Saad-Filho 2010). Indeed, as shall be made clear, neoliberalism has been used as a form of crisis management, whereby the power and scope neoliberal institutions and class relations have been entrenched and extended. The three core elements of State responses to the global financial crisis will be discussed in turn: austerity; new regulations for global finance; and fiscal stimuli, bailouts and nationalisations.

Austerity

While a strategy of fiscal stimulus was adopted by some countries, austerity soon became the norm in the advanced capitalist states. The continuities between these responses and neoliberal policy norms from the 1970s onwards lies not so much in the fact of sweeping cuts to state budgets, but rather in the class character of such cuts: the way such cuts forced the burden of adjustment onto labour. The neoliberal character of austerity was also evident in the reliance by states on policies of privatisation, marketisation, deregulation and the winding back of social protections in response to the deficits and recessionary impacts of the crisis.

In some cases these measures were forced upon states by supranational institutions, indicating that neoliberal norms remained firmly embedded within the rules and practices of such powerful institutions. For example, in return for financial bailouts from the EU, European Central Bank (ECB) and IMF, the governments of Greece, Spain and Portugal each agreed to austerity programmes. In Greece this included attacks upon social protections (such as increases to the retirement age, reduction in supplementary pensions, reductions to the minimum wage), a programme of privatisation (Laven and Santi 2012) and labour market deregulation (BBC 2012). The Portuguese government agreed to a privatisation programme (BBC 2012) and cuts to welfare programmes (Laven and Santi 2012) in addition to broader spending cuts, while in Spain, cuts to healthcare spending will see reduced healthcare benefits and cuts to the education budget will mean a significant increase in university fees (BBC 2012; Laven and Santi 2012), thus extending the marketisation of that sector and its attendant inequalities.

Other governments, however, in responding to the crisis, turned to neoliberal measures without being forced to do so by supranational bodies as a condition of bailout packages. Upon its election in 2010, Britain's Conservative Government announced a raft of neoliberal measures including the marketisation and privatisation of the NHS (extending a process already initiated by the previous Labour Government), the expansion of the market for university places with government funding of universities cut and the government authorising universities to charge students tuition fees of up to £9000 (*Guardian* 2011, 2012). Moreover, privatisation of probation services and the Royal Mail and elements of the NHS were planned, as well as an extension of PPPs for roads and motorways (Seymour 2012). The Italian government announced a programme of privatisation and widespread market deregulation (Laven and Santi 2012). In Hungary the government reduced, froze or limited sick-pay benefits, disability pension payments, student and pharma-ceutical subsidies and unemployment benefits (ibid.). The age of retire-ment was raised or is planned to be raised in Austria, Belgium and Hungary (ibid.).

In the USA, while the Obama administration has engaged in fiscal stimulus at the federal level, state and local governments have pursued a widespread austerity agenda. As the largest employer in the USA, as well as the main provider of education and healthcare and a host of other social services (Pollin and Thompson 2011: 22), this government agenda has eroded the living standards and social protections of the working class on several fronts. State and local governments shed 577,000 jobs between August 2008 and July 2011 alone (Williams et al. 2011: 4), and this figure rises when the effects of cancelled private sector contracts are added. Several states have also enforced real wage cuts on public employees and/or increased the amount they must contribute to their pension or health insurance funds (ibid.: 22–3). Cuts have also been made to state education budgets at the tertiary, secondary and elementary levels, to Medicaid as well as to a range of poor relief programmes (ibid. 2011: 11–22). It has been estimated that the combined effects of these cuts have more than outweighed the federal government's stimulus measures (Albo and Evans 2010: 291). While some states have responded to the crisis with tax cuts, these have by and large been for corporations and/or the wealthy (Williams et al. 2011: 3–4).

An indication of the continuing reliance upon neoliberal policy norms since the onset of the crisis is the extension of labour market deregulation in many countries. Perhaps the best known examples are the anti-union measures introduced by Republican Governor Scott Walker in Wisconsin, USA, which prompted a militant counter-mobilisation by workers. Yet these changes – which severely curtailed the ability and rights of trade unions to organise – were but the harbinger of a raft of similar anti-union measures introduced into state legislatures across the United States. As an International Trade Union Confederation (2012) report outlines:

> in 2011, more than 800 bills seeking to eliminate or curtail collective bargaining for public employees were introduced in state legislatures … [and] right-to-work bills that would apply to the private sector were introduced in 14 states … In addition to the flurry of right-to-work bills, 2011 saw the introduction in dozens of states of so-called 'paycheck protection' bills. Those bills … were designed to make it difficult for unions to collect dues from their members, and to use dues from members for political or advocacy purposes.

In Europe, since the onset of the crisis, labour market deregulation has been rolled out in Lithuania, Portugal, Hungary, Poland, the Czech

Republic, Greece, Romania, the Netherlands, Spain, Estonia, the United Kingdom, Bulgaria, Slovakia and Italy (Schoemann and Clauwaert 2012). Such measures include: relaxations of overtime limits; extension of time-limits and numbers of allowable renewals for fixed-term contracts; the introduction of new work contracts with denuded worker rights and entitlements; relaxation of redundancy restrictions; and decentralisation of collective bargaining (ibid.: 8–14). Consistent with the historical trajectory of neoliberalism, many of these measures have bypassed deliberative democratic arenas, such as through the use of emergency procedures in Estonia, Hungary and Slovakia and the Greek and Portuguese Governments signing up to a Memorandum of Understanding with the EU, ECB and IMF committing them to labour market deregulation (ibid.: 14). The institutionally embedded nature of such neoliberal measures is reflected in the European Central Bank's (ECB) statement that:

> Among the most urgent reform projects for most Member States are the removal of rigidities in product and labour markets … the flexibility of labour markets needs to be enhanced, given the high level of unemployment in many Member States. Wage flexibility will particularly allow the appropriate degree of wage differentiation across different types of workers and stimulate the hiring of young female and older workers. Rigidities in labour markets need to be addressed by reducing the degree of employment protection for permanent jobs. Other labour market reforms that should be pursued in order to alleviate bottlenecks and foster flexibility include the reduction of minimum wages, the elimination of wage indexation mechanisms and the strengthening of firm level agreements so that wages and working conditions can be tailored to firm's specific needs. (European Central Bank 2012: 85–6)

This statement was in the context of a discussion of the EU's Treaty on Stability, Coordination and Governance (TSCG), signed in March 2012, and clearly signalled how the ECB thought the enhanced 'convergence and competitiveness' that member states committed to should be interpreted. The IMF too has continued to advocate and require labour market deregulation as the path to economic growth among debtor states (Alexandra Peck 2012) and it is in this context that the IMF's call for 'structural reforms … to enhance growth' (IMF 2009: 17) should be read.

Overall, then, the class character of states' austerity responses to the crisis is clear: the burden of 'economic adjustment' is to be borne by labour. As Albo and Evans (2010: 286) argue:

> the working classes, directly through wage repression to boost international competitiveness, and indirectly through tax increases and public sector cuts,

should pay for the crisis and for the restoration of the economic viability of capitalist control over the financial system.

Not only does labour bear the overwhelming burden, but through austerity the power of capital is entrenched and, indeed, deepened.

Nonetheless, there is an unevenness to the extent of state reliance upon neoliberalisation as a strategy of crisis management. Neoliberal crisis responses are not unbiquitous. Indeed, the economic crisis has generated some distinctly non-neoliberal policy initiatives, even as part of the general austerity drive. This is evident, for example, with respect to taxation. While the trend in the neoliberal era has been for the reduction of top marginal tax rates and of corporate taxes in favour of flatter rates of tax, since the onset of the crisis several states have increased taxes on the wealthy and on corporations. The Belgian government has increased taxes on interest revenue, capital gains and company cars, the Czech government has increased taxes on the wealthy and removed some tax deductions, the Danish government has closed some tax loopholes exploited by multinational corporations, and the French government announced plans to increase taxes on the wealthiest households, increase capital gains tax and the property tax on non-primary residences. It also announced reducing some company tax breaks (Laven and Santi 2012). The Greek government has increased taxes on yachts and swimming pools (ibid.). In Italy the government increased taxes on banks and financial institutions and on the wealthiest income earners (ibid.). Latvia introduced a more progressive system of income taxation (ibid.). Lithuania introduced a new luxury real estate tax. Portugal increased the rate of corporate tax and the top marginal tax rate (ibid.). So, while neoliberal measures have recently dominated the responses, particularly of European states to the crisis, this is set among several distinctly non-neoliberal policy measures which, while keeping with the austerity agenda, nonetheless go against the grain of the policy norms of the neoliberal era.

New Regulations for Global Finance

Among those who viewed the global financial crisis as heralding the end of neoliberalism, much hope had been held out for a fundamental reform of the global financial system. Certainly, reform of the financial system became one of the top agenda items for major supranational organisations such as the G-20. Certainly also, since the onset of the crisis, several regulatory changes have been implemented, and commitments to further changes made, that have a distinctly non-neoliberal character. The key recommendations from supranational bodies such as the G-20, combined with international agreements such as Basel III and recommendations from international organisations such as IOSCO (International Organization of Securities Commissions), comprise four categories of broadly non-neoliberal reform, some of which have already been implemented at the national and regional level.

First, there is a move towards more extensive registration requirements for the 'shadow banking sector' and for greater disclosure requirements of financial entities (FSB 2012a, 2012b). Such measures have been recommended by the G-20 and IOSCO, and have already been implemented in some areas. At the EU level, for example, the European Parliament passed guidelines that 'require hedge funds and the private equity industry to seek government authorization to operate, hold adequate capital, and make disclosures to regulators and investors' (Eubanks 2010: 6), while the registration of the hedge fund advisers with the SEC is a requirement of the Dodd–Frank Act in the USA (Champ 2012).

Second, some countries have placed bans on short-selling. For example, both the German and Australian Governments banned naked short-selling, while in the USA the SEC placed temporary restrictions on short-selling (D'Aloisio 2009; Marshall 2009: 43; Eubanks 2010: 10).

Third, there are moves to impose greater capital and liquidity requirements on financial institutions, particularly banks. This is part of the 2010 Basel III agreement and some states, such as the United Kingdom, announced enhanced liquidity requirements for financial institutions prior to this (BIS 2010; Eubanks 2010: 14).

Fourth, there has been some movement towards states mandating changes to remuneration within financial institutions. For example, the Obama administration limited to $500,000 the remuneration of executives of financial institutions in receipt of government assistance (Marshall 2009: 38), while the EU Capital Requirements Directive imposed constraints on remuneration (Davis n.d.: 14). Finally, many states have enacted some form of bank deposit guarantee – by 2011, 48 states had enhanced their deposit protections (Davis n.d.: 23).

Having the character of restricting, limiting and placing extra obligations upon the activities of finance capital, these can legitimately be interpreted as a move away from neoliberal policy norms. However, the scope of such reforms is very limited. Moreover, the timeframes for implementation of many of the G-20 recommendations is long, leaving, as one commentator notes, plenty of 'scope for private lobbying to impede changes which might be socially warranted' (Davis n.d.: 39). Much of the financial architecture of the neoliberal era remains in place, and speculative financial activities continue within the global economy. Certainly the reforms made and mooted since the onset of the crisis do not represent a wholesale retreat from neoliberalism. Once again, the focus of analysis should properly be not on the quantity of regulation, or whether regulation is 'present' or 'absent', but rather on who benefits from the prevailing regulatory arrangements. In the years since the onset of the global financial crisis little has been done to wind back the power and freedoms that capital accrued during the neoliberal era.

Fiscal Stimuli, Bailouts and Nationalisations

Since the global economic crisis began to unfold in 2007, states across the capitalist world have poured trillions of dollars into the private economy in an attempt to shore up the profit-system. McNally (2011: 197, n. 4) estimates the total cost of the rescue packages, stimulus plans and emergency funds allocated for financial stabilisation to be about $20 trillion, 'an amount equal to almost one and a half times US GDP'. This expenditure took a range of forms, including various types of fiscal stimulus measures whereby money was pumped into the demand side of the economy and bailouts of failing firms, particularly in the financial industry, through, for example, the purchase of toxic assets. Neither bailouts of failing capitalist firms, nor programmes of fiscal stimulus, were unheard of in the neoliberal era. Whether through tax cuts, or direct transfer payments, demand-side stimulus policies were a normal part of the operation of capitalist states from the 1970s throughout the neoliberal period. Moreover, the history of the period is littered with examples of government interventions to prop up failing capitalist enterprises (Harman 2010: 234), with the US government alone bailing out carmaker Chrysler in 1979, the Continental Illinois bank in 1984, Savings and Loans corporations later that decade and the Long Term Capital Management hedge fund in 1998 (ibid.: 233–4).

But while the bailout by the state of private for-profit enterprises was not an uncommon feature of the neoliberal era, nationalisation was. As demonstrated in Chapter 2, privatisation was a defining feature of the neoliberal era. Alongside this was the development of a new neoliberal commonsense which held nationalisations to be anachronistic – an irrational and inefficient legacy of a bygone era that had become virtually unthinkable as a serious policy option. The wave of nationalisations that occurred once the global financial crisis hit in 2007 thus presented a clear challenge to the prevailing policy norms that had become virtually axiomatic in the neoliberal era.

This was compounded by the fact that such nationalisations were of some of the biggest players in the global capitalist economy, and from within its core nation-states: the US Government acquired full or partial stakes in Freddie Mac, Fannie Mae, AIG, Bank of America, Citigroup, Goldman Sachs, JP Morgan, Wells Fargo, Morgan Stanley, Bank of New York Mellon and State Street, while the UK Government nationalised Northern Rock, RBS, Lloyds, HBOS and Bradford and Bingley. Elsewhere in Europe, governments nationalised Fortis (Netherlands, Luxembourg and Belgium), Dexia (France, Belgium and Luxembourg), Landsbanki, Glitnir, Kaupthing and Straumur (Iceland) and Bankia (Spain). Moreover, the US Government acquired a 10 per cent stake in auto company Chrysler, while in what was surely the biggest break with the practices of the neoliberal era, the United Auto Workers trade union joined with the US and Canadian Governments as owners of General Motors.

However, there are some important caveats to the extent of discontinuity and rupture between these nationalisations, and the policy practices of the neoliberal era. It was not envisaged that the nationalisations would be of a lasting or durable nature. As a note by the IMF's research department pointed out, nationalisations, while generally 'undesirable' might be 'temporarily' necessary, 'until private sector solutions can be developed' (IMF 2009: 11). It was always envisaged that nationalisation was an emergency measure that would be rescinded as soon as possible and (neoliberal) business-as-usual restored. The nationalisations within the North American auto industry are also instructive. Although the UAW received a 17.5 per cent stake in General Motors, there was never 'any intention to convert GM to some larger social purpose' (Albo et al. 2010: 78). Indeed, the nationalisation package was part of a broader corporate restructure which led to job losses and cuts to wages and social protections (ibid.; Fowler 2012).

On the one hand, therefore, the sheer magnitude of the crisis and its consequences have forced state elites to depart from one of the key policy norms of the neoliberal era in the interests of systemic stabilisation. On the other hand, however, the crisis has also seen the continuation and extension of neoliberalisation. Indeed, neoliberal policies have been deployed as one of the main tools of crisis management. Far from ending the neoliberal era, the onset of the global financial crisis has led to the reproduction of neoliberalism on an expanded scale, deepening the extent of neoliberalism. This has ensured that the costs of responding to the crisis have been predominantly borne by labour as a class. Indicative of this is that by 2013, unemployment in the Euro area had risen to 12.1 per cent, and was much higher in countries including Greece (27.8 per cent),

Spain (27.3 per cent) and Portugal (18.2 per cent) (OECD 2010, 2013). Moreover, both unit labour costs and median earnings are now much lower on average in the OECD relative to pre-crisis trends. That this has occurred at a time when private sector investment growth is weak, even relative to the low growth in output, suggests that the burden of adjustment has been borne by labour, with real unit labour costs declining due to a combination of low wages and work intensification. Certainly, such measures have not ended the crisis. Indeed, by 2009, the economies of the USA and the Euro area, and the global economy as a whole (OECD economies plus Brazil, Russia, India and China) were in recession, and growth in these areas continues to be either negative or very low. Moreover, in 2013, the 'output gap' (a reasonable proxy for capacity utilisation) in the world economy was 2.8 per cent to the negative.

Nonetheless, while labour in general has suffered as a result of the crisis (and it must be noted that there is a highly uneven geographical distribution to such suffering), there are signs that the financial sector of the economy has been significantly buoyed by the enormous state assistance schemes that have flowed its way. While there has been some modest 'deleveraging' in the household sector across the OECD since the onset of the crisis in 2007, the ratio of household debt to disposable income is still higher than in 2000, and in the Euro area it is slightly higher than 2007. Moreover, while access to credit is much tighter in some countries, such as developing economies and distressed economies as with those of Greece and Spain, 'increasing risk-taking has been observed in corporate bond markets' (OECD 2013) and there has been a return to the holding of riskier financial instruments. Thus, the financialised form of capital accumulation that was so central to the economic dynamics of the neoliberal economy, remains well and truly alive since the onset of the GFC.

RESISTANCE TO NEOLIBERAL CRISIS MANAGEMENT

Across the world, resistance to neoliberal forms of crisis management have been widespread, militant and fierce. Since the onset of the crisis, millions of people have mobilised against the extension of neoliberalisation. While none of the forms taken by such mobilisations are truly new, the frequency of anti-neoliberal protests far exceeds that seen before the crisis, and the numbers of people involved are matched only by the most iconic struggles against neoliberalism before 2007.

Perhaps the most iconic 'repertoire of contention' deployed against neoliberalisation since the onset of the crisis has been the various occupations of public spaces. From Tahrir Square in Cairo, to the Puerta del Sol in Madrid, to Zuccotti Park in New York, to Taksim Square in Istanbul and hundreds of other cities across the capitalist world, people have turned out to 'occupy' against neoliberal processes of austerity, dislocation, dispossession and de-democratisation. Other forms of protest, however, have been at least as important. In opposition to neoliberal forms of crisis management people have also marched, taken strike action and, albeit less often, occupied factories and parliaments (see for example McNally 2011: 146–8).

The emergence of resistance to the extension of neoliberalisation since the onset of the global financial crisis is not surprising. As was demonstrated in the previous chapter, the social embedding of neoliberalism has been weakest in the sphere of people's experience of everyday life. The turn to neoliberalism as a form of crisis management by state elites has produced extensive popular counter-mobilisation as it has directly threatened peoples' material living conditions. Also not surprising is the particular geographical development of resistance to neoliberalisation since the crisis. Just like in the period from the 1970s until the onset of the crisis, resistance against neoliberalism has been strongest when threats to people's livelihoods have been greatest and when the threatened changes have been sudden and profound.

Anti-neoliberal movements have certainly enjoyed some success in the years since the onset of the global financial crisis. Most obviously, the broad collection of movements against neoliberalism have succeeded in putting the issue of inequality firmly on the global agenda, with the occupy movement's slogan of 'We are the 99%' perhaps the most iconic representation of this. Such movements have also asserted the principles of democracy and the commons against neoliberal processes of de-democratisation and commodification – emblematically enacted, once again, by the occupy movement.

Nonetheless, despite the significant successes that have stemmed from these strong and widespread popular mobilisations, neoliberalism remains the dominant logic of state policy making across the capitalist world. It continues to shape people's everyday lives in profound ways. Thus, while on the one hand the popular backlash against neoliberalism since the onset of the crisis highlights the fragility of neoliberalism, it should also serve as a warning of how deeply embedded it continues to be within institutional forms, ideological norms and capitalist class relations.

BEYOND EMBEDDED NEOLIBERALISM?

Having outlined how states have responded to the crisis, it is now possible to hypothesise about the future of embedded neoliberalism. What follows is a consideration of three plausible future trajectories for the global political economy emerging from the global financial crisis. Because it is my view that one of the tasks of social science is to move beyond analysis and provide the basis for desirable social change, much more space will be devoted to outlining a plausible progressive trajectory, even if it may turn out that one of the other two undesirable future scenarios becomes most likely. It is worth reiterating that speculation about alternative futures needs to be firmly grounded in an analysis of the prevailing political economy and hence it should be no surprise that antecedents of each possible future scenario are contained in the present moment of crisis.

NEOLIBERAL CONSOLIDATION

One possible future scenario is that the crisis provides the vehicle for the consolidation of neoliberalism. Clearly, many responses by states to the crisis so far have extended the scope of neoliberalisation, even as it has been checked in other ways. This reliance upon neoliberalism as one of the main forms of crisis management is likely to continue, at least in the short term.

However, while ongoing neoliberalisation will almost certainly be the norm over the short term, its emergence from the crisis in a more consolidated form is far from guaranteed. At least two criteria need to be satisfied for this to be possible. The first is that resistance to neoliberalisation would need to remain insufficiently widespread, organised or strategically deployed and thus lack the power to force or induce state elites to abandon neoliberalisation as the dominant strategy of policy making and crisis response. The second criteria is that strategies of neoliberalisation would need to be sufficient to establish the basis for a revived neoliberal regime of accumulation. To date, this has not been achieved. Growth in the global economy since the onset of the crisis has remained stagnant, and this is particularly pronounced in the core capitalist economies. On the other hand, thanks to unprecedented government handouts, the financial sector of the economy is enjoying strong profit growth. Were this extended to other sectors of the economy, then a neoliberal revival would be plausible. While it has not yet come to pass, one can imagine, for example, a situation whereby further privatisations and marketisations extend the sphere of commodification and the scope for profit-making. In such a scenario, profit rates could be boosted by wage suppression and work intensification, facilitated by further labour market deregulation, and the combination of neoliberal approaches to monetary policy and neoliberal rescue packages brokered by the IMF and other supranational institutions could force a 'shakeout' of capital in peripheral European states and the development of leaner methods of production. Thus, neoliberalism could once again be 'remade through crisis' (Peck et al. 2009: 105).

Authoritarian Economic Nationalism

Another possible trajectory for the global economy is at least as grim, possibly worse. Under this scenario, neoliberal policy responses are unable to resolve persistent stagnation in the global economy. This leads to a protracted crisis (a time of danger or great difficulty) of neoliberalism. Such a period of unresolved crisis would likely be accompanied by growing social unrest. In response, states pursue nationalistic policies that protect domestic capital accumulation, through for example further rounds of bailouts and nationalisation, tariff protections and exchange rate setting. Hence, this strategy represents a partial retreat from neoliberalism, but it would likely also entail a widespread assault upon labour conditions and freedoms in order to both stifle sources of dissent and to impose a settlement on terms favourable to capital. Alongside this, states would likely use nationalistic and racist rhetoric to scapegoat particular ethnic groups as the causes of hardship. All of this could set the scene for inter-capitalist-state military conflict (King 2012: 261–2). As Kalecki (1943: 352) pointed out in the 1940s, while big business is generally averse to:

> government spending, whether on public investment or consumption, [this aversion] is overcome by concentrating government expenditure on armaments. Finally, 'discipline in the factories' and 'political stability' under full employment are maintained by the 'new order' which ranges from suppression of trade unions to the concentration camp. Political pressure replaces the economic pressure of unemployment.

It therefore seems plausible that such a future could emerge as a form of crisis resolution. Already, concurrent with progressive mobilisations against neoliberalism has been the upsurge in support for radical Right and neo-fascist parties and movements, deploying racist and nationalistic discourses to promise security amidst the uncertainty and anxiety generated through neoliberal crisis and austerity. Indeed, the rise of far right and neo-fascist movements such as Golden Dawn in Greece, which has, as Worth (2013: 89) notes '[merged] civil violence and protest with electoral success', shows the potential appeal, and the very real threat, of this type of agenda as a form of crisis response.

DECOMMODIFICATION

A third possible trajectory for the global economy is much more desirable. However, like the other possible futures it is contingent on the outcome of struggles and compromises between different social groups. Despite the highly durable and socially embedded character of neoliberal practices, the global financial crisis does seem to have opened up opportunities for progressive political change, albeit such a move away from neoliberalism is far from guaranteed. However, the perspective outlined here shares Carroll's (2010: 169) aspiration that '[a]mid the crisis, we hope to find, within the present, elements of a more hopeful future, and to forge alliances that can leverage neoliberal capitalism's failure into a different kind of world'.

As demonstrated in the previous chapter, the dominant response by states to the crisis has been to extend neoliberalism through privatisation and deregulation and cut expenditure to services which quarantine labour from crisis and from market fluctuations, while capital has benefited from ongoing subsidies. While there have been some restrictions placed upon finance capital, these have, to date at least, been quite modest. To be sure, all of this has been rolled out unevenly, but the pattern of ongoing neoliberalisation seems clear, and Davidson (2010: 2) is surely right to argue that 'the ruling classes of the world have certainly not abandoned neoliberalism'.

Nonetheless, while neoliberalism remains the dominant logic of policy making across the capitalist world, non-neoliberal alternatives have been opened up by some of the policy responses by state elites. This is particularly true of the nationalisation of major financial institutions. Otherwise neoliberal policy making elites, for whom nationalisation has been anathema for at least two decades, moved swiftly to bring financial institutions under state ownership. While they were careful to explain that these were only temporary measures until such time as those institutions could be returned to profitability and thence private sector ownership, this break with neoliberal regulatory practices is nonetheless a significant development. As Kitromilides (2010: 157) argues:

Before the global financial crisis, the nationalization of giant banks like Citigroup, Bank of America, Lloyds TSB or even Northern Rock could not even be contemplated let alone advocated publicly. Such a proposal would have been dismissed as (a) politically naïve, (b) not technically feasible, and (c) without any theoretical basis. The crisis, undeniably, has changed these perceptions. First, it is no longer so fanciful or politically naïve to discuss the nationalization even of mega-banks some of whom are already nationalized or semi-nationalized. Politicians sense that there may be political capital to be gained from public anger against bankers and financiers. Nationalization can be presented as being in the best interest of taxpayers and as a way of punishing greedy bankers rather than bailing them out.

In this sense neoliberalism revealed its 'other' through the crisis, and gave to alternative policy practices a legitimacy they had not enjoyed for at least half a century.

However, while the crisis revealed neoliberalism's 'other', it also demonstrated quite starkly its true self. The crisis exposed the socially destructive consequences of market dependence, a cornerstone of the commodification and marketisation practices which characterised the neoliberal era. The value of retirement funds was eroded; state and municipal governments lost their invested surpluses; private providers of public services went out of business; the value of homes was decimated; workers lost their jobs. The political power of capital, which had grown during the neoliberal era, was also exposed. This is exemplified by the currency of the 'Wall Street versus Main Street' discourse in the USA. Many feel that the disproportionate influence of finance capital is evidenced by the apparent rewards granted by the state to major financial corporations, which have been in receipt of government funded bailouts, yet whose executives have continued to receive significant salaries while also appearing to be immune from sanction.

These twin dynamics of neoliberalism in crisis open up a sphere of legitimacy for progressive alternatives based upon three interconnected logics: social protection/decommodification, public provision and democratisation.

If the crisis reveals the dangers of the extension of market dependence that became a hallmark of neoliberalism, then it also suggests a non-neoliberal progressive alternative in the form of social protection and decommodification which quarantine people from market provisioning. Examples could include universally available education, childcare, healthcare, defined benefit pension schemes and social housing. Esping-Andersen (1990: 22) describes decommodification as occurring 'when a service is rendered as a matter of right, and when a person can maintain a livelihood without reliance on the market'. This means that decommodification also entails quarantining labour itself, at least to some extent, from market dependence by, for example protective labour laws and guaranteed basic income (King 2012: 263–4). As Bryan and Rafferty (2010: 218–19) argue, there is 'a need to shift to class organisations that concentrate on winning class benefits of universal goods and collective services not based on the expenditure of individual incomes or borrowing to obtain them. This involves moving towards decommodifying social relations, including labour power itself'.

Closely related to this decommodification agenda, the crisis has also given extra legitimacy to the nationalisation of private sector corporations, thus bucking the privatisation trend that was a key plank of the neoliberal era. It therefore opens up space for a more extensive programme of direct public provisioning of goods and services. In addition to the public provision of welfare services, such a programme could usefully also involve the direct public provision of other goods and services currently monopolised by the private sector – including a host of financial services, transportation, utilities and telecommunications. Even the manufacturing sector of the economy could potentially be subject to the nationalisation agenda if, as has been suggested by some (Albo et al. 2010: 114), it could thereby be converted to ecologically sustainable production. This would very likely entail the compulsory acquisition by states of at least one major corporation in each of these sectors.

Finally, if the crisis has brought to a head concerns about the growing influence of for-profit private institutions over public policy processes which had been simmering away for the last three decades due to the de-democratising processes resulting from neoliberalisation, then an agenda of economic democratisation would seem to have added traction. This would entail 'a democratic means of planning through new sets of public institutions that would enable us to take collective decisions about allocating resources for what we produce and how we will produce things we need to sustain our lives and our relationship to our environment' (Albo et al. 2010: 110). Part of this agenda would obviously be the programme of nationalisation just outlined. Crucially, however, it would differ from the most recent round of bailouts because states would take effective control over the decision-making processes of such entities – in contrast to taking majority share ownership but not exercising political control over production decisions. Beyond this, a progressive non-neoliberal agenda for economic democratisation could also usefully extend effective citizen deliberation over economic decision making to areas of urban and regional planning and monetary policy. Limiting corporate influence over economic decision making would be another means towards economic democratisation.

The global financial crisis, therefore, represents a 'political opportunity structure' (McAdam et al. 1996: 24) for progressive political economic change. This was, at least implicitly, recognised by those progressive voices who at the onset of the crisis announced it as heralding the end of neoliberalism. For many such progressives, however, it was almost an article of faith that the opportunity represented by the crisis would inevitably lead to a more progressive organisation of the global political economy. As has been detailed throughout this book, they assumed that the crisis demonstrated the flaws inherent in organising policy around neoliberal ideas and thus that it cleared the path for rational progressive ideas to trump irrational neoliberal ideas. However, as this book has been at pains to detail, neoliberalism was not primarily driven by the influence of neoliberal ideas upon policy makers. While ideational change was an important element of the broader neoliberal transformation of policy making, the context for such change was provided by contradiction, conflict and change within the global capitalist economy, as well as by institutional transformation and inertia. Indeed, the perspective under-pinning this book is that political economic change is the product of conflict and compromise, mediated by the existing institutional environ-ment and highly contingent upon the structural and associational power of labour and capital.

THE END OF NEOLIBERALISM?

Progressive political economic change, therefore, is driven by much more than simply good progressive ideas. There is a view on the Left of politics that the chief ingredient required for progressive political eco-nomic change in the neoliberal era is a new set of ideas. This view is shared by those who argue that the key to the rise of neoliberalism was the development and promotion of neoliberal ideas by neoliberal think tanks, and therefore that learning from the success of neoliberalism means developing ideas and think tanks along similar lines.

In fact, there is no paucity of good ideas on the Left about desirable progressive non-neoliberal policies. However, many of these good ideas are formulated as if they did not confront an entrenched set of class interests wedded to the expanded reproduction of neoliberalism as well as institutions rolled out during the neoliberal era that are highly resistant to change. In short, while progressive forces worldwide are overflowing with ideas about how the political economy might better be organised along more just and equitable lines, there has been little consideration given to strategic questions of how we might arrive at such an alternative society and, indeed, whether such formulations are at all realistic given the embedded nature of neoliberalism.

Many on the Left advocate the need to learn from the successes of new right think tanks and of neoliberalism more generally (George 1997). However, it is important that the correct lessons are drawn. The analysis of this book suggests that, to the extent that neoliberal think tanks have enjoyed success, it is primarily due to their discursive framing of neoliberalism and its enemies. Moreover, the radical neoliberal discourse generated by the new right think tanks not only undermined critics and opponents of neoliberalism, but also helped to shift the centre of political debate to the right which opened up spaces of legitimacy for less radical but nonetheless still neoliberal policies to be implemented by state elites. For the Left then, the lessons are clear. The role of ideas within a progressive strategy for non-neoliberal change is to articulate a set of values, arguments and images that delegitimates neoliberalism and legitimates a radical and progressive vision of society with the aim of opening up space for a less radical, but nonetheless progressive and non-neoliberal, agenda for political economic change. For such a strategy to have any traction at all, such ideas must be allied with sources of political power, much in the way that neoliberal ideas were closely allied with business interests and mobilisations.

To turn the 'crisis *in* neoliberalism' into a 'crisis *of* neoliberalism' (Saad-Filho 2010) therefore will require much more than just good ideas. It will also require political mobilisation. This point was made compellingly by Michael Kalecki in his widely cited 1943 essay 'Political Aspects of Full Employment'. Kalecki, a Marxist theorist, although one whose economics intersected with that of Keynes, argued that the achievement of full employment is much more than a technical economic feat. Indeed, he claimed that the technical knowledge to enable full employment already existed. The impediments, however, to the realisation of full employment were mobilisations against it by 'the captains of industry' (Kalecki 1943: 350).

Kalecki argues that private owners of production would oppose government programmes of full employment creation for three reasons. First, he argues such programmes would eliminate the boom and bust cycle of capitalism, thus eliminating the 'powerful indirect control over government policy' enjoyed by capitalists due to their ability to claim that 'Everything which may shake the state of [business] confidence must be carefully avoided because it would cause an economic crisis' (Kalecki 1943: 350). Second, capitalists are opposed to the specific measures required to achieve full employment. While not opposed to public investment per se – when it is 'confined to objects which do not compete with the equipment of private business (for example hospitals, schools, high-ways' (ibid.)) – the almost inevitable expansion of public investment beyond this realm into a programme of nationalisation would encroach on the profitability and prerogatives of capital. The achievement of full employment through the state subsidisation of mass consumption is also likely to be opposed because income becomes delinked from private sector employment and all of its attendant disciplines (ibid.: 351). Third, as Kalecki notes, 'under a regime of permanent full employment, the "sack" would cease to play its role as a disciplinary measure. The social position of the boss would be undermined, and the self-assurance and class consciousness of the working class grow' (p. 351). Thus, although there may be some economic benefit to capital from a regime of full employment – '[t]he entrepreneurs in the slump a longing for a boom' (p. 349) – there are broader political considerations that outweigh such obvious economic advantages.

While Kalecki wrote his essay in a different historical and political context, the broad principles he outlined remain relevant for an understanding of the problems confronting progressive forces in the context of today's global economic crisis. This book has argued that neoliberalism is embedded in a set of class relations through which the power of capital has been strengthened. Furthermore, because the profit-making strategies of business are premised upon the maintenance or extension of neoliberal forms of regulation, it is to be expected that attempts to wind these back and implement an agenda of social protection will likely encounter strong resistance from such quarters. Albo and Evans (2010: 303) are surely right to caution that contemporary resistance to neoliberalism 'confront[s] a still powerful neoliberal state and a power bloc vigorously advancing its interests nationally and internationally'. The implication is that just as capitalists were opposed to the creation of a permanent regime of full employment when Kalecki wrote in the 1940s, so are they today opposed to a progressive non-neoliberal agenda of social protection, public provision and democratisation because it would wind back their prerogatives, undermine their political and economic power, and is at odds with the accumulation strategies upon which their recent investment decisions and forward projections have been made.

It is for this reason that a broad-based and militant non-neoliberal social movement is a prerequisite for pushing state elites towards economically progressive policies. The coalition of interests supporting and wedded to neoliberal policy norms must be confronted with a commensurate mobilisation of political power. To this, of course, must be joined a vision for change and a set of ideas, values and arguments to underpin it. However such programmes and values on their own are unable to achieve the changes they envision.

While anti-neoliberal social movements are likely to form outside of traditional political parties, ultimately, if they are to be successful in embedding progressive non-neoliberal policies within a durable institutional framework, they would need to exert influence over political parties with a realistic chance of directly shaping state policy. The broad strategic considerations outlined here conform with those observed by scholars of social movements in capitalist democracies during the last century-and-a-half: '[c]umulative nonviolent action only makes a difference, in fact, to the extent that it: a) forges alliance of conscience or interest with existing members of the polity, b) offers a credible threat of disrupting routine political processes, c) poses another credible threat of direct influence in the electoral arena, and/or d) elicits pressure on authorities from external powerholders' (McAdam et al. 1996: 22).

If a progressive political economic future depends upon rolling back neoliberal regulations and institutions, then it will also be underpinned by the simultaneous roll-out of new non-neoliberal institutions. Just as neoliberal policy norms have become embedded in a durable institutional architecture, so progressive non-neoliberal policies and regulations need to be institutionally embedded in order that they develop a durable character capable of withstanding mobilisations by those social forces opposed to such measures and also able to generate support from a broad electoral base.

One necessary element of this would be the institutionalisation of working class power as a durable countervailing force to the power of capital and the inevitable mobilisations by capitalist interests against some or all of the institutional reforms proposed herein. There are many possibilities for 'increasing the effectiveness of wage earners' power resources in relation to those of business interests' (Korpi 1998: 54), but perhaps the most obvious and important is the privileging of trade unions within the workplace. Historically, there are numerous examples to draw upon, including various forms of closed shop, agency shop and union preference arrangements (Weeks 1995: 5–7). There are of course dangers with this strategy. There is no doubt that such a strategy can breed resentment among some workers, and can lead to the perception that trade unions have too much power and therefore create support for regulations to undermine the ability of workers to organise collectively. Conversely, however, there is a significant positive externality to the privileging of trade unions in the workplace in the form of reduced inequality in the economy more broadly, as research suggests a positive correlation between rates of unionisation and levels of economic equality (Hacker and Pierson 2010: 179–80).

Baldwin's (1990) analysis of the history of the welfare state concludes that the durability of universalist welfare institutions lies in their ability to cater to the interests of a diverse range of social groups. Such institutions distribute benefits and mitigate risks across income strata – they do not simply redistribute income and rewards downwards to the least fortunate in capitalist societies. He argues that '[t]he ability of the Scandinavian welfare states to cater to the middle classes as successfully as to workers has been the secret of their success' (p. 30), and concludes that '[s]olidarity, in those few instances where it has been realised, has been the outcome of a generalised and reciprocal self interest' (p. 299).

Building upon this insight, a progressive political economic strategy beyond neoliberalism would need to appeal across income strata in order to build a supportive coalition, or at least to nullify opposition. This would need to be institutionalised so that it becomes durable through the development of policy measures that meet the material self-interest of these different income strata.

In terms of a progressive agenda of social protection and decommodification, this would entail providing social services at the level demanded by the wealthy and then making them generally available. Private provision through markets could be authorised by the state in order to address concerns about consumer choice. However, if state-run services were of high quality then the private system would very likely become residualised – catering primarily to the rich and to those choosing private provision as a matter of conscience or social distinction.

In terms of public provision, this would entail the state directly providing high quality core services in the areas of finance, utilities, transportation and telecommunications. This may occur alongside the authorisation of private competitors where no natural monopoly exists. Positive externalities would derive from the state-owned company exerting price pressure on the private providers, as well as from the employment and countercyclical effects of the public provider.

It is important to note that none of these strategies can be based upon *ex-nihilo* assumptions. Any non-neoliberal progressive strategy is constrained by the institutional environment inherited from the neoliberal era. One example is that widespread financial deregulation has significantly limited the ability of monetary policy to be used to achieve full employment if a national economy is at or near full capacity utilisation. Another is that because the marketisation of social services has created a constituency of voters who have an interest in the maintenance of marketised services, any progressive programme aiming to build universalist welfare institutions would probably need to simultaneously maintain state subsidies to existing marketised programmes and draw this down over the longer term, as the increase in quality of publicly provided services enticed people back to the public sector.

Of course, such an expansionary progressive programme would need to be funded. A higher and more progressive income tax system is one option, as is an increase to corporate tax. Recent survey data suggests that majorities across several states may be developing conditional support for income tax increases where it is linked to the funding of high-quality public services. Certainly, as outlined earlier, some states have, since the onset of the crisis, managed to increase taxation levies upon corporations, wealthy individuals and luxury consumption. Whether support for a more extensive progressivisation of income tax would hold up in the face of actual policy proposals for the same, and the inevitable mobilisation against such proposals by the wealthy, remains to be seen. One area in which states might have success in raising taxation levels is sales tax. It has the advantages of being easy to collect, difficult to evade and rarely subject to the same kinds of counter mobilisations by the wealthy that beset attempts to raise income tax. The disadvantage of such schemes, of course, is that, because they are a tax on consumption, then the less one earns the more proportionately heavy the financial burden one bears, as a larger proportion of one's income is spent on consumption items (and thus subject to taxation) rather than being saved. However, if the revenue generated from such funds was exclusively used to deliver high-quality universally available services, as well as to fund other transfer payments that raised the quality of life of the less well off proportionately more than they raised the living standards of the better off, then the tax would have been directed to progressive ends, and may outweigh the regressive income effects.

Another option, which could be pursued alongside or to the exclusion of changes to income or sales tax arrangements, would be a 'socialisation of investment' programme, through which the state effectively captures economic surpluses circulating within the financial sector of the economy and directs them towards investment in socially useful infrastructure. This could be achieved through a variety of means, including fairly moderate measures such as a Tobin tax on speculation, a super profits tax on financial institutions of a certain size or, more radically, through the nationalisation of financial institutions through a Swedish-style 'wage-earner funds' (Whyman 2006) programme, or by steering existing and future pension and superannuation funds into socially productive investments (Frankel 2004; Ramsay 2004; Ramsay and Lloyd 2010). The latter could be achieved through tax benefits, or direct mandate. Given the rise of public–private partnerships and sovereign wealth funds during the late neoliberal era, the material precursors to such a socialisation of investment programme are already extant, albeit they would need to be quarantined and limited to serve particular social ends. One such end, which is very much in the spirit of Keynes' original socialisation of investment formulation (Keynes 1964: 378), is that of full employment. It has long been recognised by Keynesians and Marxists that the self-interested pursuit of profit by capitalists is unlikely, in and of itself, to produce a situation of system-wide full employment of labour, but that the state nonetheless does have the technical capacity to realise such a situation. A socialisation of investment programme could be one catalyst for full employment which would have the added positive externality of stimulating effective demand within the private sector of the economy and therefore also of increasing tax receipts of the state.

Some might argue that these proposals are too moderate – that they are more reformist than revolutionary, and indeed that the crisis prompts consideration of more radical alternatives to capitalism. Two responses are in order. This chapter has merely outlined the broad parameters of one possible progressive non-neoliberal agenda. The proposals here certainly do not preclude a more radical agenda, nor are they in conflict with such an agenda. Indeed, decommodification, if implemented extensively enough, is the antithesis of capitalism. Nonetheless it is certainly true that the proposals advocated here would very likely retain capitalist social relations in some form. These proposals are intended to be achievable in the short term, and there seems little realistic prospect of completely dismantling the system of profit-driven capital accumulation within such a timeframe. However, these proposals are conceived very much in the spirit of Chomsky's conception of goals as 'the choices and tasks that are within reach, that we will pursue one way or another, guided by vision that may be distant and hazy' (Chomsky 1996: 70).

The potential for capital flight is another possible objection. Certainly, as noted earlier, there would be *political* resistance from capital to the agenda presented here. The *economic* response by owners of capital, however, is more difficult to determine. The socialisation of investment called for here is one way to mitigate this eventuality, and it may be that prevention or further mitigation of capital flight would require broader international solidarity – whether in the form of new globally agreed regulations limiting capital movement, or direct financing of decommodification agendas by governments of other nations. It might be the case, however, that the prospects for capital flight should be less feared than is imagined. As Erik Olin Wright notes, capitalist social relations have existed alongside a large decommodifying state in Sweden for several decades, notwithstanding that country's recent neoliberalisation (Wright 2010a: 222). In either case, the possibility of capital flight simply reinforces the need for an 'organised countervailing power' (Wright 2010b: 156) to that of the coalition of interests supportive of embedded neoliberalism.

CONCLUSION

This book was motivated by dissatisfaction with conventional progressive accounts of neoliberalism and the implications of the global financial crisis for its future. By conceiving of neoliberalism in idealist terms – as reflective of and driven by fundamentalist neoliberal doctrine – they mistook regulations enacted in the wake of the crisis as a retreat from neoliberalism, and embraced a rather naïve optimism that neoliberalism was on its last legs because the ideas that drove it has been discredited.

Much of this book has been concerned to demonstrate the flaws in such idealist, or ideas-centred, approaches to neoliberalism, and to put forward an alternative conception of neoliberalism as socially embedded that offers a more fruitful interpretive frame for understanding the current conjuncture.

This chapter has shown that the neoliberal policy regime remains dominant within capitalist states globally. Indeed, neoliberalism has been used as a form of crisis response, thereby extending the scope of the neoliberal policy regime. This should not be surprising. The socially embedded nature of neoliberalism, described in previous chapters, gives it significant durability, creating structures that predispose state elites to look to neoliberal policies as the first 'go to' in times of crisis, but also ensuring that powerful groups have an interest in the maintenance and extension of the neoliberal policy regime.

Nonetheless, this chapter has also revealed significant cracks in the neoliberal edifice. Nationalisations of some of the world's biggest companies have opened up spaces for non-neoliberal policy alternatives. Moreover, neoliberal crisis responses have not been able to redress problems of low growth and high unemployment. As people's livelihoods and living standards have been variously decimated or threatened by the crisis and the neoliberal responses to it, mass mobilisations against neoliberalism have been widespread. As yet, however, while they have managed to slow the pace of neoliberalisation in some cases, they have yet to stem, or reverse the tide.

Of course, it remains to be seen whether neoliberalism will survive the current crisis. There are some grounds for optimism due to the space the crisis has opened up for non-neoliberal policy alternatives, and due to the mass mobilisations against neoliberalism. However, as Marx noted, while people make their own history, they do so not under circumstances of their choosing. We are both constrained and enabled by our inherited institutions and social relations. The highly durable character of embedded neoliberalism has, to date, shown itself capable of withstanding the most severe crisis in its history. To transform this into a just system that affords the vast majority of the human population a decent standard of living and protects them from the vicissitudes of markets will require a mobilisation, common purpose and strategic focus, the likes of which have rarely been seen in the neoliberal era.

Bibliography

Abdelal, Rawi (2007), *Capital Rules: The Construction of Global Finance*, Harvard University Press, Cambridge, MA.

Abelson, D. (2002), *Do Think Tanks Matter? Assessing the Impact of Public Policy Institutes*, McGill-Queen's University Press, Montreal.

Abouharb, M. Rodwan and David Cingranelli (2007), *Human Rights and Structural Adjustment*, Cambridge University Press, Cambridge.

Aglietta, M. (2000), *A Theory of Capitalist Regulation: The US Experience*, Verso, New York.

Albo, Greg (2002), 'Neoliberalism, the State and the Left: A Canadian Perspective', *Monthly Review*, 54(1): 46–55.

Albo, Greg and Bryan Evans (2010), 'From Rescue Strategies to Exit Strategies: The Struggle over Public Sector Austerity', in Leo Panitch, Greg Albo and Vivek Chibber (eds), *The Crisis this Time: Socialist Register 2011*, The Merlin Press, London, pp. 283–308.

Albo, G., S. Gindin and L. Panitch (2010), *In and Out of Crisis: The Global Financial Meltdown and Left Alternatives*, PM Press, Oakland.

Almeida, P.D. (2007), 'Defensive Mobilization: Popular Movements against Economic Adjustment Policies in Latin America', *Latin American Perspectives*, 34(3): 123–39.

Altvater, E. (2009), 'Postneoliberalism or Postcapitalism?, The Failure of Neoliberalism in the Financial Market Crisis', *Development Dialogue*, 51, January, 73–86.

Anderson, Tim (1999), 'The Meaning of Deregulation', *Journal of Australian Political Economy*, 44: 5–21.

Arnesen, E. (ed.) (2007), *Encyclopedia of U.S. Labor and Working Class History Volume 1*, Routledge, New York.

Auerback, Marshall and L. Randall Wray (2010), 'Toward True Health Care Reform', Public Policy Brief No. 110, March, Levy Economics Institute of Bard College, Blithewood.

Avsar, Rojhat (2011), 'Mainstream Economic Rhetoric, Ideology and Institutions', *Journal of Economic Issues*, 45(1): 137–58.

Ayers, A. and A. Saad Filho (2013), 'Democracy Against Neoliberalism: Paradoxes, Limitations, Transcendence', Paper presented to the International Initiative for Promoting Political Economy Conference, The Hague, July 9–13.

Ayers, J. (2004), 'Framing Collective Action Against Neoliberalism: The Case of the "Anti-Globalization" Movement', *Journal of World-Systems Research*, 10(1): 11–34.

Bahro, R. (1977), 'The Alternative in Eastern Europe', *New Left Review*, 106(I): 3–37.

Baker, A. and K.F. Greene (2011), 'The Latin American Left's Mandate: Free-Market Policies and Issue Voting in New Democracies', *World Politics*, 63(1): 43–77.

Baldwin, Peter (1990), *The Politics of Social Solidarity, Class Bases of the European Welfare State 1875–1975*, Cambridge University Press, Cambridge.

Barro, Robert J. and Jong-Wha Lee (2002), 'IMF Programs: Who is Chosen and What are the Effects?', Working Paper No. 8951.

BBC (2012), 'EU Austerity Drive Country By Country', available at: http://www.bbc.co.uk/news/10162176, accessed 29 November 2013.

Beder, S. (2000), *Global Spin: The Corporate Assault on Environmentalism*, Scribe, Melbourne.

Beder, S. (2001), 'Neoliberal Think Tanks and Free Market Environmentalism', *Environmental Politics*, 10(2): 128–33.

Beeson, M. and A. Firth (1998), 'Neoliberalism as a Political Rationality: Australian Public Policy Since the 1980s', *Journal of Sociology*, 34(3): 215–31.

Béland, D. and A. Waddan (2000), 'From Thatcher (and Pinochet) to Clinton? Conservative Think Tanks, Foreign Models and US Pension Reform', *Political Quarterly*, 71(2): 202–10.

Bell, Stephen (2011), 'Do We Really Need a New "Constructivist Institutionalism" to Explain Institutional Change?', *British Journal of Political Science*, 41: 883–906.

Belloc, F. and A. Nicita (2011), 'The Political Determinants of Liberalization: Do Ideological Cleavages Still Matter?', *International Review of Economics*, 58(2): 121–45.

Bellofiore, Riccardo, Francesco Garibaldo and Joseph Halevi (2010), 'The Global Crisis and the Crisis of European Mercantilism', in Leo Panitch, Greg Albo and Vivek Chibber (eds), *The Crisis this Time: Socialist Register 2011*, The Merlin Press, London, pp. 120–46.

Best, J. (2003), 'From the Top Down: The New Financial Architecture and the Re-Embedding of Global Finance', *New Political Economy*, 8(3): 363–84.

BIS (2010), 'The Basel Committee's Response to the Financial Crisis: Report to the G20', Basel Committee for Banking Supervision, Bank for International Settlements, October, available at: http://www.bis.org/publ/bcbs179.pdf, accessed 15 January 2014.

Blanchflower, David G. (2006), 'A Cross-Country Study of Union Membership', *IZA* DP No. 2016.

Bleiker, R. (2002), 'Activism after Seattle: Dilemmas of the Anti-Globalisation Movement', *Pacifica Review: Peace, Security & Global Change*, 14(3): 191–207.

Block, Fred (2003), 'Karl Polanyi and the Writing of "The Great Transformation"', *Theory and Society*, 32(3): 275–306.

Blumenthal, S. (2008), *The Rise of the Counter-Establishment: The Conservative Ascent to Political Power*, Union Square Press, New York.

Blyth, Mark (2002), *Great Transformations: Economic Ideas and Institutional Change in the Twentieth Century*, Cambridge University Press, New York.

Boccia, R. (2013), 'Cutting the U.S. Budget Would Help the Economy Grow', *Heritage Backgrounder #2864 on Budget and Spending*, available at: http://www.heritage.org/research/reports/2013/11/cutting-the-us-budget-would-help-the-economy-grow?utm_source=heritagefounda tion&utm_medium=homepage&utm_content=bottom&utm_campaign= headline131121, accessed 15 January 2014.

Bonefeld, W. (2005), 'Europe, the Market and the Transformation of Democracy', *Journal of Contemporary European Studies*, 13(1): 93–106.

Bortolotti, Bernardo and Domenico Siniscalco (2004), *The Challenges of Privatization: An International Analysis*, Oxford University Press, Oxford.

Bourdieu, Pierre (1998), 'Neoliberalism, the Utopia (Becoming a Reality) of Unlimited Exploitation', in Pierre Bourdieu, *Acts of Resistance: Against the Tyranny of the Market*, The New Press, New York.

Braithwaite, John (2008), *Regulatory Capitalism: How It Works, Ideas for Making It Work Better*, Edward Elgar, Cheltenham, UK and Northampton, MA, USA.

Brand, U. (2012), 'Contradictions and Crises of Neoliberal–Imperial Globalization and the Political Opportunity Structures for the Global Justice Movements', *Innovation: The European Journal of Social Science Research*, 25(3): 283–98.

Brenner, A. (2010), 'Preface', in Aaron Brenner, Robert Brenner and Cal Winslow (eds), *Rebel Rank and File: Labor Militancy and Revolt from Below During the Long 1970s*, Verso, New York, pp. xi–xix.

Brenner, R. (2002), *The Boom and the Bubble: The US in the World Economy*, Verso, London.

Brenner, R. (2006), *The Economics of Global Turbulence: The Advanced Capitalist Economies from Long Boom to Long Downturn, 1945–2005*, Verso, London.

Brenner, R. (2010), 'The Political Economy of the Rank-and-File Rebellion', in Aaron Brenner, Robert Brenner and Cal Winslow (eds), *Rebel Rank and File: Labor Militancy and Revolt from Below During the Long 1970s*, Verso, New York, pp. 37–74.

Brenner, N. and Theodore, N (2002), 'Cities and the Geographies of "Actually Existing Neoliberalism"', *Antipode*, 34(3): 349–79.

Brenner, N., J. Peck and N. Theodore (2010), 'Variegated Neoliberalization: Geographies, Modalities, Pathways', *Global Networks*, 10(2): 1–41.

Brown, W., Simon Deakin, David Nash and Sarah Oxenbridge (2000), 'The Employment Contract: From Collective Procedures to Individual Rights', *British Journal of Industrial Relations*, 38(4): 611–29.

Bruff, Ian (2014), 'The Rise of Authoritarian Neoliberalism', *Rethinking Marxism*, 26(1): 113–29.

Bryan, Dick and Mike Rafferty (2010), 'Deriving Capital's (and Labour's) Future', in L. Panitch, G. Albo and V. Chibber (eds), *Socialist Register 2011: The Crisis This Time*, The Merlin Press, London, pp. 196–223.

Buch-Hansen, H. and A. Wigger (2010), 'Revisiting 50 Years of Market-Making: The Neoliberal Transformation of European Competition Policy', *Review of International Political Economy*, 17(1): 20–44.

Bugaric, B. (2013), 'Europe Against the Left? On Legal Limits to Progressive Politics', *LSE 'Europe in Question' Discussion Paper Series Paper No. 61/2013*, London School of Economics, available: http://www.lse.ac.uk/europeanInstitute/LEQS/LEQSPaper61.pdf.

Burgess, J. and R. Sappey (1992), *Corporatism in Action: The Australian Pilots' Dispute 1989*, Department of Economics Research Report or Occasional Paper No. 182, University of Newcastle.

Burnham, Gilbert, Riyadh Lafta, Shannon Doocy and Les Roberts (2006), 'Mortality after the 2003 invasion of Iraq: a cross-sectional cluster sample survey', *The Lancet*, 368(9545): 1421–8.

Byrd, S. and Lorien Jasny (2010), 'Transnational Movement Innovation and Collaboration: Analysis of World Social Forum Networks', *Social Movement Studies: Journal of Social, Cultural and Political Protest*, 9(4): 355–72.

Cahill, Damien (2001), 'Why the Right uses "Class" against the Left', *Arena Journal*, 16: 151–62.

Cahill, Damien (2002), 'Funding the Ideological Struggle', *Overland*, 168: 21–6.

Cahill, D. (2004), 'New Class Discourse and the Construction of Left-Wing Elites', in Marian Sawer and Barry Hindess (eds), *Us and Them: Anti-Elitism in Australia*, Curtin University of Technology, API Network, pp. 77–95.

Cahill, D. (2008a), 'Hegemony and the Neoliberal Historical Bloc: The Australian Experience', in Richard Howson and Kylie Smith (eds), *Hegemony: Studies in Consensus and Coercion*, Routledge, New York, pp. 201–17.

Cahill, D. (2008b), 'Labo(u)r, the Boom and the Prospects for an Alternative to Neo-liberalism', *Journal of Australian Political Economy*, 61: 321–36.

Callinicos, A. (2001), *Against the Third Way*, Polity, Cambridge.

Campbell, John (2001), 'Institutional Analysis and the Role of Ideas in Political Economy', in John Campbell and Ove Pedersen (eds), *The Rise of Neoliberalism and Institutional Analysis*, Princeton University Press, Princeton, pp. 159–89.

Carroll, William (2010), 'Crisis, Movements, Counter-Hegemony: In Search of the New', *Interface: A Journal For and About Social Movements*, 2(2): 168–98.

Cato Institute (n.d.), 'Milton Friedman – Biography', *Cato Institute Website*, available at: http://www.cato.org/special/friedman/friedman/index.html, accessed 14 January 2014.

Cerny, Phil (2008), 'Embedding Neoliberalism: The Evolution of a Hegemonic Paradigm', *The Journal of International Trade and Diplomacy*, 2(1): 1–46.

Champ, N. (2012), 'Speech by SEC Staff: What SEC Registration Means for Hedge Fund Advisers', Speech given at the New York City Bar, May 11, available at: http://www.sec.gov/News/Speech/Detail/Speech/1365171490432#.UtY9K_vy0to, accessed 15 January 2014.

Chang, Ha-Joon (2002), 'Breaking the Mould: An Institutionalist Political Economy Alternative to the Neo-liberal Theory of the Market and the State', *Cambridge Journal of Economics*, 26(5): 539–59.

Checchi, D., M. Florio and J. Carrera (2009), 'Privatisation Discontent and Utility Reform in Latin America', *The Journal of Development Studies*, 45(3): 333–50.

Chomsky, Noam (1996), *Powers and Prospects: Reflections on Human Nature and Social Order*, Pluto Press, London.

Chorev, Nitsan and Sarah Babb (2009), 'The Crisis of Neoliberalism and the Future of International Institutions: A Comparison of the IMF and the WTO', *Theory and Society*, 38(5): 459–84.

Chwieroth, J. (2007), 'Neoliberal Economists and Capital Account Liberalization in Emerging Markets', *International Organization*, 61: 443–63.

Clarke, S. (1991), 'State, Class Struggle and the Reproduction of Capitalism', in Simon Clarke (ed.), *The State Debate*, St Martin's Press, New York.

Cockett, Richard (1994), *Thinking the Unthinkable: Think Tanks and the Economic Counter-Revolution 1931–1983*, Harper Collins, London.

Cohen, Nathan Joseph and Miguel Angel Centeno (2006), 'Neoliberalism and Patterns of Economic Performance 1980–2000', *The ANNALS of the American Academy of Political and Social Science*, 606(1), July, 32–67.

Cohen, N., S. Mizrahi and F. Yuval (2011), 'Public Attitudes Towards the Welfare State and Public Policy: The Israeli Experience', *Israel Affairs*, 17(4): 621–43.

Cooper, Rae and Bradon Ellem (2008), 'The Neoliberal State, Trade Unions and Collective Bargaining in Australia', *British Journal of Industrial Relations*, 46(3): 532–54.

Crouch, Colin (2011), *The Strange Non-Death of Neoliberalism*, Polity, Cambridge.

D'Aloisio, Tony (2009), 'Regulatory Response to the Financial Crisis: A Presentation by ASIC Chairman Tony D'Alosio', CPA Congress Sydney, 1 October 2009, available at: http://www.asic.gov.au/asic/pdf lib.nsf/LookupByFileName/SpeechChairman_151009.pdf/$file/Speech Chairman_151009.pdf, accessed 15 January 2014.

Dale, Gareth (2010), *Karl Polanyi*, Polity, Cambridge.

Davidson, N. (2010), 'What was Neoliberalism?', in Neil Davidson, Patricia McCafferty and David Miller (eds), *Neoliberal Scotland: Class and Society in a Stateless Nation*, Cambridge Scholars Publishing, Newcastle upon Tyne, pp. 1–89.

Davis, Ken (n.d.), 'Regulatory Reform Post the Global Financial Crisis: An Overview', A Report Prepared for the Melbourne APEC Finance Centre, available at: http://www.apec.org.au/docs/11_CON_GFC/ Regulatory%20Reform%20Post%20GFC-%20Overview%20Paper.pdf, accessed 29 November 2013.

De Angelis, M. (1999), 'Marx's Theory of Primitive Accumulation: A Suggested Reinterpretation', Section 5.3, available at: http://home pages.uel.ac.uk/M.DeAngelis/PRIMACCA.htm, accessed: 25 November 2013.

Dean, J. (2008), 'Enjoying Neoliberalism', *Cultural Politics*, 4(1): 47–72.

Dean, M. (2012), 'Free Economy, Strong State', in Damien Cahill, Lindy Edwards and Frank Stilwell (eds), *Neoliberalism: Beyond the Free Market*, Edward Elgar, Cheltenham, UK and Northampton, MA, USA, pp. 69–89.

Denham, A. and M. Garnett (1996), 'The Nature and Impact of Think Tanks in Contemporary Britain', in M.D. Kandiah and A. Seldon (eds), *Ideas and Think Tanks in Contemporary Britain, Volume 1*, Frank Cass, London, pp. 43–61.

Denham, A. and M. Garnett (1998), 'Think Tanks, British Politics and the "Climate of Opinion"', in D. Stone, A. Denham and M. Garnett (eds), *Think Tanks Across Nations: A Comparative Approach*, Manchester University Press, Manchester, pp. 21–41.

Denisova, I., M. Eller, T. Frye and E. Zhuravskaya (2012), 'Everyone Hates Privatization, but Why? Survey Evidence from 28 Post-Communist Countries', *Journal of Comparative Economics*, 40(1): 44–61.

Desai, R. (1999), 'Second-Hand Dealers in Ideas: Think-Tanks and Thatcherite Hegemony', *New Left Review*, 203: 27–64.

Dieter, H. (2005), 'The US Economy and the Sustainability of Bretton Woods II', *Journal of Australian Political Economy*, 55: 48–76.

Dumenil, G. and Dominique Levy (2001), 'Costs and Benefits of Neoliberalism. A Class Analysis', *Review of International Political Economy*, 8(4): 578–607.

Dumenil, G. and Dominique Levy (2004), *Capital Resurgent: Roots of the Neoliberal Revolution*, Harvard University Press, Cambridge, MA.

Dumenil, G and Dominique Levy (2011), *The Crisis of Neoliberalism*, Harvard University Press, Cambridge, MA.

Dunn, B. (2009), 'Accumulation by Dispossession or Accumulation of Capital? The Case of China', *Journal of Australian Political Economy*, 60: 5–27.

Dunn, B. (2011), 'Marxist Crisis Theory and the Need to Explain Both Sides of Capitalism's Cyclicity', *Rethinking Marxism*, 23(4): 524–42.

Ehrenreich, Barabara (1990), *Fear of Falling: The Inner Life of the Middle Class*, Harper Perennial, New York.

Ellem, B. (2006) 'Beyond Industrial Relations: *Workchoices* and the Reshaping of Labour, Class and the Commonwealth', *Labour History*, 90, May, 211–20.

Engels, F. (1985), *The Origin of the Family, Private Property and the State*, Penguin, Harmondsworth.

Epstein, G. (2007), 'Central Banks, Inflation Targeting and Employment Creation', *Economic and Labour Market Papers 2007/2*, Employment Analysis and Research Unit, Economic and Labour Market Analysis Department, International Labour Organization, available: http://www.ilo.org/public/english/employment/download/elm/elm07-2.pdf, accessed 15 January 2014.

Esping-Andersen, Gosta (1990), *The Three Worlds of Welfare Capitalism*, Polity, Cambridge.

Etchemendy, Sebastián (2004), 'Repression, Exclusion, and Inclusion: Government–Union Relations and Patterns of Labor Reform in Liberalizing Economies', *Comparative Politics*, 36(3), April, 273–90.

Eubanks, Walter W. (2010), 'The European Union's Response to the 2007–2009 Financial Crisis', Congressional Research Service, available at: http://www.fas.org/sgp/crs/row/R41367.pdf, accessed November 29 2013.

European Central Bank (2012), 'Articles: A Fiscal Compact for a Stronger Economic and Monetary Union', *Monthly Bulletin*, May, available at: http://www.ecb.int/pub/pdf/other/art1_mb201205en_pp79-94en.pdf, accessed 29 November 2013.

Farber, H. and Bruce Western (2002), 'Ronald Reagan and the Politics of Declining Union Organization', *British Journal of Industrial Relations*, 40(3): 385–401.

Feulner, E. (1985), 'Ideas, Think-Tanks and Governments: Away from the Power Elite, Back to the People', *Quadrant*, November, 22–6.

Fine, B. (2010), 'Locating Financialisation', *Historical Materialism*, 18: 97–116.

Foley, Duncan (2004), 'Rationality and Ideology in Economics', *Social Research* 71(2): 329–39.

Fontana, Benedetto (1993), *Hegemony and Power: On the Relation Between Gramsci and Machiavelli*, University of Minnesota Press: Minneapolis.

Foucault, Michel (2008), *The Birth of Biopolitics: Lectures at the College de France 1978–1979*, Palgrave Macmillan, New York.

Fourcade-Gourinchas, M. and S.L. Babb (2002), 'The Rebirth of the Liberal Creed: Paths to Neoliberalism in Four Countries', *American Journal of Sociology*, 108(3): 533–79.

Fowler, T. (2012), 'Does fighting back still matter? The Canadian autoworkers, capitalist crisis and confrontation', *Capital and Class*, 36(3): 493–513.

Frankel, B. (2004), 'Oils Ain't Oils and Super Ain't Super', *Journal of Australian Political Economy*, 53: 67–80.

Friedman, M. (n.d.), *Interview with Milton Friedman for The Corporation*, available at: http://hellocoolworld.com/media/TheCorporation/Friedman.pdf, accessed 10 December 2013.

Friedman, M. (1968), 'The Role of Monetary Policy', *The American Economic Review*, 58(1): 1–17.

Friedman, Milton (2002), *Capitalism and Freedom*, University of Chicago Press, Chicago.

Friedman, M. (2000), 'Commanding Heights Interview', in Lanny Ebenstein (ed.), *The Indispensible Milton Friedman: Essays on Politics and Economics*, Regenery, Washington DC, pp. 233–53.

Friedman, Milton and Rose Friedman (1980), *Free to Choose: A Personal Statement*, Penguin, Harmondsworth.

Friedman, M. and Rose Friedman (2002), 'Interview with Milton and Rose Friedman by Michael McFaul', available at: http://new media.ufm.edu/gsm/index.php?title=Interview_with_Rose_and_Milton _Friedman, accessed 15 January 2014.

FSB (2012a), 'Consultative Document: Strengthening Oversight and Regulation of Shadow Banking – An Integrated Overview of Policy Recommendations', Financial Stability Board, 18 November, available at: http://www.financialstabilityboard.org/publications/r_121118.pdf, accessed 15 January 2014.

FSB (2012b), 'Progress of Financial Regulatory Reform', 31 October, available at: https://www.financialstabilityboard.org/publications/r_ 121105.pdf, accessed 28 March 2014.

Gahan, Peter and Andreas Pekarek (2012), 'The Rise and Rise of Enterprise Bargaining in Australia', *Labour and Industry*, 22(3): 195–222.

Gamble, A. (2009), 'The Western Ideology', *Government and Opposition*, 44(1): 1–19.

Ganev, V.I. (2005), 'The "Triumph of Neoliberalism" Reconsidered: Critical Remarks on Ideas-Centred Analyses of Political and Economic Change in Post-Communism', *East European Politics and Societies*, 19(3): 343–78.

Garnaut, Ross, interview with the author, 1 October 2002.

Gemici, Kurtulus (2008), 'Karl Polanyi and the Antinomies of Embeddedness', *Socio-Economic Review*, 6: 5–53.

George, Susan (1997), 'How to Win the War of Ideas: Lessons from the Gramscian Right', *Dissent*, 44(3): 47–53.

Gill, Stephen (2001), 'Constitutionalising Capital: EMU and Disciplinary Neoliberalism', in Andreas Bieler and Adam Morton (eds), *Social Forces in the Making of New Europe*, Palgrave, New York, pp. 47–69.

Gill, S. (2002), 'Constitutionalizing Inequality and the Clash of Globalizations', *International Studies Review*, 4(2): 47–65.

Glyn, A., A. Hughes, A. Lipietz and A. Singh (2000), 'The Rise and Fall of the Golden Age', in S. Marglin and J. Schor (eds), *The Golden Age of Capitalism: Reinterpreting the Postwar Experience*, Clarendon Press, Oxford, pp. 39–125.

Glyn, Andrew (2006), *Capitalism Unleashed: Finance, Globalisation, and Welfare*, Oxford University Press, Oxford.

Gonzalez, G.A. (2001), *Corporate Power and the Environment: The Political Economy of U.S. Environmental Policy*, Roman and Littlefield, Maryland.

Gowan, P. (2009), 'Crisis in the Heartland: Consequences of the New Wall Street System', *New Left Review*, 55: 5–29.

Gramsci, Antonio (1999), *Selections from the Prison Notebooks*, trans. and ed. Quintin Hoare and Geoffrey Nowell Smith, International Publishers, New York.

Guardian (2011), 'University Funding Cuts: Which Institutions are Worst Hit?', *The Guardian*, 17 March, available at: http://www.theguardian.com/news/datablog/2011/mar/17/university-funding-cuts-institution-hefce-universities, accessed 15 January 2014.

Guardian (2012), 'University Tuition Fees to Rise in England Next Year', *The Guardian*, 26 July, available at: http://www.theguardian.com/education/2012/jul/26/university-tuition-fees-to-rise-1, accessed 15 January 2014.

Hacker, J. and Paul Pierson (2010), 'Winner-Take-All Politics: Public Policy, Political Organization, and the Precipitous Rise of Top Incomes in the United States', *Politics and Society*, 38(2): 152–204.

Hall, P. (1989a), 'Conclusion: The Politics of Keynesian Ideas', in Peter Hall (ed.), *The Political Power of Economic Ideas: Keynesianism Across Nations*, Princeton University Press, Princeton, pp. 361–91.

Hall, P. (ed.) (1989b), *The Political Power of Economic Ideas: Keynesianism Across Nations*, Princeton University Press, Princeton.

Hall, Stuart (1985), 'Authoritarian Populism: A Reply to Jessop et al.', *New Left Review*, 151, May/June, 115–24.

Hall, Stuart (1988), 'The Toad in the Garden: Thatcherism Among the Theorists', in Cary Nelson and Lawrence Grossberg (eds), *Marxism and the Interpretation of Culture*, Macmillan Education, London, pp. 35–57.

Hall, Stuart and Martin Jacques (1983) (eds), *The Politics of Thatcherism*, Lawrence and Wishart, London.

Hames, T. and R. Feasey (1994), 'Anglo-American Think Tanks under Reagan and Thatcher', in A. Adonis and T. Hames (eds), *A Conservative Revolution? The Thatcher–Reagan Decade in Perspective*, Manchester University Press, Manchester, pp. 215–37.

Harcourt, Bernard (2011), *The Illusion of Free Markets: Punishment and the Myth of Natural Order*, Harvard University Press, Cambridge, MA.

Harman, C. (2010), *Zombie Capitalism: Global Crisis and the Relevance of Marx*, Haymarket Books, Chicago.

Hartwell, R.M. (1995), *A History of the Mont Pelerin Society*, Liberty Fund, Indianapolis.

Harvey, David (2005), *A Brief History of Neoliberalism*, Oxford University Press, Oxford.

Haufler, V. (2001), *A Public Role for the Private Sector: Industry Self Regulation in a Global Economy*, Carnegie Endowment for International Peace, Washington DC.

Haupt, A.B. (2010), 'Parties' Responses to Economic Globalization: What is Left for the Left and Right for the Right?', *Party Politics*, 16(1): 5–27.

Hay, Colin and Nicola Smith (2013), 'The Resilience of Anglo-liberalism in the Absence of Growth: The UK and Irish Cases', in Vivien Schmidt and Mark Thatcher (eds), *Resilient Liberalism in Europe's Political Economy*, Cambridge University Press, Cambridge, pp. 289–312.

Hayek, F.A. (1944), *The Road to Serfdom*, Dymocks Book Arcade, Sydney.

Hayek, F.A. (1949), 'The Intellectuals and Socialism', *University of Chicago Law Review*, 16(3): 417–33.

Hayek, F.A. (1960) 'The Intellectuals and Socialism', in George B. de Huszar (ed.), *The Intellectuals: A Controversial Portrait*, The Free Press, Glencoe.

Hayek, F.A. (1973), *Law Legislation and Liberty, Volume 1: Rules and Order*, University of Chicago Press, Chicago.

Hayek, F.A. (1978), *Law Legislation and Liberty, Volume 2: The Mirage of Social Justice*, University of Chicago Press, Chicago.

Hayek, F.A. (2009), *The Constitution of Liberty*, Routledge, London.

Heclo, Hugh (2008), 'The Mixed Legacies of Ronald Reagan', *Presidential Studies Quarterly*, December, 38(4): 555–74.

Helleiner, Eric (1994), *States and the Reemergence of Global Finance: From Bretton Woods to the 1990s*, Cornell University Press, Ithaca.

Helleiner, Eric (2008), 'The Return of Regulation and What a Difference a Decade Makes', *The Globe and Mail*, 18 September, http://www.theglobeandmail.com/news/opinions/article710738.ece., accessed 15 January 2014.

Hermann, C. (2007), 'Neoliberalism in the European Union', *Studies in Political Economy*, 79, Spring, 61–89.

Hill, C. (1987), *The World Turned Upside Down: Radical Ideas During the English Revolution*, Peregrine Books, Harmondsworth.

Hinish Jr, J. (1981), 'Regulatory Reform: An Overview', in Charles Heatherly (ed.), *Mandate for Leadership: Policy Management in a Conservative Administration*, Heritage Foundation, Washington DC, pp. 697–707.

Hobsbawm, E. (1981), *Industry and Empire*, Penguin, Harmondsworth.

Hobsbawm, E. (2009), 'Socialism has Failed. Now Capitalism is Bankrupt. So What Comes Next?', *The Guardian*, 10 April, p. 33.

Hodgson, Geoffrey (2007), 'Introduction', in G. Hodgson (ed.), *The Evolution of Economic Institutions: A Critical Reader*, Edward Elgar, Cheltenham, UK and Northampton, MA, USA.

Holborow, M. (2007), 'Language, Ideology and Neoliberalism', *Journal of Language and Politics*, 6(1): 51–73.

Horsfall, D. (2013), 'There and Back Again: Convergence Towards the Competition State Plan', *Policy Studies*, 34(1): 53–72.

Hutton, Will (2008), 'A Short History of Capitalism's Rise and Fall', *The Observer* (5 October), online at: http://www.guardian.co.uk/business/2008/oct/05/creditcrunch.marketturmoil1/print, consulted 19 November 2008.

Hywood, Gregory and Mike Taylor (1986), 'ALP Unites Against Fragmented New Right', *Australian Financial Review*, 2 September, p. 4.

IMF (2004), *IMF Concessional Financing through ESAF – Fact Sheet*, IMF Website, available at: http://www.imf.org/external/np/exr/facts/esaf.htm, accessed 15 January 2014.

IMF (2009), 'G20 Meeting of the Ministers and Central Bank Governors. March 13-1 2009, Global Economic Policies and Prospects – Note by the Staff of the International Monetary Fund', available at http://www.imf.org/external/np/g20/pdf/031909a.pdf, accessed 29 November 2013.

IMF (n.d.), *IMF Data Mapper*, available at: http://www.imf.org/external/datamapper/index.php, accessed 15 August 2013.

International Trade Union Confederation (2012), *2012 Annual Survey of Violations of Trade Union Rights – USA*, available at: http://www.refworld.org/docid/4fd8891ac.html, accessed 29 November 2013.

Jacques, P.J., R.E. Dunlap and M. Freeman (2008), 'The Organisation of Denial: Conservative Think Tanks and Environmental Scepticism', *Environmental Politics*, 17(3): 349–85.

Jessop, Bob (1997), 'Survey Article: The Regulation Approach', *Journal of Political Philosophy*, 53(3): 287–326.

Jessop, B. (2002), *The Future of the Capitalist State*, Polity, Cambridge.

Jessop, Bob and Ngai-Ling Sum (2006), *Beyond the Regulation Approach: Putting Capitalist Economies in their Place*, Edward Elgar, Cheltenham, UK and Northampton, MA, USA.

Johnson, Carol (2000), *Governing Change: Keating to Howard*, University of Queensland Press, St. Lucia.

Johnston, J. and Gordon Laxer (2003), 'Solidarity in the Age of Globalization: Lessons from the anti-MAI and Zapatista Struggles', *Theory and Society*, 32: 39–91.

Jones, Evan (1984), 'Government "Intervention"', *Journal of Australian Political Economy*, 17: 53–60.

Jones, E. (1989), *Was the Post-War Boom Keynesian?*, Department of Economics Working Paper, University of Sydney.

Jordana, Jacint, David Levi-Faur and Xavier Fernandez Marin I (2011), 'The Global Diffusion of Regulatory Agencies: Channels of Transfer and Stages of Diffusion', *Comparative Political Studies*, 44(10): 1343–69.

Kalecki, Michal ([1943] 1990), 'Political Aspects of Full Employment', in Jerzy Osiatynski (ed.), *Collected Works of Michal Kalecki: Volume 1*, Clarendon Press, Oxford.

Kandiah, M.D. and A. Seldon (eds) (1996), *Ideas and Think Tanks in Contemporary Britain, Volume 1*, Frank Cass, London.

Keating, Michael, interview with the author, 5 August 2002.

Kelley, J. and J. Sikora (2002), 'Australian Public Opinion on Privatisation, 1986–2002', *Growth*, No. 50, December, pp. 54–8.

Kelsey, Jane (2008), *Serving Whose Interests?, The Political Economy of Trade in Services Agreements*, Routledge, New York.

Kerr, H. (1981), 'Labour's Social Policy 1974–1979', *Critical Social Policy*, 1(1): 5–17.

Keynes, J.M. (1937), 'The General Theory of Employment', *Quarterly Journal of Economics*, 51(2): 209–23.

Keynes, J.M. (1964), *The General Theory of Employment, Interest and Money*, Macmillan, London.

King, John (2012), 'The Future of Neoliberalism', in Damien Cahill, Lindy Edwards and Frank Stilwell (eds), *Neoliberalism: Beyond the Free Market*, Edward Elgar, Cheltenham, UK and Northampton, MA, USA, pp. 251–66.

King, S. (1997), 'National Competition Policy', *The Economic Record*, 73(222): 270–84.

Kitromilides, Y. (2010), 'The Banking Crisis, Nationalization of Banking and the Mixed Economy', in G. Fontana, J. McCombie and M.C. Sawyer (eds), *Macroeconomics, Finance and Money: Essays in Honour of Philip Arestis*, Palgrave-Macmillan, Hampshire, pp. 150–62.

Klein, N. (2007), *The Shock Doctrine: The Rise of Disaster Capitalism*, Penguin, Camberwell.

Konings, Martijn (2011), *The Development of American Finance*, Cambridge University Press, Cambridge.

Korpi, W (1998), 'Power Resources Approach vs Action and Conflict: On Causal and Intentional Explanations in the Study of Power', in Julia O'Connor and Gregg Olsen (eds), *Power Resources Theory and the Welfare State: A Critical Approach*, University of Toronto Press, Toronto, pp. 37–69.

Krippner, G. (2011), *Capitalizing on Crisis: The Political Origins of the Rise of Finance*, Harvard University Press, Cambridge, MA.

Krugman, Paul (2009), 'All the President's Zombies', *The New York Times*, August 24, available at: http://www.nytimes.com/2009/08/24/opinion/24krugman.html?_r=0.

Lafer, G. (2004), 'Neoliberalism by Other Means: The "War on Terror" at Home and Abroad', *New Political Science*, 26(3): 323–46.

Lapavitsas, C. (2009), 'Financialised Capitalism: Crisis and Financial Expropriation', *Historical Materialism*, 17: 114–48.

Larner, W. (2000), 'Neoliberalism: Policy, Ideology, Governmentality', *Studies in Political Economy*, 63: 5–25.

Lavelle, Ashley (2005), 'Social Democrats and Neo-liberalism: A Case Study of the Australian Labor Party', *Political Studies*, 53: 754–71.

Laven, Z. and Federico Santi (2012), 'EU Austerity and Reform: A Country by Country Table', The European Institute, available at: http://www.europeaninstitute.org/April-2012/eu-austerity-and-reform-a-country-by-country-table-updated-may-3.html & http://www.european institute.org/Special-G-20-Issue-on-Financial-Reform/austerity-measures-in-the-eu.html, accessed 29 November 2013.

Lebowitz, M.A. (2004), 'Ideology and Economic Development', *Monthly Review*, 56(1): 14–24.

Levien, Michael and Marcel Paret (2012), 'A Second Double Movement? Polanyi and Shifting Global Opinions on Neoliberalism', *International Sociology*, 27(6): 724–44.

Levi-Faur, David (2005), 'The Global Diffusion of Regulatory Capitalism', *The ANNALS of the American Academy of Political Science*, 598: 12–32.

Levy, P. (1985), 'The Unidimensional Perspective of the Reagan Labor Board', *Rutgers Law Journal*, 16: 269–390.

Lindblom, Charles (1977), *Politics and Markets: The World's Political Economic Systems*, Basic Books, New York.

Macartney, Huw (2011), *Variegated Neoliberalism: EU Varieties of Capitalism and International Political Economy*, Routledge, New York.

MacKenzie, Donald (2005), 'Opening the Black Boxes of Global Finance', *Review of International Political Economy*, 12(4): 555–76.

MacKenzie, Donald (2006), *An Engine, Not a Camera: How Financial Models Shape Markets*, The MIT Press, Cambridge, MA.

Maddison, A. (2006), *The World Economy*, OECD, Paris.

Madrick, J (2002), 'Economic Scene: By Some Measures, There Is Still a Need for Government to Prime the Pump', *New York Times*, April 18, available at: http://www.nytimes.com/2002/04/18/business/economic-scene-some-measures-there-still-need-for-government-prime-pump.html?pagewanted=all&src=pm, accessed 26 November 2013.

Malanga, S. (2006), 'The New New Left: The Politics of Ever-Expanding Government', Heritage Lecture #921, available at: http://www.heritage.org/research/lecture/the-new-new-left-the-politics-of-ever-expanding-government, accessed 15 January 2014.

Mann, G. (2010), 'Hobbes' Redoubt? Toward a Geography of Monetary Policy', *Progress in Human Geography*, 34(5): 601–25.

Manne, Robert (2010), 'Is Neoliberalism Finished?' in R. Manne and D. McKnight (eds), *Goodbye to All That? On the Failure of Neoliberalism and the Urgency of Change*, Black Inc, Melbourne.

Manne, Robert and David McKnight (2010), 'Introduction', in R. Manne and D. McKnight (eds), *Goodbye to All That? On the Failure of Neoliberalism and the Urgency of Change*, Black Inc, Melbourne.

Marsh, David (1995). 'Explaining "Thatcherite" Policies: Beyond Uni-Dimensional Explanation', *Political Studies*, 43: 595–613.

Marsh, David (2009), 'Keeping Ideas in their Place: In Praise of Thin Constructivism', *Australian Journal of Political Science*, 44(4): 679–96.

Marshall, J. (2009), 'The Financial Crisis in the US: Key Events, Causes and Responses', House of Commons Library Research paper 09/34, 22 April 2009, available at: http://www.voltairenet.org/IMG/pdf/US_Financial_Crisis.pdf, accessed 15 January 2014.

Martin, Stephen, interview with the author, 10 June 2003.

Marx, K. (1970), *A Contribution to the Critique of Political Economy*, Progress Publishers, Moscow.

Marx, Karl (1977), *A Contribution to the Critique of Political Economy*, Progress Publishers, Moscow.

Marx, K. (1990), *Capital: A Critique of Political Economy, Volume 1*, Penguin, London.

Marx, K. (1991), *Capital: A Critique of Political Economy, Volume 3*, Penguin, London.

Marx, K. (1992), *Capital: A Critique of Political Economy, Volume 2*, Penguin, London.

Marx, Karl and Friedrich Engels (1976), *The German Ideology*, Progress Publishers, Moscow.

McAdam, D., Sidney Tarrow and Charles Tilly (1996), 'To Map Contentious Politics', *Mobilization: An International Journal*, 1(1): 17–34.

McDonald, J. (2007), 'Legitimating Private Interests: Hegemonic Control over "the Public Interest" in National Competition Policy', *Journal of Sociology*, 43(4): 349–66.

McNally, David (2009), 'From Financial Crisis to World Slump: Accumulation, Financial Isolation and the Global Slowdown', *Historical Materialism*, 17: 35–83.

McNally, David (2011), *Global Slump: The Economics and Politics of Crisis and Resistance*, PM Press, Oakland.

Mehta, Jal (2011), 'The Varied Roles of Ideas in Politics: From "Whether" to "How"', in Daniel Beland and Robert Henry Cox (eds), *Ideas and Politics in Social Science Research*, Oxford University Press, Oxford, pp. 23–46.

Messmore, R. (2007), 'A Moral Case Against Big Government: How Government Shapes the Character, Vision, and Virtue of Citizens', *Heritage First Principles Series Report #9 on Political Thought*, available at: http://www.heritage.org/research/reports/2007/02/a-moral-case-against-big-government-how-government-shapes-the-character-vision-and-virtue-of-citizens, accessed 15 January 2014.

Miller, T. (2009), 'Testimony to The House Committee on Foreign Affairs' Subcommittee on Terrorism, Nonproliferation and Trade', available at: http://www.heritage.org/research/testimony/government-intervention-a-threat-to-economic-recovery, accessed 9 December 2013.

Mirowski, Philip (2009), 'Postface: Defining Neoliberalism', in Philip Mirowski and Dieter Plehwe (eds), *The Road from Mont Pelerin: The Making of the Neoliberal Thought Collective*, Harvard University Press, Cambridge, MA, pp. 417–55.

Mirowski, Philip (2013), *Never Let a Serious Crisis go to Waste: How Neoliberalism Survived the Financial Meltdown*, Verso, London.

Mirowski, Philip and Dieter Plehwe (eds) (2009), *The Road from Mont Pelerin: The Making of the Neoliberal Thought Collective*, Harvard University Press, Cambridge, MA.

Mitchell, D. (2005), 'The Impact of Government Spending on Economic-Growth', *Heritage Backgrounder #1831 on Federal Budget*, available at: http://www.heritage.org/research/reports/2005/03/the-impact-of-government-spending-on-economic-growth, accessed 15 January 2014.

Mitchell, William (2000), 'The Causes of Unemployment', in Stephen Bell (ed.), *The Unemployment Crisis in Australia*, Cambridge University Press, Melbourne, pp. 49–87.

Moffit, R. (2011), 'How to Roll Back the Administrative State', Heritage Center for Policy Innovation Discussion Paper #1 on Regulation, available at: http://www.heritage.org/research/reports/2011/02/how-to-roll-back-the-administrative-state, accessed 15 January 2014.

Moody, K. (2012), 'Contextualising Organised Labour in Expansion and Crisis: The Case of the US', *Historical Materialism*, 20(1): 3–30.

Morton, Adam (2007), *Unravelling Gramsci: Hegemony and Passive Revolution in the Global Economy*, Pluto Press, London.

Moseley, F. (2003), 'Marxian Crisis Theory and the Postwar US Economy', in Alfredo Saad-Filho (ed.), *Anti-Capitalism: A Marxist Introduction*, Pluto Press, London, pp. 211–23.

Mudge, S.L. (2011), 'What's Left of Leftism?: Neoliberal Politics in Western Party Systems, 1945–2004', *Social Science History*, 35(3): 337–80.

Nicol, Danny (2010), *The Constitutional Protection of Capitalism*, Hart Publishing, Oxford.

Norrington, B. (1990), *Sky Pirates: The Pilots' Strike that Grounded Australia*, ABC Books, Sydney.

Nye, J.V. (1991), 'The Myth of Free-Trade Britain and Fortress France: Tariffs and Trade in the Nineteenth Century', *The Journal of Economic History*, 51(1): 23–46.

O'Connor, J. (1973), *The Fiscal Crisis of the State*, St Martin's Press, New York.

O'Connor, James (1998), 'Capitalism, Nature, Socialism: A Theoretical Introduction', *Capitalism, Nature, Socialism – A Journal of Socialist Ecology*, (1): 11–38.

O'Connor, John (2010), 'Marxism and the Three Movements of Neoliberalism', *Critical Sociology*, 36(5): 691–715.

OECD (2010), *OECD Economic Outlook*, Vol. 2009/2, OECD Publishing, available at: http://www.keepeek.com/Digital-Asset-Management/oecd/economics/oecd-economic-outlook-volume-2009-issue-2_eco_outlook-v2009-2-en, accessed 9 August 2013.

OECD (2013), *OECD Economic Outlook*, Vol. 2013/1, OECD Publishing, available at: http://www.keepeek.com/Digital-Asset-Management/oecd/economics/oecd-economic-outlook-volume-2013-issue-1_eco_outlook-v2013-1-en, accessed 9 August 2013.

Panitch, Leo and Sam Gindin (2005a), 'Finance and American Empire', in *Socialist Register 2005: The Empire Reloaded*, Monthly Review Press, New York, pp. 46–61.

Panitch, Leo and Sam Gindin (2005b), 'Euro Capitalism and American Empire', in D. Coates (ed.), *Varieties of Capitalism, Varieties of Approaches*, Palgrave, New York.

Panitch, Leo and Sam Gindin (2012), *The Making of Global Capitalism: The Political Economy of American Empire*, Verso, New York.

Panitch, Leo and Martijn Konings (2009), 'Myths of Neoliberal Deregulation', *New Left Review*, 57: 67–83.

Park, C.M. (2010), 'Public Attitudes Toward Government Spending in the Asia-Pacific Region', *Japanese Journal of Political Science*, 11(1): 77–97.

Paton, J. (2012), 'Neoliberalism Through the Lens of "Embeddedness"', in Damien Cahill, Lindy Edwards and Frank Stilwell (eds), *Neoliberalism: Beyond the Free Market*, Edward Elgar, Cheltenham, UK and Northampton, MA, USA, pp. 90–109.

Patriquin, L. (2004), 'The Agrarian Origins of the Industrial Revolution in England', *Review of Radical Political Economics*, 36(2): 196–216.

Peck, Alexandra (2012), 'IFI Leaders Talk Jobs, But Staff Push Labour Deregulation', *Bretton Woods Project: Critical Voices on the World*

Bank and IMF, available at: http://www.brettonwoodsproject.org/art-570789, accessed 29 November 2013.

Peck, J. (1996), *Work-Place: The Social Regulation of Labor Markets*, The Guildford Press, New York.

Peck, J. (2010), *Constructions of Neoliberal Reason*, Oxford University Press, Oxford.

Peck, Jamie (2001), *Workfare States*, The Guildford Press, New York.

Peck, Jamie (2010), *Constructions of Neoliberal Reason*, Oxford University Press, Oxford.

Peck, J. and A. Tickell (2002), 'Neoliberalizing Space', *Antipode*, 34(3): 380–404.

Peck, Jamie, Nik Theodore and Neil Brenner (2009), 'Postneoliberalism and its Malcontents', *Antipode*, 41: 6.

Peet, Richard (2009), *Unholy Trinity: The IMF, World Bank and WTO*, Zed Books, London.

Petras, J. and Henry Veltmeyer (2003), 'Whither Lula's Brazil? Neoliberalism and "Third Way" Ideology', *The Journal of Peasant Studies*, 31(1): 1–44.

Pew Research (2003a), 'World Publics Approve Increased International Trade', Pew Global Attitudes Project, available at: http://www.pew global.org/2003/09/05/world-publics-approve-increased-international-trade/, accessed 15 January 2014.

Pew Research (2003b), 'Support for Free Trade', Pew Global Attitudes Project, available at: http://www.pewglobal.org/2003/11/20/support-for-free-trade/, accessed 15 January 2014.

Phelan, S. (2007), 'The Discourses of Neoliberal Hegemony: The Case of the Irish Republic', *Critical Discourse Studies*, 4(1): 29–48.

Phillips-Fein, K. (2009), *Invisible Hands: The Businessmen's Crusade Against the New Deal*, W.W. Norton, New York.

Pierson, C. (2002), '"Social Democracy on the Back Foot": The ALP and the "New" Australian Model', *New Political Economy*, 7(2): 179–98.

Piketty, Thomas and Emmanuel Saez (2006), 'The Evolution of Top Incomes: A Historical and International Perspective', *The American Economic Review*, 96(2): 200–205.

Piven, F. and R. Cloward (1972), *Regulating the Poor: The Functions of Public Welfare*, Vintage, New York.

Plehwe, Dieter (2009), 'Introduction', in Philip Mirowski and Dieter Plehwe (eds), *The Road from Mont Pelerin: The Making of the Neoliberal Thought Collective*, Harvard University Press, Cambridge, MA, pp. 1–42.

Polanyi, K. ([1944] 2001), *The Great Transformation: The Political and Economic Origins of Our Time*, Beacon Press, Boston.

Polanyi, Karl (1957), 'The Economy as Instituted Process', in Karl Polanyi, Conrad Arensberg and Harry Pearson (eds), *Trade and Market in Early Empires: Economics in History and Theory*, Free Press, Glencoe, pp. 243–70.

Pollin, Robert and Thompson, Jeff (2011), 'State and Municipal Alternatives to Austerity', *New Labor Forum*, 30(3): 22–30.

Prasad, M. (2006), *The Politics of Free Markets: The Rise of Neoliberal Economic Policies in Britain, France, Germany and The United States*, University of Chicago Press, Chicago.

Prasad, M. (2012), 'The Popular Origins of Neoliberalism in the Reagan Tax Cut of 1981', *Journal of Policy History*, 24(3): 351–83.

Pusey, Michael (1991), *Economic Rationalism in Canberra: A Nation Building State Changes Its Mind*, Cambridge University Press, Cambridge.

Pusey, Michael and Nick Turnbull (2005), 'Have Australians Embraced Economic Reform?', in Shaun Wilson, Gabrielle Meagher, Rachel Gibson, David Denmark and Mark Western (eds), *Australian Social Attitudes: The First Report*, UNSW Press, Sydney, pp. 161–81.

Radice, H. (2010), 'Confronting the Crisis: A Class Analysis', in Leo Panitch, Greg Albo and Vivek Chibber (eds), *The Crisis this Time: Socialist Register 2011*, The Merlin Press, London, pp. 21–43.

Rafferty, M. (2001), 'Corporation', in Philip Anthony O'Hara (ed.), *Encyclopaedia of Political Economy, Volume 1*, Routledge, New York, pp. 154–7.

Ramsay, T. (2004), 'The Socialization of Investment in a Contemporary Setting', *Journal of Australian Political Economy*, 53: 116–31.

Ramsay T. and C. Lloyd (2010), 'Infrastructure Investment for Full Employment: A Social Democratic Program of Funds Regulation', *Journal of Australian Political Economy*, 65: 59–87.

Reese, E. (2005), *Backlash Against Welfare Mothers: Past and Present*, University of California Press, Berkeley.

Reinhart, Carmen (2000), 'The Mirage of Floating Exchange Rates', *The American Economic Review*, 90(2): 65–70.

Richman, S. (1998), 'The Reagan Record on Free Trade: Rhetoric vs. Reality', *Cato Policy Analysis* No. 107, available at: http://www.cato.org/pubs/pas/pa107.html, accessed 14 January 2014.

Ross, Stephanie (2002), 'Is This What Democracy Looks Like? The Politics of the Anti-Globalization Movement in North America', in Leo Panitch and Colin Leys (eds), *Fighting Identities: Race, Religion and Ethno-Nationalism, Socialist Register 2003*, Monthly Review Press, New York, pp. 281–304.

Rudd, Kevin (2009), 'The Global Financial Crisis', *The Monthly*, February, 20–29.

Ruggie, John (1982), 'International Regimes, Transactions, and Change: Embedded Liberalism and the Postwar Economic Order', *International Organization*, 36(2): 379–415.

Saad Filho, A. (2007), 'Monetary Policy in the Neoliberal Transition: A Political Economy Review of Keynesianism, Monetarism and Inflation Targeting', in R. Albritton, R. Jessop and R. Westra (eds), *Political Economy and Global Capitalism: The 21st Century, Present and Future*, Anthem Press, London, pp. 89–119.

Saad-Filho, Alfredo (2010), 'Crisis *in* Neoliberalism or Crisis *of* Neoliberalism?', in L. Panitch, G. Albo and V. Chibber (eds), *Socialist Register 2011: The Crisis This Time*, The Merlin Press, London, pp. 242–59.

Saad-Filho, Alfredo (2013), 'Mass Protests under "Left Neoliberalism": Brazil, June–July 2013', *Critical Sociology*, 39: 657–69.

Sanz, Ismael and Francisco Velázquez (2007), 'The Role of Ageing in the Growth of Government and Social Welfare Spending in the OECD', *European Journal of Political Economy*, 23(4), December, 917–31.

Scharpf, F. (2010), 'The Asymmetry of European Integration, or Why the EU Cannot Be a "Social Market Economy"', *Socio-Economic Review*, (8): 211–50.

Scharpf, F. (2013), 'Monetary Union, Fiscal Crisis and the Disabling of Democratic Accountability', in Armin Schäfer and Wolfgang Streeck (eds), *Politics in the Age of Austerity*, Polity Press, Cambridge, pp. 108–42.

Schmidt, V.A. (2011), 'Reconciling Ideas and Institutions through Discursive Institutionalism', in Daniel Beland and Robert Henry Cox (eds), *Ideas and Politics in Social Science Research*, Oxford University Press, Oxford, pp. 47–64.

Schoemann, Isabelle and Stefan Clauwaert (2012), 'The Crisis and National Labour Law Reforms: A Mapping Exercise', European Trade Union Institute, available at: http://www.etui.org/Publications2/Working-Papers/The-crisis-and-national-labour-law-reforms-a-mapping-exercise, accessed 29 November 2013.

Segal, Leonie (2004), 'Why it is Time to Review the Role of Private Health Insurance in Australia', *Australian Health Review*, 27(1): 3–15.

Seymour, Richard (2012), 'A Short History of Privatisation in the UK: 1979–2012', *The Guardian*, 29 March, available at: http://www.theguardian.com/commentisfree/2012/mar/29/short-history-of-privatisation, accessed 15 January 2014.

Shaikh, A. (2010), 'The First Great Depression of the 21st Century', in Leo Panitch, Greg Albo and Vivek Chibber (eds), *The Crisis this Time: Socialist Register 2011*, The Merlin Press, London, pp. 44–63.

Shields, S. (2007), 'From Socialist Solidarity to Neo-Populist Neoliberalisation? The Paradoxes of Poland's Post-Communist Transition', *Capital & Class*, 93, Autumn, 159–78.

Silber, William (2012), *Volcker: The Triumph of Persistence*, Bloomsbury Press, New York.

Silvers, D. and Heather Slavkin (2009), 'The Legacy of Deregulation and the Financial Crisis – Linkages Between Deregulation in Labor Markets, Housing Finance Markets, and the Broader Financial Markets', *Journal of Business and Technology Law*, 4(2): 301–47.

Smith, J.A. (1991), *The Idea Brokers: Think Tanks and the Rise of the New Policy Elite*, Free Press, New York.

Smith, P. and Gary Morton (2006), 'Nine Years of New Labour: Neoliberalism and Workers' Rights', *British Journal of Industrial Relations*, 44(3): 401–20.

Starr, A. (2000), *Naming the Enemy: Anti-Corporate Movements Confront Globalization*, Zed Books, London.

Starr, A. and Jason Adams (2010), 'Anti-globalization: The Global Fight for Local Autonomy', *New Political Science*, 25(1): 19–42.

Steketee, Mike (1986), 'Young's Call to ALP: Fight the New Right', *Sydney Morning Herald*, 1 September, p. 1.

Stephen, Matthew (2011) 'Globalisation and Resistance: Struggles over Common Sense in the Global Political Economy', *Review of International Studies*, 37: 209–28.

Stiglitz, Joseph (2008), 'The End of Neo-liberalism?', Project Syndicate, 7 July, available at: http://www.project-syndicate.org/commentary/the-end-of-neo-liberalism-.

Stiglitz, Joseph (2010), *Freefall: America, Free Markets, and the Sinking of the World Economy*, W.W. Norton and Co., New York.

Stone, D. (1996), 'From the Margins of Politics: The Influence of Think Tanks in Britain', *West European Politics*, 19(4): 675–92.

Stone, D. (2007), 'Recycling Bins, Garbage Cans and Think Tanks? Three Myths Regarding Policy Analysis Institutes', *Public Administration*, 85(2): 259–78.

Strange, S. (1996), *The Retreat of the State: The Diffusion of Power in the World Economy*, Cambridge University Press, Cambridge.

Svensen, Stuart (1998), 'The Australian Wharf Lockout', *Capital and Class*, 66: 1–11.

Swank, Duane and Cathie Jo Martin (2001), 'Employers and the Welfare State: The Political Economic Organization of Firms and Social Policy in Contemporary Capitalist Democracies', *Comparative Political Studies*, October 2001, 34(8): 889–923.

Taylor, Mike (1986), 'New Push for Labour Deregulation', *Australian Financial Review*, 1 September, p. 1.

Taylor, Mike and Jenni Hewitt (1986), 'Hawke Wades Into Peko Row', *The Sydney Morning Herald*, 29 August, p. 1.

Teicher, J., R. Lambert and A. O'Rourke (2006), 'Introduction: The *Workchoices Act* as the Triumph of Neoliberalism', in J. Teicher, R. Lambert and A. O'Rourke (eds), *The New Industrial Relations Agenda*, Pearson Education Australia, Frenchs Forest, pp. 1–9.

Thatcher, M. (1987), Interview for *Woman's Own* Magazine with Douglas Keay, Margaret Thatcher Foundation Website, available at: http://www.margaretthatcher.org/document/106689, accessed 15 January 2014.

Thomas, N. (2007), 'Global Capitalism, the Anti-Globalisation Movement and the Third World', *Capital & Class*, 92: 45–78.

Thompson, E.P. (1982), *The Making of the English Working Class*, Pelican, Harmondsworth.

Thomson, S., R. Osborn, D. Squire and S.J. Reed (2010), *International Profiles of Health Care Systems*, The Commonwealth Fund, June.

Tormey, S. (2004), 'The 2003 European Social Forum: Where Next for the Anti-Capitalist Movement?', *Capital and Class*, 84: 149–57.

Turner, Rachel (2008), *Neo-Liberal Ideology: History, Concepts and Policies*, Edinburgh University Press, Edinburgh.

van Appeldoorn, B. (2009), 'The Contradictions of "Embedded Neoliberalism" and Europe's Nulti-Level Legitimacy Crisis: The European Project and its Limits', in Bastiaan van Apeldoorn, Jan Drahokoupil and Laura Horn (eds), *Contradictions and Limits of Neoliberal European Governance: From Lisbon to Lisbon*, Palgrave Macmillan, New York, pp. 21–43.

van Horn, Rob and Philip Mirowski (2009), 'The Rise of the Chicago School of Economics and the Birth of Neoliberalism', in Philip Mirowski and Dieter Plehwe (eds), *The Road from Mont Pelerin: The Making of the Neoliberal Thought Collective*, Harvard University Press, Cambridge, pp. 139–78.

Varoufakis, Yanis (1998), *Foundations of Economics: A Beginner's Companion*, Routledge, London.

Vogel, David (1996), *Freer Markets, More Rules: Regulatory Reform in Advanced Industrial Countries*, Cornell University Press, Ithaca.

Vrasti, W. (2011), '"Caring" Capitalism and the Duplicity of Critique', *Theory & Event*, 14(4): 1–26.

Vucheva, Elitsa (2008), '"Laissez-Faire" Capitalism is Finished, says France', EUObserver.com, 26 September, available at: http://euobserver.com/political/26814, consulted: 18 November 2013.

Wacquant, L. (2009), *Punishing the Poor: The Neoliberal Government of Social Insecurity*, Duke University Press, Durham.

Wacquant, L. (2012), 'Three Steps to a Historical Anthropology of Actually Existing Neoliberalism', *Social Anthropology*, 20(1): 66–79.

Walton, J. and David Seddon (1994), *Free Markets and Food Riots: The Politics of Global Adjustment*, Blackwell, Oxford.

Weeks, P. (1995), *Trade Union Security Law: A Study of Preference and Compulsory Unionism*, The Federation Press, Annandale.

White, C. (2005), '*Workchoices*: Removing the Right to Strike?', *Journal of Australian Political Economy*, 56: 66–80.

Whyman, P. (2006), 'Post-Keynesianism, Socialization of Investment and Swedish Wage-Earner Funds', *Cambridge Journal of Economics*, 30: 49–68.

Williams, E., Michael Leachman and Nicholas Johnson (2011), *State Budgets in the New Fiscal Year are Unnecessarily Harmful*, Center on Budget and Policy Priorities, Washington DC, July 28.

Williamson, John and Molly Mahar (1998), *A Survey of Financial Liberalization*, Essays in International Finance, No. 211, November, Department of Economics, Princeton.

Wilson, Shaun, Gabrielle Meagher and Trevor Breusch (2005), 'Where to for the Welfare State?' in Shaun Wilson, Gabrielle Meagher, Rachel Gibson, David Denmark and Mark Western (eds), *Australian Social Attitudes: The First Report*, UNSW Press, Sydney, pp. 101–21.

Winslow, C. (2010), 'Overview: The Rebellion from Below, 1965–81', in Aaron Brenner, Robert Brenner and Cal Winslow (eds), *Rebel Rank and File: Labor Militancy and Revolt from Below During the Long 1970s*, Verso, New York, pp. 1–35.

Wood, E.M. (2002), *The Origin of Capitalism: A Longer View*, Verso, London.

Wood, E. (2003), *Empire of Capital*, Verso, New York.

Wood, E. (2012), *Liberty and Property: A Social History of Western Political Thought from Renaissance to Enlightenment*, Verso, New York.

Worth, Owen (2013), *Resistance in the Age of Austerity: Nationalism, the Failure of the Left and the Return of God*, Zed Books, London.

Wright, E.O. (2005), 'Foundations of a Neo-Marxist Class Analysis', in E.O. Wright (ed.), *Approaches to Class Analysis*, Cambridge University Press, Cambridge.

Wright, Erik Olin (2010a), *Envisioning Real Utopias*, Verso, London.

Wright, Erik Olin (2010b), *Envisioning Real Utopias – Pre-publication Version*, available at: http://www.ssc.wisc.edu/~wright/ERU.htm, accessed 15 August 2011.

Yergin, Daniel and Joseph Stanislaw (1998), *The Commanding Heights: The Battle for the World Economy*, Simon and Schuster, New York.

Index

'This book offers the clearest, most comprehensive, detailed, readable, insightful, sensible, balanced and systematic analysis of neoliberalism available today. This is an indispensable read for anyone interested in the most important topic on contemporary capitalism.

Cahill offers the most convincing analysis of the origins, key features and limitations of neoliberalism, and the most promising examination of how it can be overcome. This book debunks myths, pierces illusions and suggests the most promising avenue for resistance against the current phase of global capitalism.'

Professor Alfredo Saad Filho
SOAS, University of London, UK

'Neoliberalism, we have learned, lives in crisis. Today, the most important questions about neoliberalism, for all its well-known flaws and limits, concern its institutional entrenchment and dogged reproduction. These are the driving questions in Damien Cahill's theoretically astute and politically savvy book. This bold and original analysis, drawing on Marx and Polanyi in equal measure, is heterodox political economy at its very best.'

Jamie Peck
University of British Columbia, Canada

'In a sobering account, Damien Cahill illuminates the true nature of neoliberalism and explains why and how it has been able to survive what some of us hoped would be its terminal crisis. His concept of "embedded neoliberalism" is indispensable for understanding the connection between ideas and class power.'

Fred Block
University of California at Davis, USA

'Damien Cahill has emerged as one of the most penetrating social scientists on the politics of neoliberalism in the advanced capitalist societies. In his new book, he brings his many years of pouring over policy documents to examine neoliberalism in the new "age of austerity". The result is an impressive survey of the history and debates about neoliberal policies. But more powerful is Cahill's hard-headed analysis of why neoliberalism may not simply be in decline, despite the great social disasters it has produced: the "Great Recession" of 2008 only being the most spectacular. Cahill insists on what many are only *beginning to realize: that a new progressive political economy will not emerge as a result of the "failure of neoliberal ideas", but only when an alternative vision of society fuses with new organized forms of social resistance.'*

Greg Albo
York University, Toronto, Canada

'Despite the global financial crisis in 2007–2008, neoliberalism has remained dominant and even informs the responses to the crisis. In his masterful analysis, Damien Cahill demonstrates that this resilience is due to neoliberalism being firmly embedded within wider class relations, institutions and ideological norms. And yet, as Cahill also argues, progressive change is possible provided it is based on large-scale political mobilisation. I most strongly recommend this book for reading.'

Andreas Bieler
Nottingham University, UK

'For those who expected neoliberalism to disappear, discredited by the global financial crisis, Cahill's penetrating analysis explains its resilience and offers a first-class account of its three decades as a socially embedded policy regime. Offering a materialist rather than idealist interpretation of neoliberalism, Cahill is able to explain why governments' apparently Keynesian responses to the crisis do not flag its demise. This is a must-read book for those who study or care about the direction of the world economy.'

Professor Verity Burgmann
Monash University, Australia

.